BMW
1975 – 2001

Model by Model

B M W
1975 – 2001
MODEL BY MODEL

LAURENCE MEREDITH

CROWOOD

First published in 2002 by
The Crowood Press Ltd
Ramsbury, Marlborough
Wiltshire SN8 2HR

British Library Cataloguing-in-Publication Data
A catalogue record for this book is available from the
British Library.

ISBN 1 86126 477 1

Frontispiece: The third generation BMW 525i was one of the
most dynamic road cars ever built and was widely hailed as the
best four-door saloon in the world at the time of its inception.

Designed and typeset by
Focus Publishing
11a St Botolph's Road
Sevenoaks
Kent TN13 1AP

Printed and bound in Malaysia by Times Offset (M) Sdn. Bhd.

Contents

Introduction

'Bavarian Motor Works' is a fairly unimaginative name for a company that, for many decades, has produced some of the world's best and most coveted motor cars. Abbreviated to 'BMW', however, the name harbours a multitude of different meanings. For some, a BMW conjures up almost everything that they see as being 'wrong' with the western world and is a status symbol representative of greed and materialism.

For others, a BMW is a reliable, safe and well-made vehicle for transporting people in unruffled comfort. For me, and many thousands like me, the cars made in Munich are for the pure enjoyment of driving. In this respect BMW have few rivals, and their only competitors are built in Stuttgart by Mercedes-Benz.

Critics – and they are surprisingly large in number – who moot the preposterous idea that the famous 'frozen-propeller' badge claims a large percentage of the purchase price of a BMW, comment from a foggy viewpoint of unforgivable ignorance. BMWs are made in an elite class which is also occupied by Mercedes-Benz and Porsche. Fords, Vauxhalls, Rovers, Nissans and the like are simply not in the same class.

Like the majority of car manufacturers, though, BMW's ride through the twentieth century has, on several occasions, proved bumpy and precarious. A stolid range of expensive saloons in the early 1950s gave way to economy Microcars at around the time of the 1956 Suez crisis; by 1959 the company was on the brink of bankruptcy. Without a large injection of cash from the Quandt family, there is little doubt that BMW would have joined the ranks of extinct makes by 1960.

Despite BMW's long history, and reputation for building cars of superb quality, many motorists continue to believe that the 'frozen-propellor' badge accounts for a hefty proportion of a BMW's purchase price...

The launch of a modern range of high-performance saloons in the 1960s saw a gradual increase in the company's fortunes. Indeed, with the introduction of the 6-cylinder 2800CS in 1968, BMW were clearly spearheading a challenge to the refined products of Daimler-Benz.

BMW's 2-litre 2002, also debuted in 1968, was among the most highly acclaimed sporting saloons of the 1970s, and correctly so, for there was nothing, with the arguable exception of comparable Alfa-Romeos, that came close to it. In terms of performance, handling and sheer drivablility, the 2002's dynamics remain impressive, even by today's standards.

As successful as the '02 range was, and in spite of its role in projecting BMW's sporting image, it was the company's deliberate policy of involvement in motor sport that began BMW's real march to the top during the latter quarter of the twentieth century.

The titanic and exciting battles fought between the big BMW coupés and Ford Capris in the European Touring Car Championship during the early years of the 1970s have rightly fallen into legend. It was a battle that BMW won.

The Munich company's powerful turbo 4-cylinder engine powered Nelson Piquet to Formula One Championship victory in 1983, and the ultimate sporting accolade came in 1999 with outright victory in the Le Mans 24 Hours. In 1995, a McLaren F1 was victorious in the French classic, also powered by a BMW power unit.

In addition to success in such high-profile events, BMW have also invested heavily in saloon car racing and rallying They currently provide engines for the Formula One Williams team and, for the past 20 years, have been at the forefront of research into hydrogen-powered engines as a potential alternative to conventional fossil fuels.

The engineering standards of both the road cars and competition machines are and, by and large always have been, state-of-the-art.

This refusal to compromise in 'architectural' integrity, and engineering refinement, was driven home to me most powerfully in recent times during a spell at the wheel of a pre-War 319. Owned by Mark Garfitt, an old pal and leading light in the Vintage Sports Car Club, this beautifully maintained example was among the first of BMW's sporting two-seaters, and fitted with an early in-line 'six'. Unlike so many open-top cars of the period, Mark's car shows no signs of fatigue, is wholly devoid of rattles, squeaks, and 'scuttle-shake', and has the performance potential of, for example, a modern MGB.

Its gear change is almost oil-smooth, the engine much the same, but arguably its most astonishing feature is a chassis that gives the handling characteristics of a modern sports car. Even within the limits of traditional cross-ply rubber, the 319 could be drifted through corners at high speed in complete safety and with completely predictable attitude with throttle application.

By comparison so many post-vintage thoroughbreds, as interesting as several undoubtedly are, feel primitive, promote anxiety under braking and cornering, and splutter along the road with the reliability record of a

... while drivers – those people who take a pride in conducting cars safely, at high speed – take just the opposite view. The BMW roundel on this modern 5 Series is complemented by a BRDC (British Racing Drivers' Club) badge.

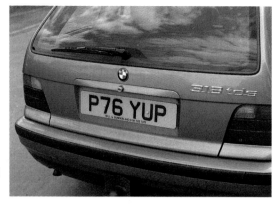

During the 'boom-and bust' days of the 1980s and 1990s, BMW owners, as this registration plate suggests, acquired a reputation for 'yuppiness' and everything that this label implied. The reputation and label quickly died away, at roughly the same rate that the desirability of these cars increased.

The late Ian Taylor, killed in a tragic accident at Spa, considered the 525i as the best all-round saloon in the world. This example, which belongs to the author, is in some ways similar to the VW Beetle 1500 – but a great deal quicker.

restaurant that occasionally 'closes for lunch'. I once drove a pre-War MG sports car (a pretty J2) which, despite its stunning mechanical condition, felt unsafe at any speed above 35mph. But the MG is far from being alone in this respect.

From the mid-1950s onwards Motor Sport's editor, Bill Boddy, rarely missed an opportunity to promote the virtues of the Volkswagen Beetle, a car he held in the highest regard for many years. 'The Bod' was heavily criticised on the grounds that an underpowered saloon had no place appearing in a journal devoted, as its title suggested, to motor sport, and for being 'unpatriotic'.

Towards the end of the 1960s, Boddy, an ardent reporter of objective facts, also discovered the many advantages of BMW motoring, expressed glowing opinions between the covers of his hallowed magazine, and was again accused of being unpatriotic. Motor Sport's Continental correspondent, Denis Jenkinson, who delighted in Porsche ownership for many years, once cited the 2002 in his 'top 10' among the world's greatest cars. He was not alone.

When it comes to assessing the worth of a motor car, I have never seen any sense in the bizarre concept of patriotism, but wholly identify with the widely-held view that Germans continue to build the best motor cars.

I once spent the day with the late Ian Taylor, a talented racing driver, who was tragically killed in a race at Spa. Ian lived for fast road and racing cars, and had driven many hundreds in his relatively short life, but considered the 525i BMW to be the best all-rounder he'd ever experienced. I asked him for his reasons. He replied, simply, 'Because that's the way it is.'

Ian was right, but the Munich company's huge success in recent years did not arrive by luck or accident. For many years Rolls-Royce marketed their cars as 'The Best in the World'. Those who have driven Stuttgart and Munich's finest appreciate that Rolls-Royce's tag was little more than a slogan. Ironically, the company who

genuinely make some of the world's best cars now own the British concern that once laid claim to this title.

BMW's dominant position today began roughly in the mid-1970s, and rode on the back of its good fortune in track racing. Journalists on both sides of the Atlantic had been extremely complimentary about the company's wonderful sporting saloons long before this time, of course, but the advent of the 3 and 7 Series cars, the introduction of the 6 Series and update, through successive marks, of the 5 Series, resulted in BMW production spiralling ever upwards. And expert motoring journalists continued to reach for ever more descriptive superlatives in an attempt to convey their increasing enthusiasm for the marque.

During the course of researching this book, I listened to the comments of several car enthusiasts, who willingly gave their views about BMW's products. By and large, BMW owners all agreed that their cars are aesthetically pleasing, extremely reliable and durable, wonderful to drive and endowed with excellent performance.

Some people I spoke to, on the other hand, expressed loathing for BMWs, despite having never driven one. They commented that BMWs are nasty aggressive cars, owned by nasty aggressive people. To support their theories, they cited sketchy anecdotal evidence such as having once been overtaken by a chap behind the wheel of a 5 Series in something of a hurry. Despite my considerable efforts, I never discovered their real motives for expressing such ridiculous opinions.

It was, however, genuinely interesting talking to my dear old pal, Nigel Phillips, a traffic policeman who, for many years, drove BMWs as 'company cars'. He considered the 528i to be an ideal pursuit vehicle, whether on a motorway, or on the twisty roads of rural Herefordshire and Shropshire. Nigel's view, that the car's performance, superb handling and sybaritic levels of comfort were without

Left: **In 1940, BMW won the Mille Miglia with a 328 similar to this example. It was the first of BMW's truly great international competition victories. In more recent times there has been huge success in motor sport at all levels, including outright victory at Le Mans in 1999.**

Below: **The author during a test session with one of his favourite BMWs, the classic 3.0CS (this example is a 1974 model); but it was the demise of this, and its closely related but less exotic sisters, that ushered in a wholly new era for BMW.**

BMW E Numbers

3 Series
E21	3 Series 1975–1982
E30	3 Series from 1983
E30/5	3 Series Touring
E30/16	Four-wheel drive 3 Series
E36	3 Series from 1991
E36/2	3 Series Coupé
E36/5	3 Series Compact (from 1994)
E36/3	3 Series Touring from 1995
E46	3 Series from 1998

5 Series
E12	5 Series from 1972
E28	5 Series from 1981
E34	5 Series from 1988
E34/16	Four-wheel drive 5 Series
E39	5 Series from 1996

6 Series
E24	6 Series Coupé 1976–1989

7 Series
E23	7 Series from 1977
E32	7 Series from 1987
E32/2	Long-wheelbase version
E38	7 Series from 1994

8 Series
E31	8 Series Coupé 1990–2000

Z sports cars
Z1	1989–1991
Z3	`1996 on

BMW Engine codes

Code	Cylinders	Capacity	Valves
M10	4	1.6, 1.8, 2.0	8
M40	4	1.6, 1.8	8
M42	4	1.8	16
S14	4	2.0, 2.3, 2.5	16
M43	4	1.8	8
M44	4	1.8	16
M41	4	1.7 diesel	8
M20	6	2.0, 2.3, 2.5, 2.7	12
M30	6	2.5, 2.8, 3.0, 3.2, 3.4, 3.5	12
M50	6	2.0, 2.5	24
M70	6	3.0	24
S36	6	3.6	24
S38	6	3.8	24
M88	6	3.5	24
M52	6	2.0, 2.5, 2.8	24
S50/B32	6	2.9 (E36 M3)	24
S50/B30	6	3.2 (E36 M3)	24
M21	6	2.4 diesel	12
M51	6	2.5 diesel	12
M57	6	3.0	24
M60	8	3.0, 4.0	32
M62	8	3.5, 4.0, 4.4	32
M73	12	5.4	24
S70	12	5.6	24
S70/2	12	6.1	48

One of the most successful of BMW's production models in modern times, the 3 Series continues to form the centre of attention among club enthusiasts throughout the world. Through several generations the cars have been modified and improved, but the sophistication of the newer cars in no way detracts from the greatness of the originals.

rival, intrigued me because his daily drive is a Mercedes-Benz.

Also during my research I spoke to a number of mechanics whose jobs involve working on many different makes of cars. On the whole they preferred Vauxhalls and Rovers to BMWs. It appears that the two British makes provide them with employment; BMWs, generally, do not!

I also sought views from my two small daughters, Lucy and Anna, about an aged but well-maintained BMW 520i that I considered buying. They looked around it, sat in the rear seats for a few minutes and, after a long silence, condemned the car as 'utterly horrible'. Neither could warm to its white paintwork, the small 'ding' in the passenger door or 'silly seats'. It was clear that they didn't approve, and I gave thanks for BMW's sake that my offspring are not members of my profession. Happily, they do approve of my 525i.

It appears that few folks with an interest in motoring are indifferent to all things BMW. You either love them or loathe them, For the former, owning a BMW is to belong to a large international 'club'. In the same way that some folks must have a Churchill 12-bore shotgun, Mont Blanc fountain pen, Rolex wristwatch, Nikon camera, or Porsche tobacco pipe, some just have to have a BMW.

In the text that follows, I have tried to convey my enthusiasm for these truly great cars. Some of my comments contain natural dollops of prejudice; I haven't spent more than 40 years of my life with cars without forming heavily biased opinions. I make no apologies for this, but hope that readers will forgive such personal indulgence.

Laurence Meredith
2001

CHAPTER ONE

BMW 3 Series

Four and Six for Three

By the mid-1970s a number of European car manufacturers were beginning to recover from the aftershocks of the politically-engineered Middle East oil crisis of 1973. The world's first production turbocharged car, the BMW 2002 turbo, was among the victims of the crisis. A fuel-thirsty sporting saloon, launched at a time when there was widespread petrol rationing in Europe, the 2002 turbo was axed from the range after the production of just 1,672 examples.

At motor racing meetings in Britain, the car parks and paddocks were almost devoid of exotic road cars and even the well-heeled were feeling the pinch. Germany's most prolific car-

maker, Volkswagen, whose huge success had been largely based on the Beetle, was on the brink of a complete change in direction.

The Beetle had had its day. Falling sales, particularly in the United States, had caused visible nervousness among members of Volkswagen's board. A new range of cars launched piecemeal from 1974, with water-cooled engines driving the front wheels, had to succeed. The alternative was unthinkable. Happily for Volkswagen, the Scirocco, Polo, Passat and Golf were immensely successful.

At the same time, Porsche launched new models that also represented a change in direction. Some senior people within the Zuffenhausen concern considered that the rear-engined 911 was becoming long in the

Production of the pretty E21 3 Series began in May 1975 in the aftermath of the 1973 Middle East oil crisis. A direct replacement for the highly acclaimed '02, the new car was well received and hailed as being superior to its predecessor.

BMW made much of the indisputable fact that the 3 Series (left) was engineered to the same quality and standards as the big, luxury 7 Series (right), launched at approximately the same time.

tooth. Despite Ferry Porsche's misgivings, the company launched the front-engined 924 and 928, and the classic rear-engined 911 went, temporarily, into decline.

While Volkswagen's board members were praying that their decision to pension off the Beetle was correct, their opposite numbers at British Leyland were in a state of almost total despair, as were the people they employed. This once respected company was engaged in what amounted to almost a feudal class war. Industrial disputes and strikes occurred on a daily basis, and car production became haphazard.

British Leyland's range of cars had become something of a sad joke; badly made, unreliable and horribly out of date. Despite huge government subsidies the company was in a state of abject decay. The foreign markets for British Leyland cars had almost completely dried up, and European car manufacturers, including BMW, made handsome capital as a result.

Volkswagen's first chief executive, Heinz Nordhoff, had once regarded British car makers as the principal competition for the products of his own company. By the mid-1970s the threat of competition from Britain had almost ceased to exist.

Beyond the obvious difference in quality between German and British cars, a new social phenomenon had been overlooked by economists in the employ of companies like British Leyland. Radical change during the 1960s had by the 1970s led to rapid expansion of the middle classes. Growing affluence among this group, in conjunction with the increase in access to financial credit facilities, created a situation whereby inexpensive, austere cars such as the Mini, for example, were no longer in demand.

By and large, western society had grown richer, and the market for plush, stylish performance cars increased dramatically. BMW were no strangers to this market, of course. Their mid-range passenger saloons had been aimed squarely at the affluent right from 1962 when production of the 1500 model got into full swing.

From the mid-1970s onwards, car makers capitalized on growing middle-class affluence, and pushed their products increasingly 'up-market'. BMW, Volkswagen, Daimler-Benz and Porsche invested heavily in broadening their customer base, and reported year-on-year increases in profits. French and Italian car manufacturers did much the same, while Saab and Volvo in Sweden continued with their solid, dependable conveyances.

By contrast, in Britain where the famous names of Triumph, Wolseley, Morris, Austin and Riley had ruled the roost for so long, a new tide swept through the country to set a future trend. By the 1990s the best of the cars manufactured in Britain were badged as Nissans, Hondas and Toyotas, while BMW's involvement with the Rover Group from the mid-1990s would end in tears for both parties.

Safe Conviction

On 2 May 1975, BMW began production of the first E21 3 Series cars. The '02 models they replaced had enjoyed an enthusiastic following for many years and the new cars would have to be good if established customers were to be impressed.

However, if BMW's engineers and marketing people had harboured reservations about the new car, they needn't have worried. By any standards it was an unmitigated success right from the start. Owners loved the car, and journalists raved about it.

316 (1975–80)

Body style	Two-door saloon: Baur cabriolet (1977–80)
Engine	
Cylinders	4
Bore × stroke	84 × 71mm
Capacity	1,563cc
Timing	Chain-driven overhead camshaft
Compression ratio	8.3:1
Carburettor	Solex 32/32 DIDTA
Max power	90bhp at 6,000rpm
Max torque	90lb ft at 4,000rpm
Transmission	
Gearbox	4-speed manual
Ratios	First 3.764
	Second 2.022
	Third 1.320
	Fourth 1.00
	Final drive 4.10
Suspension and steering	
Front	MacPherson struts, coil springs and anti-roll bar
Rear	Semi-trailing arms, coil springs and anti-roll bar
Steering	Rack and pinion
Wheels	Pressed steel 5J×13
Tyres	165SR 13 radials
Brakes	Servo assisted discs/drums
Dimensions	
Track	(front) 1,364mm/53.7in
	(rear) 1,377mm/54.2in
Wheelbase	2,563mm/100.9in
Overall length	4,355mm/171.5in
Overall width	1,610mm/63.4in
Overall height	1,380mm/54.3mm

Of the 320i (of which more later), *Car & Driver's* 1976 report commented:

The 300-series BMWs have a great deal to live up to. The 1600/2000 series enjoyed amazing success over a decade or so, and were in many ways the cornerstone of BMW's new-found pre-eminence in the upper atmosphere of enthusiast automobiles. The new cars seem to be worthy successors to that critical responsibility. They are undeniably better and more contemporary cars in every way. All of the basic pieces are recognizable to anyone familiar with the older car, but they've all been reshaped, honed and upgraded, then assembled in more sophisticated ways.

Car & Driver forcefully concluded:

This car is good-looking, sublimely comfortable, fast, safe, economical and exciting. It is also expensive, but then what isn't? To drive through any major city in North America and check its inventory of Mercedes, Jags, BMWs, Porsches, Cadillacs and Lincolns is to come face to face with the fact that there is apparently no top on the market for truly expensive cars anymore. The BMW 320i is real value-for-money, no matter how much it costs, because it's beautifully engineered and it's not boring. If that isn't reason enough to buy a car, then we'll transfer our allegiance to mass transit.

North America was, and remains, BMW's most important export market, but initially the only model available there was the 320i 4-cylinder car. On the other hand, choice in British and European markets included the 1,573cc 316, 1,766cc 318 and 1,990cc 320, all of which had 4-cylinder engines at first.

Understandably, Americans felt hard done by, especially as their 2-litre cars were not as powerful as their European counterparts. While the European-spec 2-litre car developed a healthy 125bhp at 5,800rpm, American-spec vehicles, strangled by

With its impact-absorbing safety cell, and deformable front and rear ends, the 3 Series was one of the safest passenger saloons of the mid-1970s, but this didn't prevent people from keeping the car-insurance industry on its toes. This burnt-out wreck is 'probably' beyond economic repair.

A conservatively styled three-box saloon but, with BMW's traditional hallmarks, the original 3 Series (illustrated here in 323i guise) doubled as family transport and a sports car.

And its fuel economy – 21.5mpg in our usual mileage course – is quite respectable.

Like so many, *Road & Track*'s staff failed to find beauty in the aesthetics of the 3 Series, but liked its 'basic lines', describing it as a 'clean, industrial design'. This respected magazine concluded that the designers of the new car had retained the 2002's basic character, but had made genuine improvements in key areas.

Road & Track wound up with the following:

Everything considered, the 320i is a keen sports sedan. It retains all the beloved features of the 2002 and improves on what needed improving. The price is high, but these days it's difficult if not impossible to find a car with all the 320i's attributes – excellent roadholding, compliant suspension, powerful brakes, precise steering, responsive engine and rattlefree body – for less money. It's no wonder BMWs are some of our favorite cars.

The idea that BMWs were expensive was an oft-repeated theme in magazine articles in the many years ahead, but BMW operated in a 'quality' market and were never prepared to cut corners in production. This general policy paid dividends, as sales figures for the 3 Series spiralled upwards within a short period of the car's debut despite tough competition from rival manufacturers.

exhaust-emissions equipment, pushed out 110bhp, or 105bhp in cars sold in the Californian market.

Some 200lb heavier than the 2002, the American-spec 320i was slower than its predecessor. Of this *Road & Track* commented:

Up to around 5,000rpm the engine retains much of its previous character – rather noisy but mechanically smooth and virile sounding – but it approaches its 6,400rpm redline rather unenthusiastically.

This report's writer sounded downbeat, but continued on a more optimistic note. He wrote:

Still, the 320i got to 60mph in 12 secs and covered the quarter mile in 18.7secs, and for a 2-litre car weighing 2605lb that's anything but slow.

Cracking Shell

In keeping with the '02 models, the 3 Series retained a steel 'three-box' bodyshell, naturally of modern unitary construction, with two doors. Particular attention was paid to the body's torsional rigidity, and in this respect it was improved by nearly 20 per cent over the outgoing 2002. Largely to increase rear legroom, the wheelbase was 2.5in longer, but this change also led to welcome improvements in roadholding.

Strong styling features included large circular headlamps (dual headlamps on the later 6-cylinder cars), a large glass area with the familiar 'dogleg' piece in the rear side windows, a kidney radiator grille and fluted bonnet.

The flanks were divided by prominent swage lines, and the rear was distinguished by rectangular lamps with a stylish matt black strip between them. Externally, American-spec cars were instantly recognizable by their extended bumpers, designed to absorb greater impacts at parking speeds. BMW roundels were placed on the front of the bonnet and rear bootlid.

Overall, the styling was entirely conventional but with Paul Bracq's usual touches of flair. The pressed steel wheels, for example, were designed to look like expensive alloys, a feature that added to the overall sporting look.

Primary safety was also dialled into the bodyshell, with a rigid passenger cell, deformable front and rear sections, and a bonnet designed to crumple in the middle, instead of heading through the windscreen, in the event of an accident. Regrettably, road accidents are an inevitable by-product of motoring but thanks largely to the work of Bela Barenyi for Daimler-Benz in the 1950s and 1960s, modern German cars are about as safe as they can be.

As is well known, BMWs are among the world's safest cars, and anecdotes about their drivers and passengers walking away from monumental accidents are almost legendary. My favourite concerns a couple of British policemen, whose 5 Series left the road at well over 100mph. The car travelled end-over-end several times before crashing into two trees. The BMW's bodyshell was rendered completely useless for further use, every panel having been severely bent, but the two occupants opened the doors and got out without so much as a scratch. Theirs was not a 'lucky' escape; all BMWs are built to withstand heavy, high-speed impacts.

The Interior

The cabin of the 3 Series was fundamentally designed for people who enjoy the experience of sitting behind a sports steering wheel, and booting seven bells out of a performance engine. Naturally, the adjustable seats were firmly padded in traditional German fashion, and gave excellent lateral support for thighs and back.

Writing in *Motor Sport*, January 1976, Clive Richardson commented:

> This new 320 proved one of those cars in which we felt immediately at home before we so much as started the engine.

> That facia is curved so that everything is equidistant to the eyes and within easy reach. The big speedometer, tachometer and smaller auxiliary instruments are ahead of the driver, the four separate quadrant heater/ventilation controls, rotary switch for the heater fan, cigarette lighter and quartz clock curve round to the driver's left.

Richardson went on to remark on the dazzle-free surfaces, orange, aircraft-like instrument illumination, clearly labelled controls and

Twin headlamps, 'kidney' grille and fluted bonnet were strong BMW design features carried over from the '02 series. Note that the chin spoiler on this 323i is of extremely modest proportions by comparison with its modern counterpart.

318 (1975–80)

Body style	Two-door saloon
Engine	
Cylinders	4
Bore × stroke	89 × 71mm
Capacity	1,754cc
Timing	Chain-driven overhead camshaft
Compression ratio	8.3:1
Carburettor	32/32 DIDTA
Max power	98bhp at 5,800rpm
Max torque	105lb ft at 4,000rpm
Transmission	Identical to 316 but with 3.90 final-drive ratio

Suspension, steering, brakes
and dimensions all identical to 316

efficiency of the heating and ventilation systems, but reserved criticism for the pedal layout. He wrote:

> The Germans have tried so hard to please we 'heel-and-toers' that the organ throttle pedal is a shade too close to the brake pedal.

Interestingly, this was *Motor Sport's* only criticism of the whole car, which was surprising for a magazine with a reputation for not pulling its punches in road tests.

Car & Driver was even more complimentary and remarked:

> Open the door, and the vinyl interior is just about perfect. Ours was what the British used to call 'biscuit', and the seats were – like the first exterior impression – an open invitation to drive somewhere very nice very quickly. The white-on-black instruments were neatly clustered in a semicircle framed by the top half of the steering wheel, right where the driver can see them, and at night they're indirectly illuminated by a red glow that reminds you of war movies shot in submarines.

The orange instrument illumination was something new in the motor industry, and became a talking point among BMW enthusiasts at this time. It was a sensible, practical and aesthetically pleasing piece of design that set BMWs away from the common herd. And, as usual, the herd would eventually catch up, only to find that BMW had moved on.

Car & Driver, incidentally, went on to describe the four-spoke steering wheel, with a BMW roundel in the central boss, as 'a thing of beauty', and praised it lavishly for its small diameter and for being 'raked at exactly the correct angle for serious pleasure'. The steering wheel was really quite pleasant in use, except for the horn buttons (one in each spoke) which could be difficult to locate in an emergency.

On the whole the interior was a model of spaciousness and comfort, with an aura of sportiness appreciated by those who could not warm to the Ford or Opel way of doing things. This author's personal criticism is reserved for the gear knob which, although perfectly good to use, is among the dullest and unimaginatively designed objects ever to emerge from the German car industry. As if to rub salt in the wounds, BMW produced a similarly dull knob for the second generation 3 Series.

Undercarriage and All

Springing had become entirely conventional by the mid-1970s. Independent all round, of course, with ubiquitous MacPherson struts, coil springs and anti-roll bar up front, and semi-trailing arms, coil springs and anti-roll bar at the rear.

Many drivers became wary, and even nervous, of the characteristics of the rear semi-trailing arm suspension as it was susceptible to sudden camber changes, which could result in the tail breaking away. This 'feature' can be viewed in two opposing ways but in the hands of the inexperienced or untalented, it was perceived as being potentially 'dangerous'.

For skilled, enthusiastic drivers, however, it was an inherent characteristic of a sporting car. Seasoned campaigners, brought up on conventional rear-wheel drive cars, revelled in the delights of opposite-lock motoring, the judicious application of which was essential in controlling the rear end during exuberant, fun driving.

Those who considered 'power-sliding', in other words controlling the attitude of a car in a corner by steering on the throttle, to be undesirable or dangerous, became vociferous proponents of front-wheel drive. There is no technical merit in front-wheel drive, which is just one reason why all BMWs have been driven by their rear wheels.

Of the car's drivability, *Road & Track* commented:

A responsive engine, crisp gearbox, well thought out controls and comfortable seats are just part of what makes all BMWs real drivers' machines. Driving characteristics – how it handles, steers, brakes and rides – are all of primary concern and in these areas, too, the 320i excels. Handling is typically BMW. There's neutral response until the car is pressed hard, then mild final oversteer associated with its semi-trailing arm independent rear suspension. In tight bends, the BMW lifts its inside rear wheel, effectively limiting cornering speeds.

To negate, or minimise, this tendency, BMW made a limited-slip differential available at extra cost.

Motor Sport noted that the 320's suspension was 'softer' and had greater wheel travel than the 2002's, but maintained that it was 'a beautifully balanced car'. Clive Richardson also remarked:

Traction is much improved over the 2002, especially when powering out of tight bends, although too much power on some greasy London roads had the test car's 165SRx13 Michelin ZX-shod, 5J wheels spinning and the tail twitching rather easily.

Which is exactly how a proper car should behave in such circumstances.

Steering was by ZF rack and pinion, which

---

320 (1975–77)

Body style	Two-door saloon
Engine	
Cylinders	4
Bore × stroke	89 × 80mm
Capacity	1,990cc
Timing	Chain-driven overhead camshaft
Compression ratio	8.1:1
Carburettor	Solex 32/32 DIDTA
Max power	109bhp at 5,800rpm
Max torque	116lb ft at 3,700rpm

Transmission, suspension, steering and brakes
Identical to 316

replaced the 2002's worm and roller, and it was this change that, arguably above all else, made the new 3 Series feel a better car to drive than its predecessor when driving at virtually any speed. Sensibly geared, the revised system gave precise control and quick action for a car in this class.

Braking was also improved over the 2002. The diameter of the front discs was increased from 9.45in to 10.04in, and the rear drums were also enlarged in diameter from 9.06in to 9.84in. At the same time, the Mastervac servo was also increased in size from 6in to 8in. Of the brakes *Motor Sport* commented:

> They are powerful and survived a rapid descent of Mont Ventoux without overmuch fade – though smoking more like Vesuvius – when we tried another 320 during the BMW press introduction some months ago.

Road & Track's tester was a little more enthusiastic and commented:

> These 70-profile radials with asymmetric tread not only impart a silky smooth ride to the 320i but the

Attractive cross-spoke alloys (extra-cost options in most markets) set a trend that continues to this day, and although difficult to keep clean...

tires' adhesion in cornering and braking on dry or damp pavement is little short of incredible.

Braking was, of course, one facet of car design that had improved out of all recognition in mid-range passenger saloons during the 1970s. Their progressive efficiency was as much to do with the fitting of radial tyres, the vagaries of old-fashioned cross-plies having been virtually banished for good.

A Bright Source of Power

During the 1960s many manufacturers of dull, stolid and mundane saloon cars, attempted to bring a degree of 'performance glamour' to their products in a variety of bizarre ways. A second carburettor was among the more useful additions, but 'GT' badging, go-faster stripes, 'tuned' exhaust systems and aluminium wheel trims, impressive as they were to some, did not actually enhance the performance of a 'lumpy' 4-cylinder engine found under the dreary bonnet.

Supercharging had long since gone out of fashion, BMW had yet to 'rediscover' the benefits (and several detriments) of turbocharging, and the general car-buying public endured the crudeness of their mass-produced, mostly cast-iron, engines, for the simple reason that they knew no better.

Those who sampled BMW's 4-cylinder cars during this period could scarcely believe the difference between the engines that propelled other mundane cars and the engines assembled in Munich. BMW's long tradition of designing and building technically advanced and powerful engines began in the 1930s, and continues to this day. When, for example, the South African designer Gordon Murray was given the brief to pen the McLaren F1 super-car of the 1990s, he plumped for BMW's mighty V12 to propel it. There was no other power unit in production that gave as much in bhp per litre; McLaren's outright victory in the 1995 Le Mans 24 Hours admirably demonstrated that his choice was correct.

For the E21 3 Series BMW devised two engine variants, namely, the M10 4-cylinders and M60 'sixes'. The 4-cylinder units, of 1,573cc (90bhp), 1,766cc (98bhp) and 1,990cc (109bhp), were used in the 316, 318 and 320 models respectively, while the 6-cylinder engines were available in the 320 and 323i with capacities of 1,991cc (122bhp) and 2,315cc (143bhp).

All engines followed established BMW practice in being constructed with a cast-iron cylinder block and aluminium-alloy cylinder head. A single-overhead camshaft, driven by a Duplex roller chain, was common to all units. Following the practice adopted by Mercedes-Benz during the 1950s for the 300SL 'Gullwing', the E21's engine was canted over at an angle of 30 degrees to allow for a low bonnet line.

...the latest multi-spokers fitted to the 2001 M3, while being wickedly attractive, are little better in this respect.

320i (1975–77) and US version (1976–80)

Body style	Two-door saloon
Engine	
Cylinders	4
Bore × stroke	89 × 80mm
Capacity	1,990cc
Timing	Chain-driven overhead camshaft
Compression ratio	9.3:1
Fuel injection	Bosch K-Jetronic
Max power	125bhp at 5,700rpm
Max torque	126lb ft at 4,350rpm
Transmission	Identical to 320, except for 3.64:1 final-drive ratio
Suspension, brakes and steering	
Identical to 320	
Wheels	Pressed steel 5.5J×13, or alloys at extra cost
Tyres	185/70HR 13 radials
Dimensions	
Track	(front) 1,348mm/54.6in
	(rear) 1,399mm/55.1in
Wheelbase	2,563mm/100.9in
Overall length	4,355mm/100.9in
Overall width	1,610mm/63.4in
Overall height	1,380mm/54.3in

316 (1980–82)

Body style	Two-door saloon and Baur cabriolet

Engine

Cylinders	4
Bore × stroke	89 × 71mm
Capacity	1,766cc
Timing	Chain-driven overhead camshaft
Compression ratio	9.5:1
Carburettor	Pierburg 2B4
Max power	90bhp at 5,500rpm
Max torque	101lb ft at 4,000rpm

Transmission

Gearbox	Synchromesh 4- or 5-speed manual

Ratios

	4-speed	5-speed
First	3.764	3.764
Second	2.043	2.325
Third	1.320	1.612
Fourth	1.000	1.229
Fifth		1.000
Final drive	3.91	3.91

Suspension and steering

Front	MacPherson struts, coil springs and anti-roll bar
Rear	Semi-trailing arms and coil springs
Steering	Rack and pinion
Wheels	Pressed steel 5J×13 or 5.5J×13

Brakes

	Servo-assisted discs/drums

Dimensions

Track	(front) 1,366mm/53.8in
	(rear) 1,373mm/54in
Wheelbase	2,563mm/100.9in
Overall length	4,355mm/171.5in
Overall width	1,610mm/63.4in
Overall height	1,380mm/54.3in

Twin-choke Solex carburettors were normal wear, initially, on the 4-cylinder models (Bosch fuel injection systems were fitted to the later cars) while the 320i and 323i were given fuel injection from the off. The 320 4-cylinder car is, however, not to be confused with the 6-cylinder 320 carburettor car or later 6-cylinder fuel-injected 320i.

The universal adoption of fuel injection was an inevitable response to meeting increasingly stringent laws governing exhaust emissions, particularly in North America,

and to improving performance and fuel consumption.

By contrast, the introduction of the 'small-block' 6-cylinder engines was one way in which BMW could boast a real advantage over competitors in this class sector. Although small-capacity 'sixes' were fairly common during the 1930s, the wholesale adoption of mass-production across the motor industry in the 1950s saw their popularity wane. Triumph enjoyed notable success in the 1960s with its 6-cylinder Vitesse and 2000 models but, generally, 6-, 8- and 12-cylinder engines were reserved for powerful and expensive cars which were well beyond the financial reach of the average car buyer.

BMW began work on the small-block 'sixes' as early as 1971, as their large-capacity 6-cylinder engines, employed in the big coupés and saloons from 1968, were too large to fit under the bonnets of the 3 Series. Both the 2-litre version (320) and 2.3-litre (323i) made their public debut in 1977, the former with a Solex carburettor, and the more powerful car with Bosch K-Jetronic fuel injection.

Both variants were powerful and inherently smooth. With 122bhp the 2-litre car was easily capable of nearly 115mph, while the 323i's 143bhp gave a top speed of 120mph. On the face of it, Volkswagen's contemporary 1.6-litre Golf GTi, with a top speed of 112mph, appeared to offer better value for money. Many argued that the hatchback body of the Golf was an advantage but since it was also endowed with the vagaries of front-wheel drive, motoring purists kept faith with the rear-wheel drive cars from BMW.

By comparison, Saab's 145bhp 2-litre 99 Turbo gave 0–60mph acceleration in 9secs, and was capable of just over 120mph. An impressive car by any standards, journalists loved the Swedish performance saloon, but reserved judgement about its high fuel consumption (20mpg was normal) and turbo lag. On the limit the Saab was also prone to understeer, and torquesteer and wheelspin under brisk acceleration. Well built, safe, beautifully engineered and comfortable, the Saab enjoyed a loyal and enthusiastic following, but the Swedish company's adherence to a limited model range, coupled with its reduced involvement in motor sport, eventually led to a sell-out to General Motors in the 1990s.

The 6-cylinder E21s were priced in the roughly the same bracket as cars such as the Saab Turbo, but BMW's competitors were almost exclusively fitted with 4-cylinder engines, including the recently launched Porsche 924. There was no getting away from

Left: **A model of ergonomic comfort, the leather seats of Matthew Hammond's car have nicely creased with age and use, but retain firmness and support despite having been in use for more than 180,000 miles.**

Below: **Universally acknowledged as the smoothest in-line 6-cylinder engine, this lusty power unit is buried under the complexities of fuel-injection equipment and aesthetically dull pipework.**

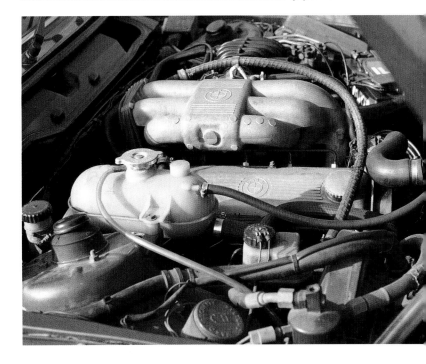

318i (1980–82)

Body style	Two-door saloon and Baur cabriolet

Engine

Cylinders	4
Bore × stroke	89 × 71mm
Capacity	1,754cc
Timing	Chain-driven overhead camshaft
Compression ratio	10:1
Fuel injection	Bosch Jetronic
Max power	105bhp at 5,800rpm
Max torque	105lb ft at 4,500rpm

Transmission
Standard 4-speed manual, plus optional 5-speed manual,
5-speed close-ratio manual or 3-speed automatic

Suspension, steering, brakes and dimensions
Identical to 316

---

the superior smoothness and vibration-free balance of the BMW 'six', and enthusiasts openly revelled in the performance and torque of these beautifully built cars.

Motor Sport's Clive Richardson, however, held reservations about the 323i, describing the gear ratios as 'adequate' and the engine as having 'less bite than I would expect from 143bhp'. He enjoyed the car's capacity to cruise comfortably at 100mph and above and the precision gear change, but was less enamoured by the 'fussy, threshing noise, apparently from the belt-driven overhead valve gear, more magnified than in the 320 six'.

With a basic purchase price of £6,249, rising to £8,000 with the inclusion of air-conditioning, electric windows and alloy wheels and so on, *Motor Sport's* 1978 report concluded that, good as the 323i undoubtedly was, £8,000 could buy 'a lot better value alternative'.

For the North American market, BMW launched a 320i in 1980 but, unlike its European counterpart, it was fitted with the fuel-injected 2-litre engine and later with the 1.8-litre unit, despite retaining its 320i appellation. With Bosch Jetronic fuel injection, compression ratio of 8.8:1 and catalytic converter, the 1.8-litre 320i developed 101bhp. Because

the 'cat' did away with the need for the exhaust gas recirculation device and air injection system of its 2-litre predecessor, the 1.8-litre car was quicker than the model it replaced, performing relatively briskly to a top speed of 110mph.

Motorists in both Canada and the US by this time were filling up with a compulsory diet of unleaded fuel and the catalytic converters demanded by legislation sapped engine power. At the same time, with a huge increase in car use in the latter quarter of the twentieth century, opportunities for high-speed road travel have diminished. In response, more and more BMW owners are joining specialist clubs in order to enjoy their machines on racing circuits, where the only restrictions on speed are the bravery and skill of the individual driver.

Stirring Stuff

Transmission experts Getrag were once again commissioned to produce gearboxes for the 3 Series, the 4-cylinder cars being fitted with a 4-speed manual, synchromesh unit from the start. The 320 6-cylinder car also had a 4-speed gearbox until 1981.

With the debut of the 323i in 1978, a 5-speed manual became available in 'standard' mode or optional close-ratio 'Sport' guise. Both types were also available at extra cost on the 320 from 1979. Down several years of development, the ratios were altered to suit both the demands of economy and performance, a point picked up by Motor Sport in its test of a 320 in 1976. The magazine remarked:

By lowering the final-drive ratio from 3.64 to 1 to 3.9 to 1 and adding 9bhp, BMW have put back the performance which an extra 2cwt over the 2002 would have lost. Indeed, this gearing makes the 320 more responsive and flexible around town, but for motorway work we would have preferred the old ratio or an overdrive 5th gear. It cruises comfortably enough, though leaving one aware that it is revving fairly hard for its living. This low gearing – abetted perhaps by carburation which was off song, displaying some hesitancy – no doubt contributed

to the disappointing fuel consumption of 21 mpg around town and a little over 23mpg during fast motorway and main road work, vastly inferior to the 2002.

In addition to the manual gearboxes, the range was optionally available with a 3-speed ZF automatic, which was notable for its smoothness in operation and the ugliness of its shift lever. The latter operated in a 'gate', which also had little aesthetic appeal, but automatics had their place, of course, and particularly found favour among customers in America.

Postage and Packing

In launching the 3 Series cars, BMW were quietly confident that they had got their sums right. The model range was extensive, with broad appeal, and built to the same high standards as the more exotic BMWs. With the

---

320 (1977–82)

Body style	Two-door saloon and Baur cabriolet

Engine
Cylinders	6
Bore × stroke	80 × 66mm
Capacity	1,990cc
Timing	Belt-driven overhead camshaft
Compression ratio	9.2:1
Carburettor	Solex 4A1
Max power	122bhp at 6,000rpm
Max torque	118lb ft at 4,000rpm

Transmission
4-speed manual or 3-speed automatic, 5-speed manual or 5-speed close-ratio manual

Suspension, steering, brakes wheels and tyres Identical to 316

Dimensions
Track	(front) 1,386mm/54.6in
	(rear) 1,399mm/55.1in
Wheelbase	2,563mm/100.9in
Overall length	4,355mm/171.5in
Overall width	1,610mm/63.4in
Overall height	1,380mm/54.3in

Circular instruments are shrouded by a 'humped' binnacle with the centre console angled towards the driver. The wood-rimmed Italian Momo steering wheel and alloy gear knob are modern, non-original additions.

debut of the Baur-bodied cabriolet, complete with its distinctive roll-hoop, the appeal of the range was extended further.

No-one considered these cars to be cheap – just the opposite – but there was no doubting that quality of this kind had to be paid for. Indeed, Clive Richardson, writing in *Motor Sport* commented on this very point. He wrote:

> In general there is no mistaking the 320 for a BMW: that feel of tautness, the aura of quality, a train-like sensation of dependability, attention to detail such as the Jensen-like automatic delay on the interior courtesy light. Added to that, this new model is comfortable, relaxing and quite extraordinarily easy and enjoyable to drive. BMW Concessionaires GB, in the past so heavily criticised for over-pricing their range, could almost be accused of charity, pricing the 320 at £3,349.

In true German tradition, the entire range was supplied in its basic, 'raw' form. Luxuries were cited as extra-cost options, a facet of BMW marketing strategy that had also long prevailed at Volkswagen, Mercedes-Benz and Porsche. A radio could be supplied and fitted by BMW, but this was never included in the list price.

For the well-heeled who wanted 'extras' there were Recaro sports seats, attractive Mahle alloy wheels, stiffer road springs and dampers, a sunroof, leather upholstery and tinted window glass. And, as always, specialist tuning companies were always willing to provide a whole lot more – at a price.

From its launch in 1975 until the end of E21 production in 1983, BMW produced more than 1.3 million variants on the 3 Series theme. Throughout its production life, sales increased rapidly year on year, reaching a high of nearly 229,000 in 1981. The lowest production figure occurred in 1983, when fewer than 34,000 cars were built, which was an inevitable response to the announcement of the car's replacement with the 'Mk2' version.

Although BMWs were mass-produced the production figures are extremely low by comparsion with those of contemporary 'mainstream' manufacturers, such as Ford, Volkswagen and Opel. This, naturally, gave BMW owners a feeling of owning fairly exclusive cars, even if this was a perception rather than reality.

Ironically, the launch of the 3 Series, more or less coincided with the advent of the classic car movement, the seeds of which were largely sewn in Britain. In the many years that have passed since, motoring connoisseurs have come to regard the 323i, in particular, as a classic design. Super performance, fine handling, precise steering, and a pleasing two-door body were part of a well-honed package that influenced a generation of sporting drivers.

The influence of the 3 Series, however, went well beyond satisfying the whims of middle class 'hooligans'. In response to the BMW's success, Daimler-Benz was moved to introduce a 'baby' to its range in the form of the 190 saloon, a surprising move for a company that, for so long, had specialised in luxury saloons and sports cars.

The 323i: Owner's View

When Matthew Hammond acquired his now pristine 1979 323i in 1996, it was something of a smoking gun, having worked hard for its living in the hands of a previous owner, a professional photographer called Richard Hammonds.

A busy chap, always in a hurry, Richard Hammonds would boot his BMW from pillar to post every day of the week and after acquiring a 628i, he passed the 323i on to its present custodian, who immediately began the unenviable task of repairing the wear and tear that it had inevitably acquired in more than 180,000 miles of hard use.

Restoration work included the replacement of the doors, wheel arches, and front and rear lids, and a complete respray. Mechanical work was confined to 'skimming' the cylinder head, fitting a new clutch and a major service. Apart from the smart wood-rimmed Momo steering wheel and stainless steel gear knob, the car is in original condition, and drives almost as well as the day it was made.

His first BMW, indeed his first car, Matthew Hammond was initially attracted to the 323i by its looks but, in five years of ownership, has come to appreciate its many other qualities.

I appreciate it more and more as the years go by. It's fast, solidly built and really nice to drive, but a little heavy on petrol by comparison with modern cars, if you boot it hard. The tail-end has a tendency to be skittish in wet weather, but you soon get used to catching it, and even enjoy it when you realise that this is just part of the car's character.

Fitted with nicely creased leather seats, which have stood the test of time particularly well, the interior is comfortable, and both looks and feels exactly how a sporting saloon should be. Even Matthew's grandmother, who travels in the car on a frequent basis, approves of its comfort and acceleration.

From time to time minor components, fatigued by old age and use, inevitably need to be replaced. For example, Matthew recently needed to buy a small plastic valve for the heating system.

I was surprised that such a small plastic component cost as much as £40 from my local BMW dealer. On the other hand some parts from main

It is worth comparing this pre-War BMW 328 2-litre 'six' with the engine in the illustration on page 23. In a straight beauty contest, the older car gets my vote every time.

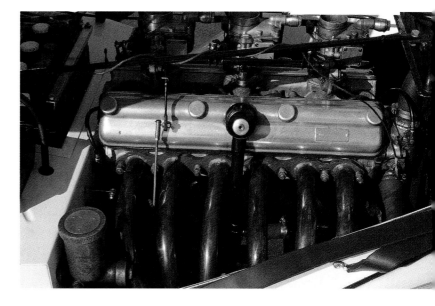

323i (1978–82)	
Body style	2-door saloon and Baur cabriolet
Engine	
Cylinders	6
Bore × stroke	80 × 76.8mm
Capacity	2,315cc
Timing	Belt-driven overhead camshaft
Compression ratio	9.5:1
Fuel injection	Bosch K-Jetronic
Max power	143bhp at 6,000rpm
Max torque	140lb ft at 4,500rpm
Transmission	
Standard 4-speed manual with usual gearbox options, and higher final-drive ratio of 3.45:1	
Suspension, steering and dimensions, Identical to 6-cylinder 320	
Brakes	
Servo-assisted discs/discs	

Parked in the grounds of Britain's largest snail farm at Credenhill, Herefordshire, Matthew Hammond's restored 323i shines in the bleak winter countryside.

dealers cost less than the ones supplied by independent specialists. With BMW parts, I've found generally that you get what you're prepared to pay for.

Out on the roads of Herefordshire, this extremely well-maintained BMW performed with the verve of a well-honed sports car, but there is no denying that by comparison with its modern-day counterparts, it is dated and unrefined.

Accelerating hard away from rest the car pulls so cleanly and strongly that it is essential to stir the gearbox as fast as you can. Engine and exhaust noise pervades the cabin, and is wonderfully intrusive – just how all sports cars should be – but it is this very cacophony that once drew criticism from *Motor Sport's* Clive Richardson and others.

Down several years of development the sporting sixes became ever quieter, principally through improved sound-proofing and exhaust 'damping', but not everyone regards this treatment as an advantage. BMWs, somehow, were meant to be raw and exciting, and Matthew Hammond's car is a good illustration of this.

With its traditional layout of the engine up front and rear-wheel drive, the handling was entirely predictable. This model acquired a reputation for tricky on-the-limit roadholding in the wet, but the tendency for the tail to step out of line never bothered skilled drivers.

An early 323i with the original 4-speed gearbox, it tends to feel 'thrashy' at high speeds, but the third gear ratio is so flexible that it allows the car to be trickled along at anything between 15 and 95mph. The gear change, incidentally, is to the traditional BMW 'no nonsense' standard; there is never any hesitation or messing around. The lever simply slots home with the satisfying 'thunk' that typifies everything that is 'meaty' and good about the best German engineering.

Roadholding is such that the chassis begs an enthusiastic driver to get involved with the whole process of high-speed cornering. As with most cars, the chassis will easily do the work for you, but high input with hand and foot delivers big rewards. It is certainly easy to provoke the tail out of line, in dry or wet weather, but for those well-versed in the art of

---

323i (1978–82)

Body style   2-door saloon and Baur cabriolet

Engine
Cylinders   6
Bore × stroke   80 × 76.8mm
Capacity   2,315cc
Timing   Belt-driven overhead camshaft
Compression ratio   9.5:1
Fuel injection   Bosch K-Jetronic
Max power   143bhp at 6,000rpm
Max torque   140lb ft at 4,500rpm

Transmission
Standard 4-speed manual with usual gearbox options, and higher final-drive ratio of 3.45:1

Suspension, steering and dimensions, Identical to 6-cylinder 320

Brakes
Servo-assisted discs/discs

US-spec 320i (1980–82)

Body style   Two-door saloon

Engine
Cylinders   4
Bore × stroke   89 × 71mm
Capacity   1,754cc
Timing   Chain-driven overhead camshaft
Compression ratio   8.8:1
Fuel injection   Bosch Jetronic, plus compulsory catalytic converter
Max power   101bhp at 5,800rpm
Max torque   100lb ft at 4,500rpm

Transmission
5-speed manual with 3.64:1 final-drive ratio

Suspension, steering and brakes
Identical to European-spec 318i but, without a rear anti-roll bar

By comparison with more modern BMWs the original shows its age a little, particularly with regard to comfort and ride quality, but cross-country performance is of an extremely high order.

opposite-lock, the only drawback to this is that the rear tyres tend to wear rather quickly.

The current tyres (Goodyear Eagle NCT) give a first class compromise between ride comfort and roadholding and, at 13in in diameter, they are not expensive to replace, unlike the 17in tyres of many modern BMWs.

Having covered more than 200,000 miles in total, which is a remarkable mileage by any standards for a performance car, Matthew Hammond's BMW stands as a glowing testament to the engineering integrity of the company who built it. It is interesting to reflect that, beyond its outstanding dynamics, the car continues to look fresh. Unlike so many three-box saloons from the same era, the 323i's aggressive-looking front end continues to radiate a degree of purpose, which is just one of the reasons why so many owners continue to warm to these cars more than 20 years after they were launched.

But It Had To Go

In keeping with modern trends, the E21 3 Series remained in production for around eight years, during which time it significantly increased BMW's clientele base. Coupled with a steady stream of international advertising campaigns, BMW's name and reputation began to reach a wider audience.

Driving enthusiasts sought ownership of the '02 range, but with the E21 BMW made a conscious effort to reach new customers, and succeeded in this aim admirably. However, on the introduction of the E21's replacement BMW would increase its efforts to reach an even wider audience, a move which would prove to have far-reaching consequences worldwide.

Racing versions sprouted large wings to aid aerodynamic stability and increase downforce, 'appendages' which in a less wild form, would eventually find their way onto special versions of the road cars.

CHAPTER TWO

BMW 3 Series:
The Second Generation

More Model Cars

Codenamed E30, BMW launched the second generation 3 Series towards the end of 1982, by which time the market for sporting saloons had become even more competitive. Volkswagen's immensely successful Golf GTi accounted for a third of all Golf sales. Vauxhall, Peugeot and others would quickly jump on the 'GTi' bandwagon, while Saab, Renault and Fiat pursued turbo technology in order to court the attentions of the sporting fraternity.

In addition Daimler-Benz had pulled off something of a coup with the launch of the

Launched in 1982 the second generation 3 Series, E30, was bigger, quicker, better appointed and had much improved handling. Models ranged from the 316i at one end of the scale to the mighty M3 at the other. Additions included a cabriolet and estate, but BMW steered clear of the contemporary trend for 'hot hatches'.

190 four-door saloon. A 2-litre car with superb build quality and the considerable prestige of the star motif, the 190 was an 'affordable Merc' and, even if its styling left a lot to be desired, it entered a niche that BMW and others simply could not afford to ignore.

Apart from high-quality engineering and a rich and successful racing record, BMW's cars held several advantages over 'the opposition'. For years, journalists the globe over had been extremely complimentary about the cars from Munich. Their message was slowly, but surely, getting through. The E21 Series had sold well on merit, and BMW's sales people had also been well supported by the company's commitment to marketing and advertising.

The amazing success of the second generation 3 Series, however, was virtually unprecedented. BMW certainly maintained an aggressive marketing policy, and kept dealers worldwide on their toes by demanding greater and greater investment in increasingly plush showrooms. This kept them in line with the company's 'up-market' image, but the association between BMW ownership and young, upwardly mobile professionals (or 'yuppies' as they became known) is best understood by reference to the prevailing political and social climate in the West.

The widespread adoption of monetarism led, initially, to booming economies and a new elite. A small minority made substantial sums in financial markets, and in many cases their preferred mode of transport was a BMW. Sales rocketed upwards; suddenly, 'everyone' identified success with BMW's products and aspired to owning one. On the other hand, Mercedes-Benz and Volvo were identified with an older generation, while Rovers and similar marques were simply unfashionable.

Devotees of marques which had a tradition of manufacturing sporting saloons, such as Alfa-Romeo, Lancia, and to a lesser extent Fiat, were beginning to become sceptical. The reputation of these cars as suffering from premature body rusting was wholly justified, and not everyone was enamoured with what journalists kindly dubbed 'cutting-edge styling'. With the benefit of hindsight, it is not difficult to appreciate the reasons behind BMW's success.

Beyond these factors, the advent of satellite television brought the company additional publicity. The German Touring Car Championship (DTM), in which BMW had a large presence and high profile, was broadcast to motor sport fans the world over. BMW's successful presence in Formula One provided the icing on the cake.

The E30's nose naturally included the grille 'kidneys' and twin headlamps, but was not as aggressively angled.

More Openings

Initially, the revised 3 Series was, like its predecessors, available with a two-door bodyshell. Within a few months of its launch, however, a four-door variant was added, and pitched into a market that included the Mercedes 190 and Alfa 75, both of which were also rear-wheel drive.

As previously, there was a Baur-bodied cabriolet with a distinctive steel roll-hoop amidships, but this model was replaced in 1985 by a new cabriolet, built by BMW, which was without a roll-hoop. The company's publicity literature and television advertising made much of the strength of the cabriolet's windscreen. This was so strong that a

Safer and more rigid than the outgoing model, the E30's bodyshell exceeded stringent US requirements. The subject of a hefty shunt, this example illustrates that the passenger cell remained intact, while the bonnet and sunroof crumpled in the intended manner.

Right: **A long held feature of BMW passenger saloons, the 'dogleg' shape of the rear side window was, and remains, a strong in-house styling characteristic.**

Below: **With revised rear suspension the E30 felt sure-footed under fast cornering. Vented steel wheels, closed with plastic hubcaps, were standard across the regular range.**

central roll-hoop had become superfluous. Most were agreed that the revised convertible's uncluttered lines were also more attractive than the Baur version.

Pre-dating the beginnings of 'hot-hatchback' era by some five years, BMW had built a 'touring' version of the '02 in the early 1970s. An eminently practical vehicle, it had enjoyed moderate success at that time. In late 1987 the E30 range was expanded with a 5-door estate, also dubbed as a Touring, but not intended to be a 'load-lugger' in the Volvo sense. Inevitably, it had more rear luggage space than its saloon counterpart but, almost endorsing 'yuppie' culture, the estate was marketed as a 'lifestyle' car. Beautifully styled, it was widely acknowledged as the best-looking estate of its day, and set something of a benchmark by which others would be judged.

In addition to the regular cars, BMW made the special M3 available from 1986, which differed externally from the standard two-door saloons in having a prominent rear wing, and much wider wheel arches, but more of this model later. The 325iX was also available in European markets (but not Britain), with permanent four-wheel drive, a move from BMW that was clearly influenced by Audi's success with the all-wheel-drive quattros.

Much in Keeping

The E30's revised styling largely kept faith with both its predecessor and its larger sisters in the extensive BMW range. Naturally, the 'kidney' radiator grille, that had given BMW such a strong identity since before the Second War, was retained, along with the 'dogleg' shape at the back of the rear side windows.

The sloping grille that had given the original 3 Series such an aggressive, although attractive, frontal appearance was changed for an upright affair, endowing the E30 with a stubby 'snout'. As before there were 'V' shaped swage lines in the bonnet of the revised car, but spaced further apart, and whereas the twin headlamps were confined to the 6-cylinder cars on the outgoing models, they were adopted across the range for the 'Mk 2'.

Large 'wrap-around' bumpers were used front and rear, there were rubber strips along the flanks, and much larger, rectangular tail-lamps with built-in reversing lights. BMW roundels appeared on the leading edge of the bonnet and trailing edge of the bootlid, model designation being denoted by a chromed

badge on the right-hand side of the bootlid.

While the track, body width and wheelbase were all increased, the length and weight of the car were reduced, the latter by as much as 40kg. Weight reduction was mainly achieved by using fewer welds in construction of the bodyshell, a move which also improved the structure's torsional rigidity.

By altering the dimensions, the designers arrived at an overall design that was fairly conservative and conventional but, with so many desirable optional 'extras' fitted, the

---

316 (1982–87)

Body style	Two-door saloon plus four-door saloon from 1983		
Engine			
Cylinders	4		
Bore × stroke	89 × 71mm		
Capacity	1,766cc		
Timing	Chain-driven overhead camshaft		
Compression ratio	9.5:1		
Carburettor	Pierburg 2B4		
Max power	90bhp at 5,500rpm		
Max torque	101lb ft at 4,000rpm		
Transmission			
Gearbox	4- or 5-speed manual or 4-speed automatic		
Ratios	**4-speed manual**	**5-speed manual**	**4-speed auto**
	First 3.76	3.72	2.48
	Second 2.04	2.02	1.48
	Third 1.32	1.32	1.00
	Fourth 1.00	1.00	0.73
		Fifth 0.80	
Final drive	3.91	3.64	3.91
Suspension and steering			
Front	MacPherson struts, coil springs and anti-roll bar		
Rear	Semi-trailing arms with coil springs		
Steering	Rack and pinion		
Wheels	Pressed steel 5J×14. 5.5J from September 1985, optional alloys		
Tyres	Radial 175/70 TR14		
Brakes	Servo assisted discs/drums with ABS anti-lock system from 1986		
Dimensions			
Track	(front) 1,407mm/55.4in		
	(rear) 1,415mm/55.7in		
Wheelbase	2,570mm/101.2in		
Overall length	4,325mm/170.3in		
Overall width	1,645mm/64.8in		
Overall height	1,380mm/54.3in		

Right: **BMW were only too pleased to offer these multi-spoke alloys – at extra cost, of course, but they were not to everyone's taste, which is why...**

Below: **...the preferred wheels of so many BMW addicts were these BBS cross-spoke alloys. Made at BBS's factory at Schiltach in southern Germany, they were expensive, but made to unrivalled standards.**

cars had a sporting appearance entirely in keeping with BMW's well cultivated image.

In order to fit larger brake units and modern low-profile tyres, the diameter of the road wheels was increased from 13in to 14in. The standard wheels were in steel, painted silver with the BMW roundel at their centres, and had a series of circular vents. Like the majority of unimaginatively styled steel wheels, they looked rather dull and many owners fitted alloys which were available from dealers at extra cost. The most desirable of all the 'after-market' alloy wheels were arguably the 'cross-spoke' alloys manufactured by BBS of Schiltach in southern Germany. The fresh and attractive design of these wheels was copied by other manufacturers, and is now regarded as a classic piece of design in the mould of the 5-spoke Fuchs alloys fitted to Porsches from 1967.

The spare wheel was housed horizontally in a well in the floor of the cavernous boot where, on the underside of the bootlid, BMW thoughtfully fitted a neat toolkit.

Changing Rooms

The car's redesigned interior was a breath of fresh automotive air. During the 1980s, many car manufacturers appeared to be in an unofficial competition with each other in an attempt to discover which could design the dullest interior. Japanese carmakers in particular were the acknowledged maestros in the field of designing 'acres' of dark grey plastic and uninspiring upholstery, whereas Volkswagen and Audi got full marks for unattractive dashboards and instrumentation. Accountants working behind the scenes were clearly giving orders to cut costs, and it was beginning to show, to the severe detriment of car design.

BMW's E30 went a long way to overturning this trend. In standard guise the seats were supportive and covered in conservatively coloured (charcoal, beige and grey predominated) cloth fabrics. Leather was an expensive option, but worth it for its comfort, appearance and ease in cleaning. The only criticism levelled by journalists about the interior was the cramped legroom in the rear. However the Mercedes 190 was exactly the same in this respect and as these seats were intended mainly for children, the journalists had rather missed the point.

Conservative styling led to unimaginative Kamm-style tail, with large, rectangular lights and chrome badging denoting model series and engine capacity, the 320i being the classic 2-litre in-line 'six'.

318i (1983–86)

Body style	Two- and four-door saloon
Engine	
Cylinders	4
Bore × stroke	89 × 71mm
Capacity	1,766cc
Timing	Chain-driven overhead camshaft
Compression ratio	9.5:1
Fuel injection	Bosch L-Jetronic
Max power	105bhp at 5,800rpm
Max torque	105lb ft at 4,500rpm

Transmission
4- or 5-speed manual with identical ratios to 316 except for 3.64 final drive: 4-speed automatic with identical ratios and final drive to 316

Suspension, steering, brakes and dimensions
Identical to 316

Although nicely rounded the bodyshell was very much along traditional styling lines, and, understandably, a number of owners personalised their cars with body kits. The bootlid spoiler is a genuine factory cost-option, and most popularly fitted to the more powerful cars in the range.

The E30's interior was not radically altered from that of its predecessor. The humped binnacle and angled centre console were slightly revised in style, but the general layout (praised for its practical advantages but criticised for its typically German austerity) remained the same. Note that the optional three-spoke, leather-covered steering wheel is fitted here.

Similar to the contemporary 5 Series BMW, the dashboard was beautifully designed and executed, a piece of modern plastic sculpture that was as ergonomically correct as it was aesthetically perfect. In these respects only the Saab 900's facia came close.

The four circular white-on-black instruments, illuminated at night by the familiar orange glow, were housed under a 'humped' and angled binnacle, with a central dashboard panel angled towards the driver.

Swivel vents for fresh air were housed at the top of the central panel with a clock, radio (optional) and heating/ventilation controls below it. A central console surrounding the gear lever included rocker switches to operate power windows (where fitted), cigarette lighter, and an ashtray. Smokers who owned these cars will remember that the ashtray had such a narrow 'mouth' that it was almost useless – possibly because its designer disapproved of smoking!

320i (1983–86)

Body style Two- and four-door saloon plus Baur cabriolet

Engine

Cylinders	6
Bore × stroke	80 × 66mm
Capacity	1,990cc
Timing	Belt-driven single-overhead camshaft
Compression ratio	9.8:1
Fuel injection	Bosch L-Jetronic
Max power	125bhp at 5,800rpm
Max torque	123lb ft at 4,000rpm

Transmission
5-speed manual with identical ratios to 318i, except for final-drive ratio of 3.45, and 4-speed automatic with identical ratios to 316, except for final-drive ratio of 3.46

Suspension, steering, brakes and dimensions
Identical to 318i except for 195/60 or 195/65 HR14 radial tyres, and optional ABS from 1983

Electrically-powered door mirrors, operated by small thumb buttons on the door armrests were extra-cost options, and offered for no good reason other than that they had been invented. For lovers of gadgetry there was a fuel economy gauge, guaranteed to produce a feeling of guilt in drivers who constantly floored the throttle pedal, a series of lights to indicate service intervals, and an onboard computer giving information that served mainly to provide a talking point at the bar.

The standard four-spoke steering wheel, with a thumb button to operate the horn in each spoke, rather let the side down. Although comfortable to use, it was fashioned from dull black plastic, and detracted from the interior's otherwise sporting feel. Naturally, a sports, leather-covered three-spoke wheel was available at extra cost, and many owners availed themselves of this expensive item. BMW's marketing machine was working well, and as intended.

As is usually the case with all newly-launched cars, the arrival of the revised 3 Series was greeted by journalists who expressed polarized opinions about its merits and less endearing points. From those who were apt to compare BMWs with Fords and Vauxhalls, there was the usual comment that the 3 Series was overpriced. Others considered that contemporary front-wheel drive cars had superior handling.

For accurate comment in those long ago days, the majority of readers turned to the respected British journal *Motor Sport*, whose editor Bill Boddy gave a fair impression of the many cars, including BMWs, he drove. Of his initial impressions of the 323i, he remarked:

Not all that number of BMWs come my way for testing these days, more's the pity, but when they do I am invariably impressed. The range of different BMWs is large but basically they do not change all that much, but where they do it is for the better.

Hard-wearing cloth fabric was used across the entire BMW range, with leather as an extra-cost option on most, but by no means all, models. Dark, sombre colours predominated during an era in which it was considered vulgar to flaunt symbols of wealth.

For instance, as soon as I got into the pleasantly hued alloy-green 3 Series fuel-injection 2.3-litre six-cylinder I was reminded of my now distant BMW days, when I drove this make regularly, by the rather awkwardly high-set ignition-key hole, which caused the key-ring to ding on the surrounds, the light clutch, the excellence of the gear change, of the lighter, revised five-speed gearbox, the commanding driving position (not quite as high as formerly, it seemed) and the hard but very comfortable seat, nicely upholstered in grey-green cloth.

Boddy left the question of the car's price tag of £9,655 (£11,277 with alloy wheels and electrical toys) to the judgement of readers. In the same issue of *Motor Sport*, Alan Henry tested the Sunbeam Lotus which, with the 0–60mph potential of 6.9secs, was viewed as a true spiritual successor to the Lotus Cortina. Henry heaped huge praise on the Sunbeam, commenting: 'On the road it's pure, uninhibited pleasure . . .'. The car retailed in 1983 at

323i (1983–85)

Body style	Two- and four-door saloons, plus Baur cabriolet

Engine

Cylinders	6
Bore × stroke	80 × 76.8mm
Capacity	2,315cc
Timing	Belt-driven single-overhead camshaft
Compression ratio	9.8:1
Fuel injection	Bosch L-Jetronic
Max power	139bhp at 5,300rpm increased to 150bhp at 6,000rpm in September 1983
Max torque	148lb ft at 4,000rpm

Transmission

Gearbox 5-speed/manual

Ratios	Standard	Sport close-ratio
First	3.83	3.764
Second	2.20	2.325
Third	1.40	1.612
Fourth	1.00	1.229
Fifth	0.81	1.000
Final drive	3.46	3.23

4-speed automatic variant with identical ratios to 320i but, with 3.23 final-drive ratio

Suspension, steering, brakes and dimensions
Identical to 320i except for rear disc brakes as standard

£7,500 but, like so many contemporary cars from similar manufacturers, body rust took a heavy toll. The high number of 'old' BMWs and their contemporary Mercs and Volkswagens still in regular use on British and European roads serves to illustrate the reasons behind the relatively high price tags for German engineering and build quality!

Cache Up Front

As with the E21, the E30 Series used a number of different 4- and 6-cylinder engines. At 'entry-level' the 316 carburettor car had a 1,596cc 'four', but all variants had fuel injection from 1987. In BMW's complex numbering system the 4-cylinder engines were known as the M10, M40 and M42, the 6-cylinder units as the M60 and M20, and the 6-cylinder diesel version as the M21.

All power units were built to the same exacting standards, and gave high output by comparison with the majority of engines from 'mainstream' manufacturers. With the exception of the 136bhp 1.8-litre 318iS and powerful M3, both of which had twin-overhead camshafts, the power units had single-overhead camshafts. The 1,766cc M10 4-cylnder unit, with its chain-driven camshaft, was to the same specification as the engines fitted to the previous model, and fitted to the 316, and early examples of the 316i and 318i. By contrast, the later belt-driven M40, which was appreciably smoother in operation, came in 1,596cc and 1,796cc guises and saw service in the 316i and later 318i.

Power outputs for the 4-cylinder engines were as follows: 100bhp at 5,500rpm (316i),

113bhp at 5,500rpm (318i), 136bhp at 6,000rpm (318iS).

The M60 6-cylinder engines had belt-driven camshafts and, fitted to the 320i 1,990cc and 323i 2,315cc cars, were the same as the power plants in the E21s. From 1985, the M20 2,494cc 6-cylinder engine debuted in the 325i and four-wheel-drive 325iX, and although never officially imported to Britain, there was an extremely economical 2,693cc unit fitted to the 325e which also saw service in the 525e.

Power outputs for the 6-cylinder cars were as follows: 125bhp, or 129bhp from 1987 (320i), 139bhp, or 150bhp from 1983 (323i), and 171bhp (325i).

Top speeds, which had become rather academic in most of Europe, and certainly in Britain by this time, ranged from 115mph for the 316i to 137mph for the 325i. In Britain, and elsewhere, much was made of the smoothness of the 'sixes', BMW boasting that it was possible for a 50p piece to be balanced on top of the camshaft cover with the engine running at 'tickover'. A test by this author demonstrated the claim to be true.

All engine variants combined good performance with refinement and excellent fuel

economy. Of the 323i he drove, *Motor Sport's* Bill Boddy commented:

> Another pleasing, and remarkable, aspect of the car is the way in which the high fifth gear, giving the very low engine speed of only 2,734rpm at 70mph cruising speed, can be retained in traffic driving, so that this and top are used in lieu of the

Although the 4-cylinder engines fitted to the 316i and 318i were nowhere near as smooth, or powerful, as the classic 6-cylinder power units, they were extremely durable and reliable. Many examples have achieved truly astonishing mileages with no apparent signs of ill health.

325i (1985–92)

Body style	Two- and four-door saloons, plus cabriolet (1986–92) and Touring (1987–92)

Engine

Cylinders	6
Bore × stroke	84 × 75mm
Capacity	2,494cc
Timing	Belt-driven single-overhead camshaft
Compression ratio	9.7:1
Fuel injection	Bosch Motronic
Max power	171bhp at 5,800rpm
Max torque	160lb ft at 4,300rpm

Transmission
5-speed manual with 3.64 final drive, 5-speed close-ratio sports box with 3.91 final drive, or 4-speed automatic with 3.46 final drive

Suspension, steering, brakes, gear ratios and dimensions
Identical to 323i

316i (1987–88)

Body style   Two- and four-door saloon

Engine
Cylinders   4
Bore × stroke   89 × 71mm
Capacity   1,766cc
Timing   Chain-driven single-overhead camshaft
Compression ratio   8.3:1
Fuel injection   Bosch L-Jetronic, Lambda probe and catalytic converter
Max power   102bhp at 5,800rpm
Max torque   101lb ft at 4,000rpm

Transmission
Gearbox   5 speed manual or optional 4-speed automatic

Ratios	**Standard**	**Automatic**
First	3.72	2.72
Second	2.02	1.56
Third	1.32	1.00
Fourth	1.00	0.73
Fifth	0.80	
Final drive	3.91	3.91

Suspension, steering and brakes
Identical to 316

316i (1987–94)

Body style   Two- and four-door saloon, plus Touring from 1989

Engine
Cylinders   4
Bore × stroke   84 × 72mm
Capacity   1,596cc
Timing   Belt-driven single-overhead camshaft
Compression ratio   9:1
Fuel injection   Bosch Motronic, Lambda probe and catalytic converter
Max power   100bhp at 5,500rpm
Max torque   102lb ft at 4,250rpm

Transmission
Gearbox   5-speed manual or optional 4-speed automatic

Ratios	**5-speed**	**Automatic**
First	3.72	2.73
Second	2.02	1.56
Third	1.32	1.00
Fourth	1.00	0.73
Fifth	0.81	
Final drive	4.10	4.45

Suspension, steering, brakes and dimensions
Identical to 316

lower ratios for much of one's driving, and this in spite of the very high-performance of this small-engined saloon.

This, and the very acceptable fuel economy – 28.6mpg overall – which has become quite a feature of the smaller, modern, fast saloons, is indicative of real progress.

It is Boddy's last point with which many BMW owners will readily identify. From the driver's seat it was readily apparent that BMW's engineers had worked extremely hard, and made real progress. Just a few years earlier, a fuel consumption figure of 28.6mpg was considered a fair achievement in a 1.5-litre Volkswagen Beetle!

In the field of improved fuel consumption, the 2.7-litre 'eta' or 'efficiency' engine represented a real leap forward in progress. A low-revving unit with a high 11:1 fuel compression ratio, and Bosch L-Jetronic fuel injection, the 325e and its larger-bodied 525e sister, were capable of returning well in excess of 30mpg. Some owners claimed that 40mpg was on the cards with gentle driving, but either way such figures for an engine of such large capacity and six cylinders were without precedent.

Transmission

With such a large variety of engine variants, it was inevitable that E30s were fitted with a bewildering number of gearboxes. The 'entry-level' 316 and early 318i had the old type 4-speed manual boxes, but were discontinued after 1986. Apart from this anomaly, a 5-speed gearbox was fitted across the range, although in effect this was a 4-speed unit with a high top gear that acted as an overdrive.

Two sets of ratios were used in the 5-speeder to suit engine characteristics, the lower set of ratios (confined to bottom, second, third and fifth) being used in the 323i and 325i. A

Captured behind the pits at Silverstone, the 325i was the only really quick member of the regular range. Accomplished racing driver, Barrie Williams, owned a similar example and considered it to be 'untouchable' as a road car.

The 3 Series, of all generations, continues to form the backbone and focus of interest for enthusiasts' clubs. Concours d'elegance are held on a regular basis.

close-ratio Sport gearbox was, as on the previous E21, available as an extra-cost option.

In addition to the manual units, there was a 4-speed automatic ZF gearbox, with a high top ratio to improve fuel consumption.

Staying Between the Hedgerows

This biggest change took place at the rear, where the trailing arms were set at 20 degrees, instead of 15 as previously. In addition the coil springs and damper units were mounted separately, and in conjunction with the wider track, these cars

handled absolutely superbly. Fitted with the M-Technic sports suspension kit, comprising stiffer road springs, gas-filled shock absorbers and wider anti-roll bars, little contemporary sporting road machinery got a look in by comparison.

I once owned a 318i from this era, a magnificent black example, with lowered suspension. Time and again it demonstrated that its chassis was far too powerful for the 4-cylinder engine, with the result that it could be thrown at corners at almost any speed in complete safety. It was possible to place the front wheels anywhere you fancied, with pin-point accuracy, bang on the throttle pedal and power out of a corner with the tail wildly, but wholly controllably, out of line.

The accomplished English racing driver, Barrie 'Whizzo' Williams, who hails from Herefordshire, owned a contemporary 325i. During a very long racing career, Williams has been, and continues to be, extremely successful. His car control is legendary, and he is known for being entirely safe. He once told me of a trip he took to Belgium and back to Britain in his 325i. In his own words it was a trip that he had to drive 'in a hurry'. Williams' idea of 'hurry' is what normal mortals would term as 'terrifying'. What impressed him most on this occasion was the performance of his BMW, commenting that nothing he had driven previously would 'live with it' in a straight line or around corners.

With remarkably few modifications the 6-cylinder 2.5-litre 325i made for a useful and competitive racing car, an ideal 'clubbie' machine capable of being driven home after an event.

Soft-Top and Estate

Porsche's erstwhile chief executive, Peter Shutz, halted the decline in popularity of the evergreen rear-engined 911 with the introduction of the first pure cabriolet version in 1983. The car had been publicly debuted as a prototype just two years earlier, and such was the response to it, that Porsche rushed ahead with production versions. It was a huge sales hit and BMW followed suit with an E30 cabriolet at the beginning of 1986.

A most elegant car, BMW's 3 Series cabriolet had clean, undramatic lines that appeared modest and subtle whether or not the top was erected. Naturally, the bodyshell had to be strengthened, reinforcements being built into the sills, windscreen surround, floorpan and scuttles. All of this resulted in an immensely strong, and torsionally rigid, structure. There was an inevitable weight penalty, which was apparent in the 4-cylinder model, but made little difference to the performance of the 6-cylinder versions.

The soft-top was in a three-layer 'sandwich', and stored in the down position behind the rear seats below a neat closing panel. As the closing panel was at roughly the same height as the bootlid, rearward vision was never impaired. This had been a long-held criticism of the Volkswagen Beetle cabriolet, whose soft-top folded back like the hood of a child's pram. Although the Beetle's arrangement was in the classic pre-War Mercedes cabriolet style, and extremely elegant, it completely blocked the driver's view of the road behind, which is hardly a passport to safe motoring in the modern era.

Like the cabriolet, the Touring very much added to the appeal of the range, and broadened BMW's potential customer base. This model was also heavier than the regular four-door saloon, due to the bodywork having been reinforced along the rear of the flanks. Self-levelling suspension was available as an extra-cost option on this model, and proved invaluable for stabilising the car when fully laden.

Of really first class proportions, the estates proved to be extremely popular, despite valid criticism that entry to the rear load area was restricted by the tail-lamps. Few owners really cared about this inconvenience; their BMW estates served a niche market and they were proud and content to be a part of it.

320i (1986–92)

Body style   two- and four-door saloon, cabriolet (1986–92) and Touring (1986–91)

Engine
Cylinders	6
Bore × stroke	80 × 66mm
Capacity	1990cc
Timing	Belt-driven single-overhead camshaft
Compression ratio	8.8:1
Fuel injection	Bosch Motronic, Lambda probe and catalytic converter
Max power	129bhp at 6000rpm
Max torque	118lb ft at 4300rpm

Transmission
5speed manual with 4.10 final-drive ratio, or optional 4-speed automatic with 4.10 final-drive ratio

Suspension, steering, brakes and dimensions
Identical to earlier 320i

Owners' Appraisal

Viv Holley's metallic silver four-door 318i, of 1986 'vintage', is a typical example of the many similar cars in daily service in Britain and mainland Europe today. Attracted to the car by its looks, and reputation for reliability, Viv, by her own admission is not especially enthusiastic about cars, citing gardening as a preferable pastime to driving.

Despite this she considers her BMW to be 'a joy to drive', despite the lack of power-assisted steering, the only facet of the car that she positively does not like. 'It's a nice, comfortable, smooth car, that doesn't rattle or bang around over bumps, and has ample performance for overtaking when I need it,' she says.

No stranger to high-speed travel, her partner, Colin Tolley, owns an ur-quattro which Viv occasionally uses for fun. 'The Audi is extremely fast – makes the 318i feel like a sluggard by comparison – but I wouldn't want to drive it every day', she says. Colin feels the same way about his venerable Audi these days, and has recently switched to BMW ownership. A driver by profession, his change of allegiance to the Munich manufacturer was largely based on a preference for rear-wheel drive. The manufacturers of front-drive cars might one day take notice that Colin is one of a growing number who care little for the understeering, wheelspinning and torque-teering antics of their boring little boxes.

Viv, by contrast, has no interest in the differences between rear- and front-wheel drive, but is adamant that she will not be returning to Ford ownership.

> Prior to buying my BMW, I owned an Escort XR3; the difference in quality between the two cars is readily apparent simply by closing the doors. The Ford made a 'tinny, clanging' noise, whereas the BMW's doors always close nicely with a solid, well-made feel. And the Escort also went rusty, which is not a problem with the BMW, despite the use it gets.

Viv has no plans to sell her car but, when the time comes, she is in little doubt that it will be replaced by another 3 Series.

From Zuffenhausen to Munich

James Booth makes a living selling new Volkswagens. Up until the spring of 2001, his

---

318i (1987–94)

Body style	Two – and four-door saloon, Touring version (1989–94), and cabriolet (1990–93)

Engine

Cylinders	4
Bore × stroke	84 × 81mm
Capacity	1,796cc
Timing	Belt-driven single-overhead camshaft
Compression ratio	8.8:1
Fuel injection	Bosch Motronic, Lambda probe and catalytic converter
Max power	113bhp at 5,500rpm
Max torque	117lb ft at 4,250rpm

Transmission
5-speed manual with 4.10 final-drive ratio, or optional 4-sped automatic with 4.45 final-drive ratio

Suspension, steering, brakes and dimensions
Identical to earlier 318i

---

daily driver was a Porsche 944 but, although impressed with the sports car's fabulous handling and seat-of-the-pants performance, he became less and less fond of its fuel consumption. Despite the disapproval of his boss, instead of plumping for a Golf, Bora, Passat, Lupo or Polo, James opted for a BMW 316i Touring.

Again, it was a natural choice for someone brought up on rear-wheel drive, but for this 25-year-old the BMW also has the kind of style which is lacking in so many contemporaries. James' Brilliant Red example, with non-standard TSW Imola 15in alloy wheels shod with wide 205/50×15 Toyo tyres, has what young people refer to as the middle-class version of 'street-cred'.

James clocks up huge mileages in his car, which is why he needs something that is both reliable and economical to run. A noise from the cylinder head recently resulted in replacement of the camshaft (as a precaution against the engine 'detonating' at high speed) but other than this the car has been entirely reliable.

James says:

Although underpowered, the car will cruise comfortably at 90mph-plus, and always feels rock-solid

and safe above this speed. The car is also very comfortable, handles perfectly, frequently returns 33mpg and gives me everything I need in a motor car. As I tend to lead a sort of 'out-of-a-suitcase' existence, I really appreciate the extra room in the back. As a single chap, it's also useful that the backrest of the rear seat folds forward. This not only increases luggage space, but can double as a bedroom on the occasions when I get stranded miles from home.

Despite being used on a daily basis for more than 15 years, and clocking up a big mileage, Viv Holley's 3 Series has proved entirely reliable. Her next car will also be a 3 Series.

318iS (1989–91)

Body style	Two- and four-door saloon
Engine	
Cylinders	4
Bore × stroke	84 × 81mm
Capacity	1,796cc
Timing	Chain-driven double-overhead camshafts with 4 valves per cylinder
Compression ratio	10:1
Fuel injection	Bosch Motronic M1/7, Lambda probe and catalytic converter
Max power	136bhp at 6,000rpm
Max torque	124lb ft at 4,600rpm

Transmission
5-speed manual gearbox identical to 318i

Suspension, steering, brakes and dimensions
Identical to 318i, except for rear brake discs as standard

Right: **A useful addition to the range, the Touring was marketed as a 'lifestyle' car – a smart, practical conveyance for combining the benefits of a shopping holdhall with traditional BMW sportiness.**

Below: **From the front the estate version is indistinguishable from the saloon. The deep chin spoiler illustrated is an 'after-market' item, while the M badge on the radiator grille is for decoration; the car is a standard 316i.**

Apart from the smart, multi-spoke alloy wheels, James' car has a full factory-fitted M-Technic body kit, comprising a deep chin spoiler, side skirts and a skirt around the rear bumper. Under the skin, there are M-Technic road springs and shock absorbers, which contribute significantly to the firm feel of the car, and its superb handling. M-Technic badging is applied to the seats and steering wheel, adding a sporting ambience to the interior which, although a trifle pretentious in view of the modest output from the standard 4-cylinder engine, is all part of brightening up one man's motoring scene.

Unlike so many estates, the 3 Series Touring was beautifully designed, the back having been integrated and executed perfectly into the saloon's original lines. 'Smoked-out' lenses and . . .

Like so many BMW owners, James has given up fitting BMW-badged caps to the tyre valves, because they are stolen on a regular basis.

Despite the practical advantages of James Booth's 318i Touring, he openly admits to missing the corrupting effect of his Porsche 944's acceleration and exhilarating top speed. However, not all is lost, as he keeps a 2.2-litre Porsche 911 tucked away for use on high days and holidays.

'In the BMW and Porsche 911, I have my ideal pair of cars,' he says, and there's little doubting that he has a very good point.

The Opposition

Apart from the quite superbly made, if 'frumpy-looking' Mercedes-Benz 190, there was no shortage of competition for 3 Series. At nearly £10,000 in 1983, Ford's Sierra XR4i V6, appeared to give the in-line BMW 'sixes' a run for their money. With a

. . . black-painted 'kidneys' are popular modern touches aimed at presenting a 'cooler' more sporting image.

325e (1985–86)	
Body style	Two- and four-door saloon, plus Baur cabriolet
Engine	
Cylinders	6
Bore × stroke	84 × 81mm
Capacity	2,693cc
Timing	Belt-driven single-overhead camshaft
Compression ratio	11:1
Fuel injection	Bosch Motronic, Lambda probe and catalytic converter
Max power	122bhp at 4,250rpm
Max torque	166lb ft at 3,250rpm
Transmission	
5-speed manual	
Ratios	First 3.83
	Second 2.20
	Third 1.40
	Fourth 1.00
	Fifth 0.81
	Final drive 2.93
Suspension, steering, brakes and dimensions Identical to 320i	

325e (1985–86)	
Body style	Two- and four-door saloon, plus Baur cabriolet
Engine	
Cylinders	6
Bore × stroke	84 × 81mm
Capacity	2,693cc
Timing	Belt-driven single-overhead camshaft
Compression ratio	11:1
Fuel injection	Bosch Motronic, Lambda probe and catalytic converter
Max power	122bhp at 4,250rpm
Max torque	166lb ft at 3,250rpm
Transmission	
5-speed manual	
Ratios	First 3.83
	Second 2.20
	Third 1.40
	Fourth 1.00
	Fifth 0.81
	Final drive 2.93
Suspension, steering, brakes and dimensions	
Identical to 320i	

In a market dominated for so long by the Volvo estate, the Touring does not shape up to traditional estate values. Access to the load area is compromised by the intrusive rear lights.

top speed of 130mph, 25mpg, and a best 0–60mph time of 7.8secs, the Sierra was quick and reasonably economical, but the styling was initially controversial and the standard suspension was heavily criticized for being far too soft for performance motoring.

Interestingly, the XR4i's facia was similar in conception to the BMW's, with the central panel angled towards the driver, but the Ford's internal appearance was clearly not in the same league as the Munich car. Love it or hate it, the Ford provided reasonable value for money, but rust would claim a good number of these cars in a surprisingly short period.

Audi's mid-range 80 saloon was an obvious contender for the 3 Series, the quattro version boasting permanent four-wheel drive as a distinct advantage for some. At more than £11,000 in 1983, it wasn't cheap, but there was a new 2,144cc 5-cylinder engine under the bonnet developing a useful 136bhp, and a respectable top speed of 120mph. The Audi was well made, if blandly styled, and let down by its plain, slightly austere interior but, supported by a successful international rallying programme, the Ingolstadt company was in ascendance.

It would take a further 15 to 20 years for Audi's four-rings motif to be taken seriously in the company of the Mercedes star and BMW aeroplane propeller, but that was the aim of the company's helmsman, Dr Ferdinand Piëch, and he can rightly claim to have succeeded.

In addition to formidable progress from Audi, Volkswagen were in ascendance with the Golf GTi, an acknowledged classic which in revised Mk2 format was a serious contender against the 4-cylinder BMWs. The Golf provided spacious 'family' accommodation, demanded little in the way of driver input, and performed well. It clearly led the hatchback class, but its lack of class would maintain BMW's client loyalty long into the future.

Alfa-Romeo enjoyed an enviable reputation for making sporting family cars. Both the twin-cam and V6 versions of the rear-drive 75 were quick, competent and stylish although the angular body was not to everyone's taste, but usually came with a dose of unreliable electrical components and, despite claims to the contrary from their makers, an unrivalled inability to resist corrosion. Committed Alfa owners, and there were thousands throughout Europe, were an understanding, devoted bunch who appreciated their cars when they worked properly, and shrugged their shoulders philosophically when they did not.

With a superb and versatile range of cars that began with the 316i, and ended with the luxury 7 Series (and exotic M1 for those involved in motor racing), BMW remained confident in all sectors, with good reason.

'M' for Pillar and Pinnacle

At the top of the E30 tree, the M3 made its public debut in 1985 and became available to the car-buying public just a year later. Its arrival was timely; western society had 'never had it so good', and international motor sport was going through one of its high points. The Group C sports car programme and Group B rally regulations led to the creation of some of the world's fastest, most powerful and exciting cars. The M3 was a roadgoing 'spin-off' from this heady era, and although it was expensive to buy and run, there was no shortage of takers.

The car was a product of BMW's Motorsport Division, founded in 1972 to run

---

325iX four-wheel drive (1985–92)

Specification identical to regular 325i, except in the following:

Running gear
Permanently engaged four-wheel drive; central differential allowing for a torque split of 37/63 per cent front-to-rear wheels. Viscous limited-slip differential rear and centre

Final drive
3.91 ratio with 5-speed manual and 3.73 with optional 4-speed automatic

Suspension and steering
Steering	Power-assistance as standard fitting
Wheels	Steel 6JY14, or optional alloys
Tyres	195/65 VR14, or 200/60 VR365 tyres if fitted with alloy wheels

Brakes	ABS anti-lock braking fitted as standard

Dimensions
Track	(front) 1,420mm/55.9in
	(rear) 1,416mm/55.7in
Overall height	1,400mm/55.1in

Quick, elegant and sure-footed, the Touring makes for a genuine 80mph cross-country car. That it continues to be highly prized is reflected in high residual values.

the works touring cars and support private BMW racing teams, the M appellation standing for 'Motorsport'. A wholly separate entity, with house colours in red, blue and purple, and later with a chromium-plated 'M' being added to this colourful logo, the Motorsport 'M-badged' cars were marketed as a brand in their own right, and quickly became identified with high performance.

Competition for the M3 came principally from the 2.3-litre 16-valve Mercedes-Benz 190E, a quick piece of machinery with a special cylinder head developed by Keith Duckworth's Cosworth company based at Hylton Road, Worcester. Battles in the German Touring Car Championship

James Booth reckons that his Touring is among the soundest of many cars he's owned, including his 1967 Porsche 911: praise indeed from someone who sells Volkswagens for a living!

between the Mercs and BMWs were 'hotting-up' during this period, and the heat in the respective company's showrooms was no less intense.

Race Pedigree

Intended as a racing car, the roadgoing M3, although based on the standard E30 two-door bodyshell, was substantially different from the normal range. With the exception of the bonnet, virtually every other panel had to be specially fashioned for the car, including the wide wheel arches and sills. Many parts of the shell were redesigned to allow a rollcage to be fitted to the racing versions, the angle of the rear window was altered to allow air passing over the car to be directed to the rear aerofoil more efficiently, and a deep chin spoiler conspired to create an overall impression of a most purposeful, if aggressive, road rocket.

The interior of the standard M3 was, in the tradition of true sporting machinery, impressively dull. Hip-hugging seats, a three-spoke sports steering wheel, and discreet 'M' badging sat between the principal instruments, but the usual luxury items found in expensive cars were only available as extra-cost options.

BMW could easily have dropped one of their powerful 6-cylinder production engines into the M3, but the majority of people involved with this special project were agreed that a 'six' would have been too heavy, and therefore compromise the car's handling and roadholding.

As usual, the engine project was initially overseen by BMW's tuning guru, Paul Rosche, who used an enlarged version of the 2-litre 4-cylinder power unit. With a bore of 93.4mm and stroke of 84mm, there was an overall capacity of 2,302cc. The 16-valve cylinder head was to the same design as the unit used on the 6-cylinder cars which, with Bosch Motronic fuel injection, resulted in an engine developing 200bhp at 6,750rpm.

M3 (1986–89)

Body style	Two-door saloon and cabriolet	
Engine		
Cylinders	4	
Bore × stroke	93.4 × 84mm	
Capacity	2,302cc	
Timing	Chain-driven double-overhead camshafts	
Compression ratio	10.5:1	
Fuel injection	Bosch Motronic ML	
Max power	200bhp at 6,750rpm (195bhp at 6,750rpmwith cat version)	
Max torque	177lb ft at 4,750rpm (170lb ft at 4,750rpm with cat version)	
Transmission		
Gearbox	5-speed sports close-ratio	
Ratios	**Euro-spec**	**US-spec**
First	3.72	3.764
Second	2.40	2.40
Third	1.77	1.77
Fourth	1.26	1.26
Fifth	1.00	1.00
Final drive	3.25	4.1
Suspension and steering		
Front	MacPherson struts with coil springs and anti-roll bar, all modified from standard	
Rear	Semi-trailing arms with coil springs and anti-roll bar modified for performance	
Steering	Rack and pinion	
Wheels	7J×15 alloys	
Tyres	205/55 ZR15	
Brakes		
Servo-assisted discs with standard ABS		
Dimensions		
Track	(front) 1,412mm/55.6in	
	(rear) 1,414mm/56in	
Wheelbase	2,562mm/100.9in	
Overall length	4,345mm/171in	
Overall width	1,680mm/66.1in	
Overall height	1,370mm/53.9in	

The unit was mated to a 5-speed Getrag close-ratio gearbox, with a 'dogleg' first, similar to the Porsche Carrera 'lightweight', and the other 'cogs' in normal H pattern. A ZF limited-slip differential was standard wear, and performed an admirable job of controlling wheelspin under hard acceleration.

Also beneath the sheet metalwork were beefy brakes from the 5 Series, ABS, altered suspension geometry and Boge gas-filled shock absorbers, quick steering rack, and a set of wide BBS cross-spoke alloy to a 5-bolt, rather than 4-bolt, fixing.

All examples were built in limited numbers with left-hand drive, and developed through several Evolution models to keep pace with the demands of homologation racing rules. Initially capable of 143mph and a 0–60mph

The M3 distinguished itself in track events and international rallying alike, and utilised a special version of BMW's 4-cylinder engine. A 'six' was considered too heavy for this finely balanced car.

A homolgation special produced under the guidance of BMW's Motorsport Division, the limited edition M3, used extensively in national and international competition, was a 3 Series 'look-alike', virtually every panel differing from the standard car. Note the flared wheel arches, complex chin spoiler, and large rear wing.

A classic among classics, the M3 is eminently collectable today, this shining white example sitting between standard road cars at a BMW club test session at Castle Combe. With increasing traffic congestion on public roads, more and more BMW enthusiasts are taking to racing circuits.

Hugely successful for BMW, the E30 is still a familiar sight on the roads of Britain and mainland Europe. Used examples in top condition can be bought for just a few hundreds of pounds; build quality and reliability are beyond question.

320iS (Italian market only)	
Engine	
Cylinders	4, with 4-valve-per-cylinder cylinder head
Bore × stroke	93.4 × 72.6mm
Capacity	1,990cc
Max power	192bhp at 6,900rpm
Transmission	
5-speed manual only	
Brakes	
Discs all-round, drums on rear of European-spec cars	

time of slightly less than 7secs, enthusiasts snapped these cars up quickly, and enjoyed them for what they were.

In 1990, the M3 Sport Evolution 111 appeared with a 2.5-litre engine developing as much as 238bhp, despite the presence of a power-sapping catalytic converter. This incarnation was an extraordinary representation of engineering progress. With a top speed of close to 150mph, it was as fast as the 2.7-litre Porsche Carrera of the 1970s, the Stuttgart projectile having been specially developed, and stripped of all superfluous weight, to reach such velocity.

In addition to the regular 'tin-tops' BMW also built 786 M3 cabriolets, with an electrically-powered soft-top, the latter representing something of an engineering tour de force in itself.

Conclusion

The E30 models had proved enormously successful but by the end of the 1980s they had had their day, by which time BMW had established itself as an equal to Mercedes-Benz. Many considered that BMWs were superior to the acknowledged maestros from Stuttgart, and BMW did nothing to dispel this reputation in the years ahead.

CHAPTER THREE

BMW 3 Series: The Third Generation

E-number 36

The third generation 3 Series was launched in 1990 against a motoring background that was returning to normality after a long period of complete insanity. During the 1980s, so many 'mainstream' cars, particularly of Japanese origin, had become dull and the car-buying public lodged one unofficial 'protest' after another.

During the same period there had been an unforseen boom in the growth in interest in classic cars, mainly from the 1950s and 1960s. Speculators invested huge sums in old cars, prices were hiked upwards and values soared to the point where even quite mundane machinery began to change hands for huge sums. Apart from being responsible for the creation of a worldwide restoration and parts industry worth millions, the classic car movement had sent a clear signal to the motor industry that it was time for the latter to pull its finger out. Enthusiasts loved the aesthetics of old cars, and frequently expressed their contempt for the looks of new ones.

In 1989, however, the classic car bubble suddenly burst. Within just a few months, the bottom dropped out of the market and values tumbled. Many speculators got their financial fingers badly burnt, and a hardcore of enthusiasts breathed a huge sigh of relief that 'normality' had returned.

Despite this, manufacturers of modern cars clearly began to react to criticism. The message had hit home that the money that had been directed at restoring and running old cars might otherwise have been spent on new cars. The industry had lost out, and in consequence automotive designers began to look to the past for inspiration.

At the beginning of the 1990s the Rover Group, for example, launched a modern version of the Mini-Cooper, and a long-overdue Mini cabriolet. At roughly the same time Porsche, Daimler-Benz and BMW began work on new designs for 'retro-look' sports cars that would eventually materialise in production as the Boxster, SLK and Z3 respectively.

Launched in 1990, the third generation 3 Series (the E36) was a bolder, more aerodynamically efficient car, that broke away from traditional styling tenets, while at the same time retaining BMW's famous hallmarks.

A piece of pure BMW styling innovation, the aerodynamically fashioned door mirrors were mounted on double stalks.

A four-door saloon was the staple of the range, which continued to include both standard 4- and powerful 6-cylinder engines.

During this final decade of the second millennium, BMW's designers were well aware that the cars they had created hitherto, both the saloons and sporting machines, were already being hailed as classics. BMW's profits, along with car production, had risen sharply. BMW clubs throughout the world were increasingly gaining members and, as the economic boom of the mid to late 1980s subsided, 'yuppy' slowly began to disappear from English vocabulary.

For the third generation 3 Series, BMW incorporated features from previous designs, naturally, but apart from increasing the size of these cars, they also aimed them at the family motorist. Although the revised saloons were every bit as sporting in nature as their illustrious forerunners, the staple of the range was a four-door saloon, in which guise they were also raced in European and British Touring Car Championships.

In addition to the 'booted' four-door saloon there were two-door coupé, convertible, estate (Touring) and Compact variants, the latter being a two-door, similar in appearance to the expensive coupé, and designed to compete head on with inexpensive cars from Ford, Vauxhall and Volkswagen.

The design of the new car was bold, and hugely improved in many respects over the outgoing E30, even if its aggressive frontal appearance failed to capture the imagination of several Mercedes-Benz owners.

A practical useful two-door hatchback, the Compact bore a strong resemblance to the regular coupé, even if it didn't go like one.

Cheating the Wind

Few traditionalists criticised the E30's styling; although conservative, it was probably correct for its day. During the same period Audi launched their 100 saloon. With its wind-cheating body and low drag-coefficient, it looked modern and hinted at the future, but was too advanced for reactionary car buyers, whose psyche was deeply entrenched in the idea that a bluff-fronted three-box saloon was correct. It clearly was not. For years wind-tunnel tests had demonstrated this to be the case, but it was only the bravest manufacturers such as Audi and Citroën who had launched cars with bodies shaped according to scientific principles.

316i (1990–98)

Body style	four-door saloon, two-door coupé and Compact (1994–98)
Engine	
Cylinders	4
Bore × stroke	84 × 72mm
Capacity	1,596cc
Timing	Belt-driven single-overhead camshaft
Compression ratio	9:1
Fuel injection	Bosch Motronic with Lambda probe and catalytic converter
Max power	100bhp at 5,000rpm (102bhp at 5,500rpm from 1993)
Max torque	102lb ft 4,250rpm (110lb ft at 3,900rpm from 1993)

Transmission

Gearbox: 5-speed manual or optional 4-speed automatic

Ratios	5-speed manual	4-speed automatic
First	4.23	2.40
Second	2.52	1.47
Third	1.77	1.00
Fourth	1.26	0.72
Fifth	1.00	
Final drive	3.45	4.45

[end table]

Suspension and steering

Front	MacPherson struts, coil springs and anti-roll bar
Rear	BMW multi-link system with coil springs and anti-roll bar

Coupé versions differ in that they have 'Z-axle' with semi-trailing arms and separate springs and shock absorbers

Steering	Rack and pinion, power-assistance standard from summer 1992
Wheels	6J×15 or 7J×15 on coupé versions
Tyres	185×15 or 205×15 on coupé versions

Brakes

Servo-assisted discs/discs

Dimensions

Track	(front) 1,418mm/55.8in
	(rear) 1,431mm/56.3in
Wheelbase	2,700mm/106.3in
Overall length	4,433mm/174.5in
Overall width	1,698mm/66.8in
Overall height	1,393mm/54.8in

The 3 Series was the only car to take part in the British Touring Car Championship with rear-wheel drive. Steve Soper and 'Smokin' Jo Winkelhock were star drivers in the 1990s.

The E36 was designed in such a way that it took account of sound aerodynamic principles, while at the same time retaining hallmarks of classic BMW styling. Naturally, the kidney radiator grille and twin circular headlamps were retained, but the frontal aspect and windscreen were steeply raked to allow cleaner airflow over the body, and the headlamps were enclosed under pieces of glass, also aimed at wind-cheating.

The door handles and window glass were

flush with the contours of the sheet metalwork in contemporary 1990s fashion, and the huge door mirrors were shaped much along the lines of the items fitted to Group B sports racing cars. Exterior trim, incidentally, was in matt black; brightwork had long since gone out of fashion, a move that was made initially by Lamborghini in 1967 with the launch of the mid-engined Miura.

With the aim of smoothing airflow over, and around, the flanks, there was a deep front air dam below the bumper, shaped side skirts along the sills (rocker panels), and a large wrap-around bumper at the rear contoured to keep turbulence behind the car to a minimum. In standard form, the bumpers and side skirts were coloured in dark grey, which contrasted markedly with all body colours and, in conjunction with steel wheels and plastic wheel trims, the car's aesthetics did not live up to BMW's reputation for creating dramatic, sporting visuals.

When the first cars were made available to journalists, I was struck in particular by the car's size. The wheelbase alone was 5in longer than the old model's, bootspace appeared to be cavernous and the cabin felt spacious even by the standards of the 5 Series.

BMW, Mercedes-Benz and Opel fought searing battles in the German Touring Car Championship, but the DTM descended into something of a shambles, and BMW turned their attentions elsewhere.

318i (1990–98)	
Body style	Four-door saloon, convertible from 1993 and Touring from 1995
Engine	
Cylinders	4
Bore × stroke	84 × 81mm
Capacity	1,796cc
Timing	Belt-driven single-overhead camshaft
Compression ratio	8.8:1
Fuel injection	Bosch Motronic, Lambda probe and catalytic converter
Max power	113bhp at 5,500rpm (115bhp at 5,500rpm from 1993)
Max torque	117lb ft at 4,250rpm (124lb ft at 3,900rpm from 1993)
Gearbox, suspension, steering, brakes and dimensions Identical to 316i, except for power-steering as standard	

The increase in wheelbase gave improved ride quality, and in conjunction with changes to the rear suspension, improved roadholding, but there was an inevitable weight penalty which led to criticism in some quarters that the car felt less crisp and less exciting. On the 'flip-side' the bodyshell was stronger, more torsionally rigid, and gave improved crash protection.

Vorsprung Durch Plastic

Although bright, airy and spacious, the redesigned cabin was representative of change for the sake of it, and made no ergonomic improvements over the E30's layout. The instruments were to the usual circular design and shrouded under a curved binnacle. The standard steering wheel had four spokes (a three-spoke sports steering wheel was available at extra cost) and all the controls were in easy reach of the driver. However, the extensive use of moulded plastic, although inevitable in mass-produced cars, was justifiably criticised for being excessive.

On the earliest cars there was also a problem over the quality of some interior components, including the cloth upholstery, many owners complaining vociferously that they did not expect to pay BMW money to experience the kind of problems that had endured for years in cars made in Britain. Unlike British manufacturers, though, BMW agreed that standards were not up to par, and quickly made amends. Cars made from early in 1991 were much improved, and criticism died away.

This episode was an unfortunate one, and a situation to which no manufacturer is immune, but it gave vent to the views of those who had always considered that BMWs had always been the over-priced products of clever 'spin-doctors'. Interestingly, the

The revised rear end included a concave depression in the rear panel, a refreshingly curvaceous shape for the lamp clusters – a fresh look for the 1990s.

contemporary 5 Series, manufactured from 1988, enjoyed an almost unrivalled reputation for superior build quality.

Below Decks

As in the past the E36's suspension relied on MacPherson struts, coil springs and an anti-roll bar at the front. At the rear, though, changes aimed at dialling out oversteer included a multi-link set-up, in conjunction with trailing arms, coil springs and an anti-roll bar.

Standard road wheels were increased in diameter to 15in, allowing for an increase in brake size, and while the 4-cylinder cars were equipped with front discs and rear drums, the more powerful 'sixes' got discs all round.

Steering, which was power-assisted across the board, was by modern rack-and-pinion, of course, but with a higher ratio than previously to give improved directional precision and control under cornering.

320i (1990–96)

Body style	four-door saloon, coupé from 1992, cabriolet from 1993 and Touring from 1995

Engine

Cylinders	6
Bore × stroke	80 × 66mm
Capacity	1,991cc, with 4 valves per cylinder
Timing	Belt-driven single-overhead camshaft with VANOS variable valve timing from September 1992
Compression ratio	11:1
Fuel injection	Bosch Motronic M1.7, Lambda probe and catalytic converter
Max power	150bhp at 5,900rpm
Max torque	140lb ft at 4,700rpm

Transmission

Gearbox	5-speed manual and 5-speed automatic	
Ratios	**5-speed manual**	**5-speed automatic**
First	4.23	3.67
Second	2.52	2.00
Third	1.77	1.41
Fourth	1.26	1.00
Fifth	1.00	0.74
Final drive	3.45	4.45

Suspension and steering
Identical to 316i except for 6.5J×15 wheels on saloon, or 7J×15 wheels on coupé, and 205/60VR 15 tyres

Brakes	Ventilated front discs, solid rears and ABS fitted as standard

Dimensions

Track	(front) 1,408mm/55.4in
	(rear) 1,421mm/55.9in
Wheelbase	2,700mm/106.3in
Overall length	4,433mm/174.5in
Overall width	1,698mm (saloon), 1,710mm/67.3in (coupé)
Overall height	1,393mm/54.8in (saloon), 1,366mm/53.8in (coupé)

A much larger car than the model it replaced, the E36's wheelbase was a full 5in longer, giving vastly increased legroom for rear-seat passengers.

Power Plus

The engines fitted to the E36 range were to the same general pattern as the past model, in that there were 4- and 6-cylinder variants in both petrol and diesel guise. The M40 4-cylinder units in the 100bhp 1.6- and 113bhp 1.8-litre 316i and 318i respectively produced the same output as they had in the E30 model equivalents, but development had resulted in improved fuel consumption and smoother running. Bosch Motronic management systems saw service on both these 4-cylinder units.

Already famous for their power output and smoothness, the 6-cylinder engines (150bhp 1,991cc in the 320i and 192bhp 2,494cc in the 325i) were further improved with four, instead of two, valves per cylinder. Top speeds also rose to 133mph for the 2-litre car and a quite astounding 145mph for the 2.5-litre model.

Just as astonishing was the top speed of 120mph from the 2,498cc turbocharged 6-cylinder diesel engine, hitherto unheard of performance for an oil-burner.

From autumn 1992, the petrol-engined 'sixes' were also treated to the VANOS system

Twin headlamps were retained, of course, but these were placed under clear lenses, just one of many new features that reduced aerodynamic drag.

of variable valve timing, which improved the power units spread of usable power across the entire rev range. In 1996, BMW debuted two new M52 6-cylinder engines, which also had the VANOS variable timing set-up. The revised power units, which broke with tradition in having alloy, rather than cast-iron, cylinder blocks, also boasted four valves per cylinder and twin-overhead camshafts.

Producing 170bhp the 2,494cc unit was fitted, confusingly, into the 323i, and the 193bhp 2,793cc engine went into the new 328i. The latter model revived a famous BMW serial number from pre-War days, which went unno-

The magnificent two-door coupé (captured here in the sleepy town of Zuffenhausen where Porsche have made cars since 1950) was among the most exciting sports saloons of its day, correctly hailed as an overnight classic.

The cabriolet version was every bit as attractive as the coupé, but typical British weather is not always conducive to 'wind in the face' motoring.

ticed by the vast majority of BMW's customers, many whom were unaware of the company's great sporting achievements of the 1930s.

New 5-speed gearboxes were fitted across the entire range, with revised ratios that took account of the more sporting nature of the new range. To this end the fifth gears were not in the nature of overdrive ratios. Automatic transmission was an extra-cost option, with 4-speed gearboxes in the 4-cylinder cars, and 5-speeders in the 'sixes'.

Much More in the M3

For the majority of people, even the most enthusiastic, the standard 328i provided for exhilarating motoring. By any standards it was quick, held the road superbly and had a braking system second to none. The M3 version, though, went several steps further.

Based on the stunning two-door coupé, the car was late in arriving. Perhaps oddly the M3 version of the E30 cabriolet

325i (1990–95)	
Body style	Four-door saloon, two-door coupé from 1992, and two-door convertible from 1993
Engine	
Cylinders	6
Bore × stroke	84 × 75mm
Capacity	2,494cc
Timing	4 valves per cylinder, belt-driven single-overhead camshaft with VANOS variable valve timing from September 1992
Compression ratio	10.5:1
Fuel injection	Bosch Motronic M1.7, Lambda probe and catalytic converter
Max power	192bhp at 5,900rpm
Max torque	177lb ft at 4,00rpm
Transmission	
5-speed manual with 3.15 final-drive ratio, or optional 5-speed automatic with 3.15 final-drive ratio	
Suspension and steering	
Identical to 316i apart from standard power-assisted steering and 7J×15 wheels	
Brakes	
Identical to 316i apart from vented front discs, standard rear discs and ABS	

remained in production until the summer of 1991, 'overlapping' the E36 range by quite some margin, but the new E36 M3 remained at the development stage while its less powerful sisters were being snapped up by eager customers.

There is no doubt that BMW was playing its cards close to its chest. As noted elsewhere, the early standard E36 cars suffered from a whole host of problems that resulted in warranty claims. BMW was forced to foot the bill for problems of its own making. To have allowed the same situation to arise with the M3 would have been inexcusable. It would have also tarnished the company's reputation, and given Porsche owners something to crow about, and BMW simply could not allow this to happen.

The M3 made its public debut at the 1992 Paris Motor Show, and reaction to it was much as BMW expected, for the car not only looked sensational, but went like a politician in search of a clue. Tin-top and convertible versions were available (along with a four-door saloon from 1994), and British customers warmed to right-hand drive variants, a novelty in view of the fact that the E30 M3s had all been left-hookers.

At the heart of the M3 was a mighty 3-litre (2,990cc) in-line 6-cylinder engine, employing twin-overhead camshafts, two valves per cylinder and a compression ratio of 10.8:1. In European-spec it produced 286bhp at 7,000rpm, and a full 46bhp less in US versions. Astonishingly, there was 236lb ft of torque at 3,600rpm, which allowed for elephantine acceleration all the way to the top of the rev range.

A top speed in excess of 150mph was, of course, entirely academic, for there was nowhere in the world that this could safely be achieved on public roads. In Germany, autobahns were becoming more restricted by speed limits, and those that remained unrestricted were choked by dense traffic. Many M3 owners, therefore, lived in despair, while a lucky few were able to enjoy their cars on the safety of a racing circuit.

An extraordinary piece of engineering planning in itself, the cabriolet's electrically-operated soft-top is child's play, and takes less than a minute to fold away or erect.

The top folds itself backwards...

...the closing panel opens upwards . . .

...swallows the hood...

...and the closing panel shuts neatly over the top – just one example of German engineering efficiency and know-how.

In keeping with engine power, the suspension was stiffened, the brakes increased in size and stopping power, and the power-steering was altered to give the driver better 'feel' of the road at high touring speeds.

Externally, the M3 was unmistakable as a sports car, but a lot more discreet than it might have been. At the front there was the 'statutory' chin spoiler, incorporating a meshed grille and protruding front lip, aerodynamically shaped side skirts, and a deep rear bumper from the standard car. Alloy wheels were to a striking five-spoke design, 17in in diameter and, needless to say, eye-wateringly expensive but, for those who failed to notice that this wasn't an ordinary 'Bee-em', there was a discreet M3 badge on the bootlid.

Inside the cabin, the picture was one of simple good taste and, apart from the sports front seats and sundry 'M' logos, was much the same as the standard E36. As usual, BMW offered a host of toys at extra cost, the nicest and most sensible of which was the leather-covered three-spoke steering wheel containing a central airbag.

Owners Speak Volumes

Sheila Jones is among the many thousands of women whose preferred form of transport was manufactured in Munich. An E36 2.5-litre 323i coupé, she has owned her car for more than four years, and sees no future in parting

318iS (1992–95)	
Body style	Two-door coupé
Engine	
Cylinders	4
Bore × stroke	84 × 81mm
Capacity	1,796cc
Timing	Four valves per cylinder, chain-driven single-overhead camshaft
Compression ratio	10:1
Fuel injection	Bosch Motronic M1.7, Lambda probe and catalytic converter
Max power	140bhp at 6,000rpm
Max torque	129lb ft at 4,500rpm
Transmission	
Identical to 316i	
Suspension and steering	
Suspension	Identical to 318i
Wheels	7J×15
Tyres	205/60VR 15
Brakes	Identical apart from ABS and rear discs as standard
Dimensions	
Track	(front) 1,408mm/55.4in
	(rear) 1,421mm/55.9in
Wheelbase	2,700mm/106.3in
Overall length	4,433mm/174.5in
Overall width	1,710mm/67.3in
Overall height	1,366mm/53.8in

Instrumentation was typically clear and uncluttered. M badge identifies this example as the powerful M3.

with it. This is her third consecutive BMW, and she is apt to compare them with cars she's driven previously.

Sheila laughs:

My second BMW was smashed up in an accident, forcing me to use a hired Vauxhall Corsa for six weeks. The Corsa was utterly horrible. I found it extremely difficult to use the gears, and changed it for an automatic, which creaked and rattled and threatened me on several occasions with a loss of steering control over bumps in the road.

The Ford Escort XR3i she once owned shaped up in much the same way. She comments:

I really hated the Ford. It felt rough by comparison with BMW's standards and, because of the position of the boot spoiler, it was difficult to see clearly through the back window.

Like the Corsa she hired, her current BMW is also an automatic. In the same mould as many folks who eschew manual gearboxes in favour of autos, Sheila would never want to return to the 'chore' of shifting a stick, particularly in heavy traffic.

Above: **The E36's dashboard was curved, in contemporary vogue, and nicely styled, but criticised in some quarters for such heavy use of dull-looking plastic.**

Left: **The sports leather-covered, three-spoke steering wheel has superb grip and feel. Note the continued use of aircraft-style orange illumination for the instruments.**

328i (1994–98)		
Body style	Four-door saloon, two-door coupé and Touring	
Engine		
Cylinders	6	
Bore × stroke	84 × 84mm	
Capacity	2,793cc	
Timing	4 valves per cylinder, chain-driven double-overhead camshafts, VANOS variable valve timing	
Compression ratio	10.2:1	
Fuel injection	Bosch Motronic, Lambda probe with catalytic converter	
Max power	193bhp at 5,300rpm	
Max torque	206lb ft at 3,950rpm	
Transmission		
Gearbox	5-speed manual or optional 5-speed automatic	
Ratios	**5-speed manual**	**5-speed automatic**
First	4.20	3.67
Second	2.49	2.00
Third	1.66	1.41
Fourth	1.24	1.00
Fifth	1.00	0.74
Final drive	2.93	4.45
Suspension, steering, brakes and dimensions Identical to 323i		

The mighty M3 3-litre develops 286bhp at 7,000rpm. Costing considerably more to buy than the regular range, these supercars were capable of giving contemporary Ferraris and Porsches a run for their money.

Drawn to BMWs by their aesthetics she describes her coupé as 'good looking' – 'a neat compact design' – but also appreciates its high level of useful equipment. Sheila cannot fault the car's performance either, and with leather-covered seats and steering wheel, she has nothing but praise for the car's comfort.

The seats are very firm, but most comfortable over long journeys, and in contrast to the discomfort I used to suffer in the days I owned rubbish cars.

Having chosen a two-door car on the grounds of safety (her grandchildren are frequent rear-seat passengers) Sheila's only complaint is the inconvenience of having to reach so far back for the seatbelt, but recognises that this as a small price to pay. When the children are older she might consider swapping her coupé for a four-door, but whether with two or four doors, the new car will definitely be a BMW.

And a Thorney Viewpoint

In this author's experience, secondhand car dealers are of a breed that are difficult, or even impossible, to warm to, but there are exceptions, that include an old chum, Rocky Thorne.

Honest, upstanding and hardworking, Rocky and his brother and business partner Gary have been in the motor trade since they

were teenagers. With a wealth of mechanical knowledge behind them, they have both settled for long-term BMW ownership; Rocky has an M3 Evolution and Gary drives a 325i cabriolet, and their reasoning is impeccable.

The M3 is a 3.2-litre 24-valve car, developing 321bhp, with a 6-speed gearbox and every conceivable 'whistle and flute'. Naturally, it goes like a farmer in search of government compensation, looks utterly wonderful in its smart, black livery, and makes for a particularly pleasant conveyance on sunny days with

The M3's deep chin spoiler was derived from motor racing experience, and worked in collaboration with the unusual side skirts and large rear wing.

M3 (1992–95)	
Body style	Two-door coupé, two-door convertible from 1994, and four-door saloon from 1994
Engine	
Cylinders	6
Bore × stroke	86 × 85.8mm
Capacity	2,990cc
Timing	4 valves per cylinder, chain-driven double-overhead camshafts, VANOS variable valve timing
Compression ratio	10.8:1
Fuel injection	Bosch Motronic M3.3, Lambda probe and catalytic converter
Max power	286bhp at 7,000rpm, or 240bhp for US-spec version
Max torque	231lb ft at 3,600rpm
Transmission	
Gearbox	5-speed manual
Ratios	First 4.20
	Second 2.49
	Third 1.66
	Fourth 1.24
	Fifth 1.00
	Final drive 3.15, or 3.23 on US-spec version
Suspension and steering	
Suspension	Identical to 325i
Steering	BMW variable-ratio
Wheels	7.5J×17, 8.5J×17 or 8.5J×17
Tyres	`235/40ZR 17
Brakes	Identical to 325i
Dimensions	
Track	(front) 1,482mm/56in
	(rear) 1,444mm/56.8in
Wheelbase	2,700mm/106.3in
Overall length	4,433mm/174.5in
Overall width	1,710mm/67.3mm
Overall height	1,366mm/53.8in

Former Ford owner but a committed BMW enthusiast, Sheila Jones cites her 6-cylinder coupé as the best car she has ever driven.

Apart from being sufficiently practical for ferrying grandchildren between 'Toys R Us' and Burger King, Sheila Jones reckons that her coupé is one of the best styled cars to emerge from BMW.

the electrically-operated soft-top folded away.

Rocky and brother Gary arrived at BMW ownership principally as a result of experiences with so many other cars. Rocky comments:

I find the M3 easy to service, easy to work on and cheap to run. When it reached 60,000 miles, I put it on my hydraulic ramp to inspect the underside; there wasn't one drop of oil, or any other fluid, leaking from anywhere. I've also discovered that replacement parts, although you don't need them too often, are a lot cheaper than most people think. Some Ford and Vauxhall parts, for example, cost a lot more, and generally tend to be needed more often.

In our business we see Japanese cars that are reliable and give good service, but have awful styling, and cars from British manufacturers who have clearly lost the plot. Audis and Mercedes-Benzes are built to exemplary standards, and rarely go wrong, but I see the Merc in particular as a car for an older generation, which is why they don't yet appeal to me.

Injection pipework and associated plumbing is naturally complex but, in traditional racing style, it presents a classic and utterly wonderful under-bonnet picture.

M3 Evolution (1995–98)

Engine

Cylinders	6
Bore × stroke	86.4 × 91mm, US-spec 86.4 × 89.6mm
Capacity	3,201cc, US-spec 3,152cc
Timing	4 valves per cylinder, chain-driven double-overhead camshafts, double-VANOS variable valve timing
Compression ratio	11.3:1, US-spec version 10.5:1
Fuel injection	BMW MSS 50, twin Lambda probes, and catalytic converter
Max power	321bhp at 7,400rpm, US-spec 243bhp
Max torque	258lb ft at 3,250rpm, US-spec 236lb ft at 3,800rpm

Transmission

Gearbox	6-speed manual for Euro-spec, 5-speed manual from previous M3 for US-spec version
Ratios	First 4.23
	Second 2.51
	Third 1.67
	Fourth 1.23
	Fifth 1.00
	Sixth 0.83
	Final drive 3.23

Suspension, brakes, steering and dimensions
Identical to previous M3, apart from 225/45 17 front tyres, and 245/50 17 rear tyres.

The 3.2-litre version of the M3, illustrated in cabriolet guise, was virtually peerless as a seriously quick sporting saloon. This immaculate car is used on a daily basis by motor trader, Rocky Thorne, who claims that the only superior car is a Porsche 911.

The M3's 3.2-litre 24-valve 'six' pushes out 321bhp, but top speed is limited to a 'sensible' 155mph.

A dynamic car with superlative roadholding and handling, acceleration form corners is electrifying, but care needs to be exercised with the throttle pedal in the wet.

Rocky Thorne's views are frequently echoed across the board among BMW owners; they tell the same very old story – that you get top-notch performance in a car that costs no more to run than a run-of-the-mill plodder. Curiously the M3 cabriolet regularly returns in excess of 25mpg, despite occasionally being booted hard. As Rocky pointed out, 'a less-than-exciting Rover returns about the same,' and asks, 'so why have a Rover?'

Brother Gary is adamant that German engineering has not yet been equalled.

Pound for pound, it's virtually impossible to beat a Volkswagen Golf. They're extremely reliable and durable, give really good performance and don't depreciate in the manner of most cars. For me, though, the BMW is a better vehicle. It has more than adequate performance, is supremely good looking, and the 6-cylinder motor is a beautiful jewel of engineering at its very best. In addition the roadholding is first class, although far from fool-proof – the tail can easily be kicked out of line – if you play around with the throttle pedal, especially in wet weather. There's nothing I don't like about it – BMW have just got everything so absolutely right.

Despite regular use for their intended purpose, the Thornes' cars show few signs of wear and tear. Water and wax makes them shine like new, testament to the manner in which they were originally screwed together, but it is inescapable that BMW residual values continue to trail someway behind those of Daimler-Benz's products.

Despite sizzling performance when it's needed, Rocky Thorne enjoys the entirely functional aspect of the car's comfort and ability to seat four adults.

Cream leather seats are not especially easy to keep clean, but when you've got a car capable of accelerating from 0–60mph in less than 7secs, who cares?

From BMW's first car in 1928 (an Austin 7 made under licence and dubbed Dixi), via near bankruptcy in 1959, to supercar manufacturer by the 1990s is almost unprecedented in the history of motor manufacturing. Like all good things, though, production of the third generation 3 Series had to come to an end. It made way for a genuinely improved fourth generation 3 Series.

Secondhand Values

By the mid-1990s, there had been many changes in western society that would have been inconceivable just 20 years earlier. With the arrival of the Internet (invented as long ago as 1971 at the height of the Cold War) it was predicted that more and more people would work at home, leading to a decline in dependence on the motor car. This prediction has not yet proved to be correct.

In the western world, intellectuals on both sides of the Atlantic regularly warned of the 'dangers' of increasing consumerism and materialism. Yet consumerism and materialism increased measurably.

For many, the acquisition of a BMW, rightly or wrongly, became an outward symbol of their success. More than any other car of the latter quarter of the twentieth century, a BMW had become the archetypal middle-class conveyance, and the Munich company's profits soared once again.

A New Nose Job

In 1996 the 3 Series received a wholly insignificant facelift, a total nonsense in which the front of the car was slightly revised. The chromium-plated bands around the 'kidney' parts of the radiator grille were made broader, and there was an awkward, angled panel placed next to the inner edges of the headlamp lenses which, from a styling viewpoint, brought the 3 Series into line with the contemporary 5 Series.

Those who noticed these small changes were few and far between, and those whose eyesight was good enough did not really care. A new model was shortly on the way, and many had heard that it purported to be the finest 3 Series car to date.

CHAPTER FOUR

BMW 3 Series:
The Fourth Generation

Trouble at the Top

By the time of the launch of the fourth generation E46 3 Series in 1998, BMW's board members were collectively shaking their heads, and seriously beginning to regret becoming involved in Rover's affairs. The Germany company owned the English one, and it had become apparent to the German side of the operation that there were irreconcilable differences between the two companies.

BMW's post-War operation had been successful since the early 1960s. The company had clearly got the formula for success down to a fine art. Rover were trying very hard in the same sort of markets, and failing dismally. The British manufacturer's cars had a poor image, styling to which many were indifferent, poor build quality to which no-one was indifferent, and an abysmal reliability record.

With poor management, a lack of investment stretching back decades and a ghastly range of cars, Rover's fortunes went from bad to worse, while at the same time, BMW's got better and better. Interestingly, BMW originally acquired the entire Rover Group for considerably less than it cost to develop the then current 5 Series BMW. By the end of the 1990s, the German giant would discover the reasons for this.

The current 3 Series is arguably the best of the breed, a benchmark in safety, engineering integrity, performance, comfort and style. Despite having put on weight down the years, these cars are anything but 'flabby' but, in terms of technical complexity, are very far removed from the original mid-1970s concept.

The unique design of the narrow 'wave-like' piece at the base of the headlamp cowls pleasantly softens the otherwise aggressive frontal appearance.

Arguably the best looking of all the 3 Series cars, the E46 was larger than previously, and once again a four-door saloon formed the initial staple of the range. A stunningly beautiful coupé followed 12 months later, with a convertible (with optional hard-top), Compact, Touring and M3 tagging along behind. The increase in body size was by less than 2in in width, height and length, but the overall effect was of a car of vast proportions. Volkswagen had similarly increased successive generations of the Golf and their sales, particularly in Europe, demonstrated that this was the correct strategy.

Some commentators predicted that the size of the 3 Series, together with the usual BMW attributes, would be responsible for eating into sales of the 5 Series. This was a reasonable assumption, but it did not materialize.

Apart from having a larger body, the latest incarnation was considerably stiffer and safer, with particular attention having been paid to the car's primary safety. Although BMW had always made exceptionally safe passenger saloons, the company had never emphasized this aspect of design in its many marketing campaigns. Safety had been taken for granted but the marketing men dwelt a little on this during the late 1990s after it had become apparent that Volvo and Saab were selling more and more cars on their well-worn safety theme.

Although aesthetically similar to the contemporary 5 Series, and bearing undertones of its predecessor, the E46 was considerably more rounded than previous generations, and hailed as 'pretty' by BMW devotees. Arguably the strongest new styling innovation was the 'wavy' line below each of the headlamp clusters that followed the contours of the bases of each lamp. This was but one example of German styling beating the Italians at their own game, notwithstanding a new range of Alfa-Romeos which, despite in built 'Italianesque', and the inherent vagaries of front-wheel drive, looked stunning.

Despite Rover's difficulties, and BMW's attempts to put a brave face on the situation, the launch of the E46 was one of many motoring highlights of the mid to late 1990s. Porsche, Daimler-Benz, BMW and Lotus had suddenly reawakened the interests of driving enthusiasts, who had hitherto begun to question whether the automotive industry had wholly lost the plot. Exciting and affordable sports machines from these manufacturers rejuvenated a motoring world that had become grey and dull. For BMW fans, the Z3 two-seater and new 3 Series saloons were cars to which they could look forward.

The New E46 – So What?

In the outgoing 3 Series BMW had made something of a rod for its own back. The car had been a huge success and many owners regarded it as being so good as to be beyond improvement. However arch-rivals Mercedes-Benz had gone a step further with the C class range, and BMW could not afford to drag its feet. The E36 was a good car – extremely good – but progress had been made in certain areas of design, and for BMW the result was the E46.

Sleek, well-balanced, neat and seductive, the superb lines of the bodywork are perfectly complemented by large-diameter alloy wheels.

A Spell Inside

Apart from improving roadholding, the revised car's longer wheelbase also increased legroom for rear-seat passengers. Many considered that this had at long last addressed a long-standing 'problem', but the past criticism of the 3 Series' lack of legroom was, of course, another dollop of journalese nonsense. The vast majority of passenger saloons are used by one person – the driver. When the owners of 3 Series BMWs fill their cars to capacity, the rear seats are usually occupied by children, as borne out by market research, so the vitriol aimed by professional commentators was yet another example of unfounded and shallow thinking.

Interior styling was in contemporary German style, with elliptical shapes used for the instrument binnacle, and door panels. The instruments were circular and the central panel was angled towards the driver – nothing new here – but the upper surface of the dashboard gave an impression of a designer's terminal obsession with plastic, and detracted slightly from what was otherwise a statement of confident quality.

It goes without saying that the seats were firmly padded, the three-spoke steering wheel and gear lever were perfect, and that wood

trim and leather upholstery were available to the well-heeled. However the most notable features were related to modern technology.

Apart from the ubiquitous on-board computer giving information about fuel consumption, average speed and the rest, there were Car Memory, Key Memory and satellite navigation (optional) systems to play with. The Memory systems allowed a whole host of functions to be programmed in advance, while satellite navigation negated the need for a traditional road atlas. The latter also gave infor-

The driving environment is ergonomically perfect, and most stylish, but critics continue to groan about the 'acres' of dull plastic for the dashboard.

mation about journey distances to and from any destination on the globe with pin-point accuracy. In addition, there was a 'synthetic' voice to guide drivers when travelling alone.

That a beam can be directed from a satellite in space, circumnavigating the globe on an hourly basis, to a car's ABS brake sensors, and into a dashboard-mounted screen via a CD-Rom housed in the boot, is a marvel of man's ingenuity. The real test of man's ingenuity, however, will be those occasions when 'gremlins' creep into such systems and repairs are needed, which is when these high-tech gadgets may yet prove to be more trouble than they are worth.

In addition to the 'toys' the E46 was equipped with a system of airbags for front and rear passengers (optional in the rear) which, although greatly improving the chance of survival in serious impacts, have shown their shortcomings in a number of high-profile cases. With a deployment speed of close to 300mph, airbags are known to be capable of inflicting severe injuries, particularly on small children, but their benefits overall undoubtedly contribute to reducing uncomfortable statistics.

If It Ain't Broke . . .

For the suspension system, there was no getting away from tried and tested components. MacPherson struts, coil springs and an anti-roll bar were employed up front, while the multi-link system, in conjunction with coil springs and anti-roll, bar were retained at the rear.

Disc brakes were fitted all round as standard, and for those occasionally caught napping, ABS was also standard across the range. Steering was by rack and pinion and power-assisted, and the more powerful models also came with traction-control, an electronic device that has virtually replaced the old-fashioned limited-slip differential as a means of keeping the tail in line under hard acceleration.

Although the same basic 'chassis' was retained, the E46 handled slightly better than its predecessors. The increase in wheelbase and track gave inherently better stability and, in conjunction with the engine position, which was moved further back towards the front bulkhead, the front-to-rear weight distribution was just about perfect.

The result of these changes is a sporting saloon, that held the road, and handled in state of the art fashion – a precision piece whose designers produced a perfect compromise between the demands of sporting drivers, and the requirements of comfort made by their passengers. Taut, yet lively, and arrow-straight at high speed, the chassis is a rear-wheel drive marvel, and exactly how a late 1990s machine should be.

Power You Nit

Although the revised cars retained the same model designations as previously (mostly for marketing reasons) there were changes in engine capacity that served to confuse. At entry level, there were the 4-cylinder 316i and 318i, which were both powered by the same 1,895cc engine, but in different states of tune. The former, despite power output of 105bhp, was capable of 125mph, while the 118bhp 318i could almost nudge 130mph.

The 6-cylinder cars, with four valves per cylinder and double-overhead camshafts, were placed in the 320i, 323i and 328i with capacities of 1,991cc (150bhp), 2,494cc (170bhp) and 2,793cc (193bhp) respectively. In addition to the classic petrol engines, there was the usual spate of 'oil-burners', including a new 4-cylinder 2-litre unit, but these are beyond the scope of this book; this author

316i (1999–)

Body style	four-door saloon, two-door coupé, two-door convertible and Touring

Engine

Cylinders	4
Bore × stroke	83.5 × 85mm
Capacity	1,895cc
Timing	Chain-driven single-overhead camshaft
Compression ratio	9.7:1
Fuel injection	BMW 46 system, Lambda probe, catalytic converter
Max power	105bhp at 5,300rpm
Max torque	122lb ft at 2,500rpm

Transmission

Gearbox	5-speed manual or optional 4-speed automatic	
Ratios	**5-speed manual**	**4-speed automatic**
First	4.23	2.40
Second	2.52	1.47
Third	1.66	1.00
Fourth	1.22	0.72
Fifth	1.00	
Final drive	3.23	4.44

Suspension and steering

Front	MacPherson struts, coil springs and anti-roll bar
Rear	BMW multi-link system, coil springs and anti-roll bar
Steering	Power-assisted rack and pinion
Wheels	6.5J×15
Tyres	195/65R 15

Brakes	Servo-assisted vented front, solid rear discs with ABS

Dimensions

Track	(front) 1,481mm/58.3in
	(rear) 1,488mm/58.5in
Wheelbase	2,730mm/107.5in
Overall length	4,471mm/176in
Overall width	1,739mm/68.5in
Overall height	1,415mm/55.7in

Top-of-the-range M3 coupé boasts 3.2-litre 343bhp race-derived 6-cylinder power unit. Capable of 0–60mph in 5secs, and astonishingly good looking, it fails to rouse much interest at a VSCC meeting.

being firmly of the conviction that diesel-engine use should be discouraged on health and environmental grounds.

The performance of each model within the E46 range was, to say the least, quite astonishing, although not by BMW's standards, of course. Despite the presence of catalytic converters (a legal requirement in many countries) each model was capable of knocking spots off virtually every contemporary from rival manufacturers. The range-topping 328i, for example, was capable of a wholly academic 150mph, and even more once it had been 'breathed on' by specialist tuning companies.

Beyond performance, however, was the improved smoothness and torque of the engines across the board. Double-VANOS variable valve timing improved engine characteristics, while catalytic converters housed inside the exhaust manifolds not only decreased the time it took for the engine to reach its optimum operating temperature but also reduced power loss, inherent in all catalytic converters, to a minimum.

Engine characteristics were also matched extremely well to gearbox ratios. Standard across the range was a 5-speed manual with close ratios, and a 4-speed automatic was available as usual as an extra-cost option. In addition, there was a 5-speed 'Steptronic' system, which allowed manual, or automatic, shifting.

318i (1999–)

Identical to 316i except for the following:

Engine
Max power	118bhp at 5,500rpm
Max torque	133lb ft at 3,900rpm

Transmission
5-speed manual with 3.38:1 final-drive ratio

320Ci (1999–)	
Identical to 318i except for the following:	
Engine	
Cylinders	6
Bore × stroke	66 × 80mm
Capacity	1,991cc
Timing	4 valves per cylinder, chain-driven double-overhead camshafts with Double-VANOS variable valve timing
Compression ratio	11:1
Fuel injection	BMW DMS 46, twin catalytic converters
Max power	150bhp at 5,900rpm
Max torque	140lb ft at 3,500rpm
Brakes	Vented rear discs

Owner's View

Despite having reached the mature age of 75, retired estate agent Major Bill Rollings has lost none of his long-held enthusiasm for cars, driving, and BMWs in particular. For many years he ran Peugeots and there was a spell behind the wheel of a Triumph 2.5 PI but, having bought his first BMW (a 733i) in 1976, he never again wanted for anything other than a car built in Munich.

When on one occasion he and his wife were touring in the Triumph through Germany and Switzerland, the only cars that overtook were BMWs, and this 'audacity' naturally aroused Bill's curiosity. That first 733i more than a quarter of a century ago made a huge impression.

> It's very dated now, but in its day it was absolutely great in every way. That car, although far too big to hustle quickly along country lanes, was a marvel. It handled like no car I'd driven before, there was comfort in abundance, and the performance just seemed so effortless, especially during motorway cruising. From a very early stage, it occurred to me that although BMWs were impressive from the outside, what you were paying for was the engineering on the inside.

Bill's 733i was followed by four further examples of the 7 Series in a row, with a variety of 6-cylinder engine variants. He enjoyed each to the full, citing their quietness, smoothness and comfort as strong points, and sheer size as a disadvantage for his purposes.

Bill recalls:

> There is no doubt that the big cars handled extremely well, and bodyroll was minimal – like a nimble sports car in some respects – and braking was superb but, if you met another car in a narrow lane, you had to stop, wait and waste time in manoeuvring past. The ridiculous thing about the 'Seven', almost above everything else was, that for such performance, fuel consumption was so astonishingly good – between 26–30mpg was quite normal.

After the Sevens, he had a couple of 5 Series cars in a row; the first a classic straight-six and the second a 3-litre V8.

Vents in the front wings, to allow hot air from the engine bay to escape, distinguish the M3 from 'lesser' models.

323Ci (1999–)

Identical to 320Ci except for the following:

Engine

Cylinders	6
Bore × stroke	75 × 84mm
Capacity	2,494cc
Timing	4 valves per cylinder, chain-driven double-overhead camshafts with Double-VANOS variable valve timing
Compression ratio	10.5:1
Fuel injection	BMW DMS 46
Max power	170bhp at 5,500rpm
Max torque	181lb ft at 3,500rpm

Major Bill Rollings, 75, has owned a number of important BMW models, including 5 and 7 Series cars, but cites his 323i as the finest all-rounder.

The 530i was an especially good car, the smoothness of the V8 engine excelling the brilliance of the 6-cylinder model. It was with the 5 Series that I also came to realise that with a BMW you get the same build quality and immaculate paint finish across the range. The 'Five', being that much smaller than the 7 Series, was also a lot nimbler in corners – a car you could really fling around without worrying, if you wanted to.

Major Bill enjoyed the 530i so much that, unusually for him, he kept it for six years, and was loathe to part with it. However, as one of BMW's long-standing customers, he was naturally tempted by his local dealer to consider other models in the range, and inevitably considered buying a V12 850i.

In many ways the V12 makes for the ideal Grand Touring car and, as someone who makes long sojourns to continental Europe, it would be absolutely perfect. The car is undeniably powerful, comfortable, quiet and has a huge luggage space below the bootlid, but a test drive con-

vinced me that I didn't need one. I didn't like the driving position, and couldn't see the end of the bonnet or wings, which I could imagine giving a few difficulties when parking in tight spaces. A few years ago, I tried a 635CSi and experienced the same difficulties, in addition to having to reach back a long way for the seatbelt buckle.

When the E46 3 Series was launched, Bill, like so many others, just had to have one. Similar in proportions to the outgoing E34 5 Series, but even prettier in his view, he rushed out and 'chopped in' his 530i for a 'fully-loaded', metallic silver, 2.5-litre 323i. For a while, Bill viewed it, all things considered, as the best (for his purposes) BMW he had owned.

> It's spacious, powerful, economical, holds the road as well as anything I've driven previously, is well equipped – I especially like the satellite navigation system – and looks absolutely stunning.

However, as I sat in the passenger seat of Bill's car, as he demonstrated the technological wizardry of the satellite screen, he expressed a rare tinge of regret, and another of quiet excitement. In the manner of a naughty schoolboy, yearning to swap his blazer and grey flannels for a T-shirt and shorts, Bill forcefully remarked:

> Yep, this is a great car . . . but I want a cabriolet – a soft-top version of this. It would be absolutely perfect, but just wasn't available when I rushed off and bought this tin-top.

Having retired from business five years ago at the age of 70, Bill has never been in the habit of looking back. Cars have played a big part of his life, and he maintains an infectious zest and enthusiasm for driving his BMW at every opportunity. As an ex-military man his cars are always in spotless condition, and maintained in the manner that their makers intended. And Bill Rollings is but one example of a chap who has swayed slightly against

Leather interior is an expensive extra-cost option, but arguably more worthwhile than the...

the grain. It is often said that sporting motorists prefer BMWs, but change to a Mercedes as they mature, but Stuttgart's best is not for Bill, as he explains.

> Like lots of European taxi drivers, I've driven Mercs and found them to be perfectly satisfactory. They're well screwed together, the engineering quality is beautiful, but I've never especially warmed to their styling, and find them to be very austere inside.

...satellite navigation system. You pays your money.

The under-bonnet picture of Bill Rollings' 6-cylinder car is as aesthetically dull as the dashboard, but at least the electronic complexities discourage Sunday morning tinkerers.

But, whether he retains his current mount, or scorches off to acquire a convertible, he is in no doubt that his future destiny lies in travelling at the wheel of a BMW through countries he knows well and loves. France, Germany, Switzerland and Austria are personal favourites for soaking up the miles, but Eire is also a priority.

Southern Ireland is a country I especially enjoy. Apart from uncluttered roads, the place is like a time-warp. There's no evidence of vandalism, anywhere, and you can leave your car unlocked, with valuables so overtly on display, safe in the knowledge that no-one will take anything.

Like the cars he has owned over the past 25 years or so, Bill Rollings has grown up with successive generations of BMWs, and considers each new development to be in the nature of genuine improvement; the engineers at BMW feel much the same way!

Conclusion Without End

Through four successive generations of the 3 Series, BMW have created a sporting saloon in a niche market by which all others have come to be judged. That the 3 Series is a class leader, since its inception, is not in doubt. With development each generation has become more powerful, more sophisticated, and despite inevitable gains in weight, the BMW has not become 'flabby'.

The car has evolved steadily, maintaining rear-wheel drive, and other BMW hallmarks throughout. Sales have increased, in some instances most dramatically, as the BMW word spreads further afield. There is a case for arguing that the latest sophisticates, in the form of the E46, have lost the raw edge held by the '02 and first generation 3 Series, but this, if it is true, is an inevitable part of 'growing up'. Demands of safety by world legislatures alone play a large part in the way any car takes shape over a long period; where BMW's engineers and designers score well is in keeping well ahead of the bureaucrats, accountants

The Touring version is arguably the most dynamic of all estates; Audi vehemently disagree, of course.

328Ci (1999–)

Identical to 318i except for the following:

Engine

Cylinders	6
Bore × stroke	84 × 84mm
Capacity	2,793cc
Timing	4 valves per cylinder, chain-driven double-overhead camshafts with Double-VANOS variable valve timing
Compression ratio	10.2:1
Fuel injection	BMW DMS 46, twin catalytic converters
Max power	193bhp at 5,500rpm
Max torque	207lb ft at 3,500rpm

Transmission

Gearbox   5-speed manual, or optional 5-speed automatic

Ratios	**5-speed manual**	**5-speed automatic**
First	4.21	3.67
Second	2.49	2.00
Third	1.66	1.41
Fourth	1.24	1.00
Fifth	1.00	0.74
Final drive	2.93	3.07

Wheels and tyres   7J×16 alloy wheels with 205/55R 16 tyres

Dimensions

Track	(front) 1,471mm (57.9in)
	(rear) 1,478mm (58.1in)

and breeds of pressure groups who have a natural tendency to call for changes to be made when they run out of others to blame for their miserable, insignificant lives.

Sitting pretty at the top of the tree, as BMW's products certainly do, has been achieved by hard work and constant vigilance. There are rivals aplenty, not least Daimler-Benz, Volkswagen and Alfa-Romeo, and in no sense can anyone at Munich afford to sit back and congratulate themselves for having performed a 'marvellous job' yet again.

Japanese manufacturers have eaten healthily into European markets but it cannot be coincidence, though, that so many new models from the styling houses of the Far East, closely resemble existing designs from Munich, Stuttgart and Wolfsburg!

Among BMW enthusiasts the 3 Series forms a backbone of interest, particularly among the members of specialist clubs. Their interest is growing, tangibly, as so many models become acknowledged as classic pieces of design. Older cars are being restored in increasing numbers, and there is strong evidence of a growing market in customising and tuning.

Despite this interest in past models, however, the people in Munich are at work on a fifth generation of the 3 Series. As good as the E46 undoubtedly is, its successor will be different, and in some respects improved. The new car's specification, for the time being, remains wrapped in secrecy, and only those who continue to loathe BMWs will remain oblivious to its public debut. Long may they remain in ignorance.

CHAPTER FIVE

BMW 5 Series

'Probably the Best Car in the World'

The immortal 5 Series (the 'Fünfer', as it is affectionately known in Germany), was originally launched at the 1972 Olympic Games, hosted in that fateful year in Munich. The great sporting occasion ostensibly provided a great 'backdrop' for BMW to launch their new saloon in a blaze of international publicity. Unfortunately, things didn't turn out as planned.

What should have been a great competitive event between sporting nations, developed into a tragedy when Palestinians executed a number of Israeli athletes. For days the international media understandably focused its attention on the catastrophe, and few noticed that a new BMW had appeared. A year later, the Middle East oil crisis resulted in fuel rationing in many European countries, including Britain, and almost everything in the civilised motoring world threatened to become 'pear-shaped'.

Along with a number of other German manufacturers, BMW rode this economic storm well and survived, which was surprising in view of the luxury, sporting nature and lofty purchase price of the new 5 Series machine. Right from the start of production, it was obvious that the 5 Series was a superior machine to the 2000 saloon range it replaced.

As early as 1975, respected American journal *Road & Track* commented:

The 530i is everything a luxury-sports sedan should be. It's comfortable, practical in the extreme and with good measure of performance, ride and handling thrown in. It's no wonder we had little trouble choosing it as one of the world's ten best cars.

The current 5 Series stands as a beacon of dynamic engineering ability, a technical *tour de force* arrived at through several generations that started in 1972. Hailed for many years as the world's best all-round saloon, BMW's 'Fünfer', as it is known in Germany, is a sports car for 'grown-ups'.

For people who have never driven, or ridden in, one of these splendid cars, it's difficult to impart in words the way in which the BMW works so well and competently. Those who have pre-conceived notions about, but absolutely no experience of, Rolls-Royce motoring, might like to substitute in their minds the idea of a 5 Series instead.

One dark, foggy damp evening during the dismal autumn of 1997, I boarded a British Airways flight from Atlanta, Georgia, bound for London's Heathrow Airport. After the aeroplane (an aged DC10) had reached 38,000ft and 'levelled-out' the Captain, Bill Mullens, dutifully ventured out of the flight deck to speak to his passengers. Intrigued by the 'mysteries' of powered flight, I enquired of our Captain what it was like to fly a DC10. He explained that he loved the aircraft, had flown them for over 20 years and said, without hesitation that, from the helmsman's seat, it was almost identical to driving a BMW 528i – a car of which he was a huge fan.

This was extremely interesting, for Mullens further explained that a DC10 was so manoeuvrable that, like a 528i, it was possible to kick the tail out of line simply by applying loads of throttle. In reply to his enthusiastic meanderings, I remarked that I believed him one hundred per cent, but forcefully expressed the wish that he wouldn't seek to prove his claim while I was aboard! I assume that he complied, because I fell asleep for the entire flight.

The E12

Built between 1972 and 1981, the first of the 5 Series generation was intended as an 'up-market' four-door saloon. BMW had attempted to acquire Lancia during the late 1960s but, having failed against Italian giant Fiat, was left with little choice but to tread a path of its own. Styled by Paul Bracq who, during his time at Daimler-Benz had been

responsible for the radical 'Pagoda' SL sports cars of the 1960s, the new car was representative of heavy investment, but with equally 'heavy' potential.

Designed to accommodate both 4- and 6-cylinder power units, the revised car utilised many tried and tested components from the Munich parts bin and, mechanically, was almost entirely conventional. By initially adopting this policy, BMW would inevitably save money that could be usefully employed elsewhere.

Regrettably, the majority of the original Fünfers have either disappeared, or languish in a state of terminal decay.

During the 1970s BMW's bonnet roundel meant little to 'Joe Public', but the Munich company's aim of toppling Daimler-Benz in the luxury market would be just a few years ahead.

Designed to Last

Although narrower and shorter in height than the outgoing 1800 to 2000 range of cars, the E12 was some 3in longer, and weighed almost 300lb more than the old model. Despite the additional length, aimed at enhancing rear legroom and boot space, Paul Bracq's styling was a classic piece of masterly understatement, with overtones of sporting prowess that would live and remain fresh and exciting in the many years ahead.

Twin headlamps were used at the front (a strong styling feature of the big CS coupés launched in 1968) along with the 'obligatory' kidney radiator grille. The latter 'ate' marginally into a small bonnet 'bulge' from 1976 which, in combination with the sharply raked angle of the grille, gave the frontal appearance of BMW's classic 'friendly-shark' look.

The flanks were 'broken' by a prominent swage line, leading from the sides of the bonnet through to the rear, and rubbing strips were fitted lower down to protect the four doors from the usual antics of careless folk in supermarket car parks. Naturally, on the grounds of both safety and aesthetics, the car retained BMW's long-standing commitment to providing a large glass area. The 'dogleg' piece was incorporated into the rear side windows and, to add to the car's sporting appeal,

both the large panoramic windscreen and rear window were sloped at a steep angle.

In the manner of contemporaries from Mercedes-Benz and Volkswagen, the Fünfer's bodyshell comprised a rigid passenger cell with front and rear zones designed to absorb shock effectively and crumple in the event of a collision. This was largely in response to US safety legislation, and very long overdue. Sometimes referred to as the 'father of passive safety', Bela Barenyi, who worked for Daimler-Benz for many years, had pioneered many safety features that had been incorporated in Mercedes' since the 1950s.

His inventions included side-impact beams in doors, and the famous 'Pagoda' roof, which was capable of withstanding the sort of weight more normally associated with the aircraft industry. Barenyi was a rare talent, way ahead of his time, and thought little of driving from Stuttgart to southern Italy and back during the course of a weekend merely to test a new component. He lived for motor cars and driving. His pioneering work has saved thousands of lives worldwide, but it was not until the 1970s that the rest of the automotive world would begin to learn from his example.

The Fünfer's cabin also broke new ground in that the central control panel containing the heating and ventilation functions was angled towards the driver. This, along with

518 (1974–81)

Body style   Four-door saloon throughout production

Engine
Cylinders   4
Bore × stroke   89 × 71mm
Capacity   1,766
Timing   All models with single-overhead camshaft
Compression ratio   8.6:1
Carburettor   Solex
Max power   90bhp at 5,500rpm
Max torque   104lb ft at 3,500rpm

Transmission
From 1974 to 1975
Gearbox   4-speed manual
Ratios   First 3.764
                                Second 2.02
                                Third 1.32
                                Fourth 1.00

From September 75
Ratios   First 3.764
                                Second 2.043
                                Third 1.320
                                Fourth 1.00

From September 75, optional 3-speed automatic
Ratios   First 2.52
                                Second 1.52
                                Third 1.00

From September 1979, optional 5-speed manual
Ratios   First 3.822
                                Second 2.202
                                Third 1.398
                                Fourth 1.00
                                Overdrive fifth 0.813

Suspension and steering
Front   MacPherson struts and anti-roll bar
Rear   Semi-trailing arms, coil springs and optional anti-roll bar
Steering   ZF worm and roller, optional PAS
Wheels   Pressed steel 5.5J×14
Tyres   175SR 14 radials

Brakes   Servo-assisted discs/drums

Dimensions
Track   (front) 1,406mm/55.3in
                                (rear) 1,412mm/55.3in
Wheelbase   2,636mm/103.7in
Overall length   4,620mm/181.9in
Overall width   1,690mm/66.5in
Overall height   1,425mm/56.1in

Like the contemporary 3 Series, the 5 Series was conservatively styled.
A conventional 'three-box' saloon, but embracing the usual BMW styling features, the 5 Series became an automotive paragon coveted by the middle-classes in the whole of Europe.

Twin headlamps, 'kidney' radiator grille in fashionable matt black, and deep chin spoiler were carried over from the previous 2500/2800 saloons which...

the novelty of instrument illumination in orange, were major features that would serve for many future BMW designs. While the cloth-covered seats were fully adjustable, smart in appearance and comfortable, they were firmly padded (in traditional German fashion), and made for a sensible compromise between touring-style comfort and the needs of sporting drivers who liked to conduct their cars through corners with the wing mirrors firmly in contact with the tarmac.

---

520 (1972–77)

Identical to 518 except for the following:

Engine

Cylinders	4
Bore × stroke	89 × 90mm
Capacity	1,990cc
Compression ratio	9:1
Carburettor	Stromberg 175 CDET
Max power	115bhp at 5,800rpm
Max torque	119lb ft at 3,700rpm

Transmission

Gearbox 4-speed manual or optional 3-speed automatic

Ratios	4-speed manual	3-speed automatic
First	3.764	2.52
Second	2.02	1.52
Third	1.32	1.00
Fourth	1.00	
Final drive	4.11	4.11

Suspension
Rear anti-roll bar fitted as standard

Rear track	1,442mm/56.8in

520 (1977–81)

Identical to original model except for the following:

Engine

Cylinders	6
Bore × stroke	80 × 66mm
Compression ratio	9.2:1
Carburettor	Solex 4A1
Max power	122bhp at 6,000rpm
Max torque	118lb ft at 4,000rpm

Transmission

Gearbox: 4-speed manual or optional 3-speed automatic

Ratios	4-speed manual	3-speed automatic
First	3.764	2.56
Second	2.043	1.52
Third	1.320	1.00
Fourth	1.00	
Final drive	3.90	3.90

Suspension and steering
Rear anti-roll bar not fitted as standard

Modern and airy in every respect, but without the host of electrically-operated toys to be found in the later cars, the cabin was spacious and intended to impress four adults, or five at a push. In effect, the car gave notice to Daimler-Benz that BMW were serious about challenging, and ultimately toppling, their Stuttgart rivals in the luxury saloon market once and for all.

Bits That Move and Bits That Don't

Under the new bodywork of the 5 Series was a suspension system comprising the usual MacPherson struts, coil springs and anti-roll bar at the front, with semi-trailing arms, struts, coil springs and anti-roll bar at the rear, although not all models were fitted with the rear anti-roll bar.

Braking was by servo-assisted discs up front and drums at the rear, steering was the old-fashioned ZF worm-and-roller type, but reliable and dependable, and the standard 5.5J×14 road wheels were in steel closed with hubcaps. These wheels did little for the car's sporting image, which is why multi-spoke alloys were eventual-

ly made available at extra cost. Radial tyres were standard in all markets, the cross-plies of yesteryear having been mercifully consigned to the suspicions and curiosity of history.

In the early days of production the 5 Series was available with a limited choice of 4-cylinder engines, although it had been engineered to accept more powerful 6-cylinder units from the off. At entry level, the 518 had the 1,766cc motor which, with a single Solex 38 PDSI carburettor and compression ratio of 8.6:1, developed a gentlemanly 90bhp at 5,500rpm. As with all future generations of the 5 Series fitted with a 1.8-litre engine, this early model was heavily criticised for being underpowered, particularly as it had a comparatively heavy body to lug around.

The 2-litre 4-cylinder car was available in both single carburettor 115bhp guise (the 520), or with fuel injection in which format it developed 130bhp. All variants at this stage had a 4-speed manual gearbox, or 3-speed automatic transmission as an extra-cost option.

As a development of the 1800–2000 series of the 1960s, the new 5 Series was seen as a refined improvement, and readily welcomed

520i (1972–77)	
Identical to 520 except in the following:	
Engine	
Cylinders	4
Bore × stroke	89 × 90mm
Capacity	1,990cc
Compression ratio	9.5:1
Fuel injection	Kugelfischer PL04
Max power	130bhp at 5,800rpm
Max torque	131lb ft at 4,500rpm
Modifications from September 1975	
Compression ratio	9.3:1
Fuel injection	Bosch K-Jetronic
Max power	125bhp at 5,700rpm
Max torque	126lb ft at 4,350rpm

...like the early Fünfers are also becoming rarer. This example has suffered the fate of so many, and is now beyond economic restoration.

by BMW aficionados. Just a year later the company launched the long-awaited 525, fitted with the twin-carburettor 2.5-litre 6-cylinder engine that had already seen service in the beautiful 2500 saloon.

Its launch was timely as the company's racing coupés were notching up one victory after another in the European Touring Championship. Developing 145bhp (150bhp from 1976), the 525 had taller gearing for unflustered high-speed cruising, all-round disc brakes and a top speed well in excess of 120mph. With such impeccable credentials it was just about peerless.

Background

In some respects this was among the most exciting motoring eras. In the USA Porsche were all-conquering in the Can-Am sports racing series with their fearsome Spyder version of the 917. With 1,100bhp, the world had never witnessed a faster or more powerful racing machine. In Europe, Matra and Ferrari were battling it out in the international sports car championship, with Matra comprehensively winning the battle for Le Mans. In the 'dazzling' world of Formula One, wee Jackie Stewart (or Jock McArmco as *Motor Sport's* Denis Jenkinson unkindly dubbed him after the Scot's campaign to make motor racing safer) was sawing away to claim his third Drivers' Championship title in one of Ken Tyrrell's Cosworth-powered 'kit-cars'. Stewart retired at the end of the 1973 season, and for many this brought an end to one of the most interesting periods of Grand Prix racing.

Among production cars the late 1960s and early 1970s were years of great innovation among designers. Ferrari had the last of its great front-engined V12s (the 174mph 365GTB 'Daytona') and the pretty Dino 246, Porsche launched the 2.7-litre 'lightweight' Carrera in 1972 (the most competent of all cross-country racing 'rockets') and among

Grand Touring cars the Maserati-engined Citroën SM was the most radically styled object that had been seen for a long time.

Daimler-Benz were two years into the production of the third generation of SL sports cars, BMW's 3.0CS was hailed as one of the most elegantly styled sports coupés ever built, and Rolls-Royce were attempting to recover from a serious financial crisis. British Leyland, on the other hand, were actively engaged in producing some of the world's worst ever motor cars. The Allegro, Maxi, Princess, Marina, Stag and Dolomite and so on would seal the fate of this ailing company for good, and make way for a British motor industry entirely dominated by Japanese manufacturers.

By contrast, the British-built Ford Escort continued to dominate the international and national rallying scene, where its light weight,

predictable handling and excellent power-to-weight ratio saw off tough competition from traditional sources.

The 1973 oil crisis, though, brought huge changes in the motor industry at all levels. Fuel consumption became a major issue, and many of the great and exciting cars of the pre-1973 era eventually died away. In their wake came dozens of dullards; the uninspired Boxer Ferrari, for example, replaced the Daytona, and Citroën's mighty SM was history by 1975. BMW 2002 turbo ceased production in 1973 as a direct result of the oil crisis, and Volkswagen hit rock-bottom when the Wolfsburg giant launched an 'economy' version of the 1200 Beetle. This car was devoid of all superfluous trim, including the traditional hubcaps, full headlining and external brightwork. Erwin Komenda's classic design, completed definitively by 18 January 1936, had

525 (1973–81)

Identical to 520 except for the following:

Engine

Cylinders	6
Bore × stroke	86 × 71.6mm
Capacity	2,494cc
Compression ratio	9:1
Carburettor	Zenith 32/40 INAT
Max power	145bhp at 6,000rpm
Max torque	153lb ft at 4,000rpm

Modifications from August 1976
Carburettor	Solex 4A1
Max power	150bhp at 5,800rpm

Transmission

	4-speed manual or optional 3-speed automatic	
Gearbox		
Ratios	4-speed manual	3-speed auto
First	3.855	2.56
Second	2.202	1.52
Third	1.401	1.00
Fourth	1.00	
Final drive	3.64	3.64
[end table]

Brakes   Servo-assisted discs/discs

Suspension
Rear track   1466mm/57.7in

been reduced to a dreary, dull-looking oddity. The Beetle had had its day and by 1974 production had completely ceased at the Volkswagen's main plant in Wolfsburg, German production finishing altogether in January 1978.

As a result of the oil crisis, BMW's 518 was selling reasonably well, customers making the incorrect perception that the 1.8-litre engine was more economical than the 2-litre. It wasn't but customers knew better, and BMW carried on building more and more cars.

Dust Settled

By the mid-1970s engineers, working behind the scenes, were slowly developing the motor

car. Improving passenger safety and engine efficiency had become matters of the moment, but this didn't mean that cars were about to become dull – far from it. In 1975, BMW launched the 528, a mighty 165bhp version of the 5 Series with a similar 6-cylinder engine fitted to the 2800 saloon.

At the same time the 5 Series was launched for the first time in North America. Badged as the 530i it was fitted with BMW's 3-litre 'six', developing an impressive 176bhp at 5,500rpm. *Car & Driver*'s Patrick Bedard road test of the new car, headed as 'a compact without the stigma of low price', described the new car as 'a middle child, halfway between the nimble 2002 sport sedan and the executive commuter 3.0Si.'

---

528 (1975–77)

Identical to 520 except for the following:

Engine

Cylinders	6
Bore × stroke	86 × 80mm
Capacity	2,788cc
Compression ratio	9:1
Carburettors	Twin Zenith 35/40 INAT
Max power	165bhp at 5,800rpm
Max torque	186lb ft at 4,000rpm

Modification from August 1976

Carburettor	Solex 4A1
Max power	170bhp at 5,800rpm

Transmission

Gearbox	4-speed manual or optional 3-speed automatic	
Ratios	**5-speed manual**	**3-speed automatic**
First	3.855	2.56
Second	2.202	1.52
Third	1.401	1.00
Fourth	1.00	
Final drive	3.64	3.64

Steering
Servo assistance fitted as standard

Wheels	6J×14
Tyres	195/70HR 14

Dimensions

Track	(front) 1,422mm/56in
	(rear) 1,470mm/57.9in

528i (1977–81)

Identical to the 528 except for the following:

Engine
Fuel injection   Bosch L-Jetronic
Max power   176bhp at 5,800rpm
Max torque   173lb ft at 4,300rpm

Modification from September 1978
Compression ratio   9.3:1
Max power   184bhp at 5,800rpm
Max torque   173lb ft at 4,200rpm

In his usual style Bedard naturally compared the BMW to contemporary Mercedes' and commented:

BMWs are, first and foremost, finely tuned machines. They encourage participation from their drivers and offer smooth and accurate response as a reward. They are agile where Mercedes are heavy, exhilarating where Mercedes are stolid. It's significant that nearly half of the 3.0Si models imported to the US have manual transmissions, an incredible statistic for a car with a base price approaching $14,000. Detroit has nothing in its plethora of models for this brand of driver. Even Mercedes eschews manual transmission in anything more costly than its 4-cylinder diesel. So for drivers who want to count their revs, choose their gears and engage their clutches – and can afford to do it in the finest surroundings – there is no other sedan but a BMW.

By European standards the 5 Series was anything but 'compact' but, as Patrick Bedard went on to point out, the 530i was a full eight inches shorter than the Ford Granada, shorter than the 280-series Mercedes-Benz, and about the same size as the 262 Volvo. His only observations that remotely approached criticism was the old chestnut, that the interior, although well finished in top-quality materials, did not quite match the car's purchase price.

There were vinyl seats, a no-nonsense dashboard, there were no planks of wood and no gadgets, which had been BMW's way of thinking for years. The interior was functional, roomy and comfortable, and if you didn't like it BMW were big enough to consider that this was your problem and not theirs. Accepted by American enthusiasts as something of a cross between the

530i (1975–78) US-spec

Identical to 528 except for the following:

Engine
Cylinders   6
Bore × stroke   80 × 88.9mm
Capacity   2,985cc
Compression ratio   8:1
Fuel injection   Bosch L-Jetronic
Max power   176bhp at 5,500rpm
Max torque   185lb ft at 4,500rpm

Dimensions
Overall length   4,823mm/189.9in
Overall width   1,706mm/67.2in
Rear track   1,460mm/57.5in

agile, sporting nature of the 2002 – a much-loved car in America – and the comfort and luxury of the outgoing 3-litre Bavaria model, the 530i was an instant hit, despite sales suggesting that it was in a very small, niche market.

In North America, the 2002 accounted for roughly three quarters of all BMW sales during the mid-1970s, and it had become obvious by this time that, try as they might, the Bavarian cars were just about beyond criticism. *Car & Driver* considered the 530i to be the best car in its class, reserving a fair quantity of vitriol for its radio. Of this the magazine commented:

> How they can do all that good stuff and then screw it up with one of those incredible Blaupunkt radios is a little hard to imagine, but that's what they did . . . It was maybe the dumbest radio anybody ever stuck in an automobile, like all Blaupunkt and Becker radios, yet the Geman car makers – for reasons unknown – continue to use them.

Despite the passage of more than 25 years since this criticism was published in *Car & Driver*, a period in which advances in global communications have astonished even committed technophiles, car radios still leave a lot to be desired. During the past many years, I have owned a number of quite wonderful cars from Volkswagen, Saab and BMW, and discovered each time that their radios simply do not work properly.

A Small Cut and Tuck

Within just four years of the car's launch the 5 Series was subjected to a minor facelift. There were larger tail lamps, a four-choke Solex carburettor in place of the twin Zeniths for the 2.5- and 2.8-litre cars (a move that increased power output to 150bhp and 170bhp respectively) and the frontal appearance was improved by the increased height of the 'kidneys' in the radiator grille. This latter change resulted in a reshaped bonnet, and a most purposeful-looking 'bulge' that gave the car a more sporting appearance.

A year later BMW launched their 520 'baby six', the 2-litre 6-cylinder car to replace the original 4-cylinder 2-litre. With development this power unit would become the 'benchmark' power unit in the 2-litre class, for it was the smoothest and most refined of its type. That it was initially underpowered did not go unnoticed, but BMW's engineers would quickly address criticism in their usual manner.

At the same time the mighty 528 was fitted with Bosch L-Jetronic fuel injection, rebadged as a 528i, and boasted a 6bhp gain in power to give a top speed in the region of 130mph. Clearly, the oil crisis of a few years earlier had been forgotten! It is also interesting that BMW continued to view the three-pointed star as its arch rival. However, it had become apparent to students of the 'old school' that Daimler-Benz had forgotten more

Attractive cross-spoke alloy wheels were desirable extra-cost options, and perfectly complemented the clean lines of the bodywork.

M535i (1980–81)

Identical to 528i except for the following:

Engine
Cylinders	6
Bore × stroke	93.4 × 84mm
Capacity	3,453cc
Compression ratio	9.3:1
Fuel Injection	Bosch L-Jetronic
Max power	218bhp at 5,200rpm
Max torque	228lb ft at 4,000rpm

Transmission
Final-drive ratio 3.25 or 3.07

---

about making great cars than the majority of manufacturers were ever likely to know.

In 1954 the Stuttgart company launched the 300SL 'Gullwing', a production sports car based on the racing cars that had so convincingly finished first and second in the 1952 Le Mans 24 Hours. Fitted with a fuel-injected 3-litre in-line 6-cylinder engine, the production Gullwing was capable of 155mph, which was completely unrivalled in this capacity class during the mid-1950s. Expensive to buy and run, the Gullwing was discontinued in 1957 in favour of the 300SL Roadster. Fitted with the same engine the revised car (a 'ragtop' and, therefore much heavier) had a top speed of around 130mph, which many regarded in some respects as a step backwards. Thirty years on, the BMW 528i had comparable performance to the 300SL Roadster; the difference, though, was that whereas the Merc had been a two-seater sports machine, the BMW was a four-door saloon which anyone could comfortably use for a Sunday afternoon trip. Progress was being made in the motor industry but, on the face of it, it was taking an awfully long time.

'M' for More Power

By the end of the 1970s the world was on the brink of a rude awakening. In the West, premiers Reagan, Thatcher and Schmidt, who broadly shared the same political ideology, swept hard brooms through outdated systems. The 'every-man-for-himself' philosophy, promoted by Margaret Thatcher in particular as 'self-reliance', would lead to greater poverty on the one hand, and even greater wealth on the other.

'Fat cats' working for financial institutions made fortunes and, believing that they had worked hard for their money, headed quickly in the direction of Ferrari, Porsche, Mercedes and BMW showrooms. Manufacturers were only too happy to oblige the 'nouveau riche', who were equally happy to enjoy their powerful cars. One man known to this author, an accountant, in one sense typified the period. He got happy and rich and bought an M535i BMW. He then got greedy and spent a significant length of time languishing at the pleasure of Her Majesty the Queen. But it was not BMW's fault that such people gave the cars, and the company who made them, something of an image problem.

In 1979, BMW added to the Fünfer range with the M535i, which was publicly debuted at the Frankfurt Auto Show in the autumn of this same year. By this stage the E12 had been in production for seven years, and was due for replacement, and a powerful version was seen by BMW's Motorsport Division as a means of boosting the model's image.

The formula for the 'M-powered' car was simple; the 6 and 7 Series cars were powered by a 3.5-litre 6-cylinder engine, a high-performance version of which was also running in the M1 supercar. A versatile, flexible and powerful unit, it was ideal for the Fünfer. With Bosch L-Jetronic fuel injection, and a compression ratio of 9.3:1 the car developed 218bhp at 5200rpm.

With its cross-spoke BBS alloy wheels, deep chin spoiler, bootlid aerofoil and M logos, it resembled a road-legal racing car and, with a top speed of 138mph, it almost went like one. A close-ratio 5-speed gearbox, Recaro sports seats and sports steering were all part of a lightning package that inspired BMW fans to new heights for the car was a driving machine par excellence. From BMW's point of view it made sense, was something of a marketing coup, and relatively cheap and profitable to make.

Interestingly, the M535i didn't have a great deal in the way of competition, except, of course, from other models in the BMW range. In Britain, Jaguar's powerful 12-cylinder XJS was coveted by those who lived in an automotive world governed by misplaced English patriotism. Rover's 3500 V8 SD1, loosely styled along the lines of the Ferrari 365GTB4A Daytona, was a rust-bucket, and not especially reliable on occasions. Its old-fashioned pushrod engine, despite huge displacement, also gave lacklustre performance, which British police forces who used these cars as pursuit vehicles frequently discovered to their cost.

Contemporary Mercs were as beautifully built, dependable and reliable as ever, and appreciated by an increasingly large and extremely loyal clientele, but just as many people regarded them as truck-like barges with out-of-date styling and a flabby gait. This aside, it was only a fool who thought that Daimler-Benz's days were numbered.

Lancia devotees were beginning to lose hope with their perennial battle against rust, while Alfa-Romeo fans traded rust for the joy of caning their twin-cams and V6 jewels. France's traditional manufacturers, Renault, Peugeot and Citroën, continued to produce the 'sensible shoes' of the saloon world which, with the possible exception of Citroen's range-topping CX, held little or no interest for motoring enthusiasts.

By the beginning of the 1980s, BMW was very well poised to spearhead an all-out attack against the opposition, the foundations of which had been laid in the early 1970s. The company simply built on its growing reputation for finely made and stylish sporting saloons. In this ill-defined category, BMW was actually at the top of the tree; the problem for them was that many potential customers disagreed.

And, from 1980, a threat appeared to BMW's future supremacy from Ingolstadt, where Dr Ferdinand Piëch was gearing up for the launch of the Audi quattro rallying programme. Initially, the quattro rally cars, and production counterparts, were not taken too seriously. Permanent four-wheel drive was perceived in some quarters as an unnecessary novelty, an ephemeral product of fashion that would quickly fade away.

At this time, the Audi's four-rings motif and illustrious motor racing history of the 1930s had been largely forgotten. Piëch set forth on a mission to reverse the company's fortunes; by 1985 the Audi quattro had become all-conquering on the international rallying stage and a trend-setter that paved the way for others. In conjunction with success in various Touring Car Championships in the years ahead, the ascending name of Audi could not be ignored.

Beyond this there was the ever-present threat from Japanese manufacturers, who appeared to be in competition to produce the ugliest and dullest cars. That BMW remained on top was firm evidence of their commitment not to return to the dark days of 1959 when the Quandt family's money rescued the company from almost certain financial oblivion.

CHAPTER SIX

BMW 5 Series:
The Second Generation

Development Brisk, Without Fear of Risk

When the E12 bowed out it was replaced by the E28 Fünfer that, to casual observers and journalists who didn't look further than the reshaped bonnet, initially appeared to be much the same car. Ostensibly, BMW had erred on the side of caution, particularly in the styling department, but the revised car was in many respects substantially different from the model it replaced.

By 1981, when the E28 went into production, BMW's marketing people had done their homework thoroughly. As a result, they knew who their customers were, and what they sought in a BMW. Broadly, BMW's 5 Series customers were largely conservative, middle class males (women inclined more towards the 3 Series) of 40-plus years for whom a Mercedes-Benz was simply dull. A member of BMW's board of directors once expressed a sincere view of Mercedes in asking: 'Who would want to drive a car that was like a truck?' BMW's clientele was of much the same sentiment.

The Munich company's publicity literature, which in true German tradition was never in the habit of making extravagant or exaggerated claims, summed up the new 5 Series accurately. It claimed:

> The BMW 5 series is a progressive car through and through, without trying to look revolutionary.

It went on:

> In the world of motoring, the true signs of progress are genuine substance and quality, and not merely prestige and status at the wheel . . .

However, despite BMW's commitment to practical motoring requirements leaving aside imaginative but unrealistic styling concepts, we have succeeded, through a process of constant aerodynamic refinement, in setting new standards in modern streamlining and achieving a low drag coefficient.

Large, rectangular tail-lamps were unimaginatively styled, but wholly in keeping with the car's conservative image. The badge identifies the engine as a 2-litre 'six'.

Behind the prosaic lyricism of the copywriters, however, was an altogether more serious message, and this message was coming directly from the engineers and designers – the people who really count in car manufacturing. The oil crisis of 1973 had certainly been forgotten but, as fuel prices rose inexorably upwards throughout Europe, economy and reduced exhaust emissions had become ever more important.

To this end, BMW's people had trodden the most obvious path to improving the fuel mileage of the 5 Series, and it was glaringly apparent that the bodyshell had been subjected to major, but subtle, revisions in an attempt to reduce wind resistance.

To quote from the company's publicity literature again, BMW commented:

The entire body of the new BMW 5 Series has been designed for maximum smoothness through and through. The aerodynamic styling of each body element combined with the smooth transitions between the individual panels provides an ideal basis for minimum air resistance and optimum streamlining. A further improvement is provided by the new plastic wheel covers standard on all vehicles fitted with steel wheels.

Although at 0.38 the revised car's drag coefficient was certainly an improvement over the

518 (1981–84)

Engine

Cylinders	4
Bore × stroke	89 × 71mm
Capacity	1,766cc
Compression ratio	9.5:1
Carburettor	Pierburg 2B4
Max power	90bhp at 5,500rpm
Max torque	

Transmission

Gearbox	4-speed manual or optional 5-speed manual	
Ratios	**4-speed**	**5-speed**
First	3.764	3.822
Second	2.043	2.202
Third	1.32	1.398
Fourth	1.00	1.00
Fifth		0.813

Suspension and steering

Front	MacPherson struts and anti-roll bar
Rear	Semi-trailing arms and coil springs
Steering	Power-assisted (optional) worm and roller
Wheels	5.5J×14
Tyres	175SR 14

Brakes

	Servo-assisted discs/drums

Dimensions

Track	(front) 1,430mm/56.3in
	(rear) 1,460mm/56.3in
Wheelbase	2,625mm/103.3in
Overall length	4,620mm/181.9in
Overall width	1,700mm/66.9in
Overall height	1,415mm/55.7in

outgoing car's figure of 0.44, it still lagged behind the contemporary Citroën CX and Audi 100. However, overall the revised shape was within perfectly acceptable aerodynamic goals, but more important to most was the superb 'razor-sharp' styling.

The two-door 3.0CS coupés of the 1970s were acknowledged classics, and among the most striking and aesthetically beautiful designs of all time. In some respects, the E28 kept faith with the big coupés; the sloping radiator grille and twin headlamps were both retained, the former in fashionable matt-black plastic, with chromium-plating being discreetly confined to the perimeters of the centrally-located 'kidneys'.

Below the front bumper there was a chin spoiler, which added to the car's sporting appearance and naturally aided high-speed stability. All four wheel arches were flared, the flanks were broken by swage lines and rubber 'rubbing' strips, and the 'dogleg' shape (a distinctive BMW hallmark) was retained along the trailing edge of the rear side windows. At the rear, there were large, rectangular tail-lamps, a huge boot with the tool kit fitted to the underside of the lid, and in BMW tradition each model was identified by a chromed badge on the right-hand side of the bootlid.

The old adage that something 'which looks right is right' was especially apt for the new Fünfer, and it has become apparent in recent

times that these cars have stood the test of time extremely well. BMW enthusiasts continue to cherish and maintain them in perfect order, many having reached 'galactic' mileage without enduring major surgery.

The standard cloth-covered seats in Kevin Evans' 520i are in tip-top condition after more than 180,000 miles.

Cabin Cruiser

Like all BMWs, the E28's interior gave a first class driving environment for people who cared about driving, and something for sybarites to moan and groan about because of the absence of strips of polished wood across the dashboard and door cappings. For those

---

518i (1984–87)

Identical to 518 except for the following:

Engine

Compression ratio	10:1
Fuel injection	Bosch L-Jetronic
Max power	105bhp at 5,800rpm
Max torque	105lb ft at 4,500rpm
Final-drive ratio	4.10

Dimensions

Wheels	6J×14
Tyres	175HR 14

---

who wanted for nothing more than well-shaped, firm, comfortable seats, there was durable cloth upholstery, while leather was offered as an extra-cost option. M-Technic sports seats were also available at extra cost.

Despite the use of lightweight plastics in the interior, the dashboard, central console, pyramid-shaped instrument shroud and door cappings were tastefully finished and of exceptional quality. Only the standard four-spoke steering wheel, with its four horn buttons integrated into the spokes, cast doubt over the aesthetics. Made of textured plastic, with a harsh 'grainy' finish, the wheel's gawky appearance was accentuated by its large diameter but, for those who preferred a more sporting item, BMW provided a three-spoke version (at extra cost, naturally!)

Instrumentation (speedometer left, tachometer right and combination gauges in the centre) was circular and to BMW's usual white on black with orange illumination during darkness. Built into the base of the tachometer there was a new innovation: a fuel-function, giving instant information about the quantity of fuel being consumed at any one time. Although useful in some circumstances many owners found it to be a source of irritation and guilt. Bang the throttle pedal to the floor and the needle would instantly disappear from the scale, indicating to the driver that the car was doing 2mpg or worse. BMW motorists with 'a conscience' kept a constant watch on this gauge, and drove for economy, which in one sense defeated the object of owning a sporting saloon.

In addition there was also an on-board computer giving information about eight different functions, and the usual array of electrically-operated toys to be found in a car of this nature. BMW's summary of the interior was that it:

520i (1981–87)

Identical to 518i except for the following:

Engine

Cylinders	6
Bore × stroke	80 × 86mm
Capacity	1990cc
Compression ratio	9.8:1
Fuel injection	Bosch K-Jetronic
Max power	125bhp at 5,800rpm
Max torque	119lb ft at 4,000rpm

From September 1986
Optional model with Lambda probe and catalytic converter

Compression ratio	8.8:1

Gearbox

	4-speed manual (discontinued in September 1982, 5-speed manual or optional 3-speed automatic

Suspension and steering
Optional rear anti-roll bar

Steering	ZF Kugelmutter system with servo-assistance
Wheels	5.5J×14 (6J×14 from August 1985)
Tyres	175HR 14 (195/70HR 14 from August 1985)

Brakes
ABS anti-lock system optional from April 1982
Rear discs from February 1986
ABS standard from August 1986

525e (1984–87)

Identical to 520 except for the following

Engine
Cylinders	6
Bore × stroke	84 × 81mm
Capacity	2,693cc
Compression ratio	8.5:1
Fuel injection	Electronic Bosch Motronic, Lambda probe and catalytic converter
Max power	129bhp at 4,800rpm
Max torque	166lb ft at 3,200rpm

Transmission
Gearbox: 5-speed manual or optional 4-speed automatic

Ratios	**5-speed manual**	**4-speed automatic**
First	3.83	2.48
Second	2.20	1.48
Third	1.40	1.00
Fourth	1.00	0.73
Fifth	0.81	
Final drive	3.25	3.46

Suspension and steering
Suspension	Optional rear anti-roll bar
Steering	ZF Kugelmutter
Wheels	6J×14
Tyres	195/70HR 14

Brakes Rear discs, and optional ABS

offers a new system of instruments, controls and technology that does the thinking for you – to an unprecedented standard. The new environment gives the driver a great deal of extra freedom to make his own decisions – and therefore hails the advent of a more rational and disciplined approach to modern motoring.

Power-assisted steering was fitted as standard across the entire range, and was well weighted to take account of road 'feel' at both low and high speeds. With the traditional BMW policy of adhering to a large glass area, and improved rear legroom and headroom, the cabin was something approaching a modern masterpiece of interior design.

However, despite claims that the Fünfer was well protected against theft, BMWs became something of a target for theives and insurance premiums crept ever upwards. This

problem would be addressed in future years, but not entirely eradicated.

Spring Cleaning

Although along the lines of past BMWs, the E28's suspension system was modified in small ways to improve roadholding, comfort and safety. At the front there were MacPherson struts (nothing else was considered) and coil springs. However, instead of conventional wishbones or single links, there were two links for location purposes. This gave, in BMW's words:

a small positive steering radius. This means that when applying the brakes whilst the left-hand and right-hand wheels are running on different surfaces, directional stability will remain true and the car will not pull to one side.

In conjunction with anti-dive geometry, the car also remained safe under heavy braking from high speeds. To a unique design the front suspension also had an improved anti-roll bar fitted directly to the spring strut positioned behind instead of in front of the front axle line. This helped to reduce weight and, in conjunction with the deformable parts of the bodywork, reduced the effects and possibility of injury in the event of frontal impacts.

At the rear there was BMW's traditional semi-trailing arm set-up but with revised rubber bushing to reduce noise filtering through to the cabin and modifications to minimise dive under acceleration and deceleration. Across the range the E28 was optionally available with BMW's sports suspension kit, with gas-filled dampers also available as extra-cost options on the 528i. The latter, incidentally, came as standard on the range-topping 535i.

With so much cockpit space, and large panoramic windscreen, the driver gets a commanding view of the road. Seating is typically firm, supportive and comfortable.

In making these modifications the car was endowed with almost unrivalled ride quality, although British journalists cited the XJ6 Jaguar as the best car in this particular respect, and predictable roadholding and handling. There was the usual hoard of dissenters, though, who argued, without convincing the majority of owners, that the car was prone towards undesirable quantities of oversteer.

For the majority of driving enthusiasts, brought up on a traditional diet of rear-wheel-drive cars like BMWs, oversteer was part and parcel of the fun and skill of conducting a well-honed steed at high speed. Oversteer was not only desirable, but an inherent characteristic of most powerful cars with rear-drive. Those who claimed otherwise had wholly missed the point. In addition, it is also this author's experience, that in the absence of foolhardy driving, or a hefty right foot in low gears, the reality is that it is actually quite difficult to 'lose' the rear of an E28.

Head on the Block

At 'entry-level' the 518i was the only 4-cylinder car in the range. Displacing 1,766cc and fitted with Bosch L-Jetronic fuel injection, it developed 105bhp at 5,800rpm with a relatively high compression ratio of 9.5:1. Although said by many to be underpowered, this sentiment needs to be put into a realistic context.

The car was capable of accelerating from 0–62mph in 12.6secs, a top speed of 109mph and performing the standing-start kilometre in 34secs. With an overdrive 5-speed gearbox, it was also capable of returning an astonishing 46.3mpg at a constant 56mph, and 35.3mpg at 75mph. These figures are worth digesting. Just 15 years earlier Colin Chapman's definitive roadgoing sports saloon of the mid-1960s, the Lotus Cortina 1.6-litre twin-cam, was capable of a top speed 105mph and accelerating from 0–60 in approximately 10.5secs.

The 518i's close rival from Sweden, the Saab 900 2-litre 4-cylinder, was capable of 107mph, and performing the benchmark 0–60mph dash in 13.7secs. Volkswagen's contemporary Golf GTi Mk2, in fuel-injected 1.8-litre guise, could reach 60mph from rest in under 8secs and sprint to around 115mph. In company like this the BMW 518i shaped up extremely well, and those who criticised it were apt to do so as a result of comparing it with the more powerful cars in the BMW range. Set against a 525i, for example, the 518i inevitably felt tame but, with both cars sharing a similar chassis, the 4-cylinder car's great strength lay in its roadholding capabilities, which were truly astonishing.

All other Fünfers in the line-up had 6-cylinder power units and began with the 2-litre (1,990cc) 520i. To BMW's predictable and classic layout this single-overhead camshaft engine, with its seven-bearing crankshaft, was widely acknowledged as the smoothest 'six' to be found anywhere. With a compression ratio of 9.8:1 it developed 125bhp at 5,800rpm and, in addition to the 5-speed manual version, was also offered with a 4-speed automatic as an option. With a top speed of 117mph (114mph automatic) and a 0–62mph best of 11.4secs, the 520i was arguably the definitive, benchmark 2-litre saloon of its day, and a most popular choice among those who might have otherwise chosen to buy a Ford or Vauxhall.

Although weighing 70kg (155lb) more than the 520i, the more powerful 2.5-litre 150bhp 525i was capable of a perfectly respectable 125mph and 30.7mpg at 75mph. Many regarded this model as the pick of the range, for it combined top-level performance with exquisite road manners and good fuel economy.

525i (1981–87)

Identical to 520i except for the following:

Engine

Cylinders	6
Bore × stroke	86 × 71.6mm
Capacity	2,496cc
Compression ratio	9.6:1
Fuel injection	Bosch L-Jetronic
Max power	150bhp at 5,500rpm
Max torque	155lb ft at 4,000rpm

Transmission

Gearbox: 4-speed manual, 5-speed manual (ratios as for 518), or optional 3-speed automatic

Ratios	4-speed manual	3-speed automatic
First	3.855	2.48
Second	2.202	1.48
Third	1.402	1.00
Fourth	1.000	
Final drive	3.45	3.45

Suspension and steering

Suspension	Optional rear anti-roll bar
Steering	Servo-assisted ZF Kugelmutter
Wheels	Pressed steel 5.5J×14, or optional 6J×14 alloys
Tyres	175SR 14, or optional 195/70 VR 14 with alloys

Brakes: Optional ABS, discs at rear

Burning Little Gas

Confusingly, BMW also produced the 525e (e for eta) which, despite its model number was fitted with a special 2693cc version of the 6-cylinder engine. This car had been under development at Munich for quite some time, and dispelled the myth that a performance car could not also be economical.

The Greek 'eta' was used to reflect high efficiency. A high compression ratio of 11:1, and small changes to the shape of the combustion chambers, ensured that the fuel/air mixture was burnt as efficiently as possible. There were small modifications to valve timing, and inlet manifolds which were longer than standard to ensure that the combustion chambers were filled efficiently. By using a low-revving, large-capacity engine the general philosophy behind this car was to reduce the power unit's friction coefficient, so that performance comparable to that of the 2-litre 520i could be gained, but not at the expense of fuel economy.

There was nothing especially new in this philosophy, of course. Many pre-War cars utilised 'lazy', long-stroke engines of large capacity to produce reasonable output and good fuel mileage but, typically, BMW brought the concept up to date. The 525e's maximum output of 125bhp, modest for a 2.7-litre car by any standards, allowed for low-tension valve springs, which reduced friction between the rocker arms and cams, and the number of camshaft bearings was reduced from seven to four. This was engineering refinement, extended to the use of the Digital Motor Electronics system, which aided cold starting. Another advantage included more economical use of fuel when the engine was cold, by the simple expedient of decreasing the time that it took for the engine to warm up.

BMW claimed that the car would return 37.7mpg at a steady 75mph, and 24.6mpg during the loosely defined urban cycle. With a high final-drive ratio (2.93:1) the 525e had the same top speed as the 520i but, with better low-speed torque it was quicker from 0–60mph at an unflustered 10.5secs. Interestingly, the car was only available with 4-speed automatic transmission.

A technically interesting exercise and a popular one among fuel-thrifty customers, the car's major drawback was its purchase

Instrumentation is characteristically clear, comprehensive and easy to read, but aesthetically dull without illumination.

528e (1982–83) US-spec

Identical to 525e except for the following:

Engine

Compression ratio	9:1
Fuel injection	Bosch L-Jetronic
Max power	121bhp at 4250rpm
Max torque	170lb ft at 3250rpm

Transmission

Gearbox	5-speed manual
Final-drive ratio	2.93

Wheels and tyres

Wheels	6.50J×14
Tyres	195/70SR 14

Dimensions

Overall length	4,800mm/189in
Track (rear)	1,470mm (57.9in)

price. In 1983, British dealers quoted a list price of £11,495, and although the car came with a high specification, and lots of 'goodies', it was some £1,300 more to buy than a standard 520i. Those who stood the most to gain from such hefty investment were generally business users covering a high annual mileage.

The British journal *Motor Sport* concluded its road test of the 525e by remarking:

The 5 Series BMW recipe remains pretty well unchanged, a high level of basic specification being further enhanced on our test car by the addition of an electric sunroof (579), alloy wheels (£557), central locking (£197), one of those irritating onboard computers (at £499 a waste of the writer's money, at least) and electric windows (£528). An interesting car, well worth thinking about for the owner who has to think carefully about his petrol bills without wanting to dispense with all his performance aspirations.

Ironically, a good example of a 525e can be bought secondhand today for roughly the same price as a new set of alloy wheels back in 1983.

Beyond the considerations of this economy model the 528i, fitted with the 2.8-litre (2,788cc) 6-cylinder engine, was an out-and-out performance machine with ostensibly few concessions to fuel thriftiness, despite BMW's claim of 40.4mpg at a constant 56mph. Developing 184bhp at 5,800rpm the 528i was capable of 133mph and 0–60mph in 8.4secs which, in a car weighing 1,300kg (2,900lb), was impressive to say the least.

A superb all-rounder by any standards, and fitted with the 5-speed gearbox as standard (4-speed auto was optional), this model was both expensive to buy and run, and although naturally popular among BMW's growing international 'club' of owners, particularly in mainland Europe, some British journalists questioned the car's true value.

Ford provided large-capacity 6-cylinder Granadas and Capris, with similar performance to the 528i but, at a fraction of the cost of the BMW. In Britain, there was a growing sense that BMW's growing stature was the result of 'hype'. Many felt that the BMW did not represent 'value for money', whereas the Fords were a better bet in this respect. It was an old chestnut, that for many had been set-

---

528i (1981–87)

Identical to 525i except for the following

Engine

Cylinders	6
Bore × stroke	86 × 80mm
Capacity	2,788cc
Compression ratio	9.3:1
Fuel injection	Bosch L-Jetronic
Max power	184bhp at 5,800rpm
Max torque	173lb ft at 4,200rpm

Transmission

Gearbox	5-speed manual (ratios as for 518), optional 3-speed automatic, or 4-speed automatic from September 1983	
Ratios	**3-speed automatic**	**4-speed automatic**
First	2.48	2.48
Second	1.48	1.48
Third	1.00	1.00
Fourth		0.73
Final drive	3.25	3.45

Suspension and steering

Suspension	Standard rear anti-roll bar
Steering	ZF Kugelmutter with servo-assistance
Wheels	Pressed steel 5.5J×14, or optional 6J×14alloys
Tyres	175SR14, or 195/70VR 14 with alloys

Brakes	Optional ABS (standard from August 1986), standard rear discs

---

tled during the 1970s, when the Ford Capris from Cologne and BMWs from Munich had slugged it out on the race tracks. BMW came out on top, full stop. But the idea that a 528i was comparable to a V6 Ford was, of course, a total absurdity, despite the wide price margin between the two.

The BMW was a sophisticate, beautifully built, smooth and possessed drivability that remained unequalled in its class, and this was reflected heavily in BMW's marketing policy in North America where the only Fünfer available was the 528e. This was virtually to the same specification as the European 525e, and fitted with the 2.7-litre engine. Americans were well used to large-capacity engines that drank fuel as if it was going out of fashion. They had also become accustomed to potentially powerful cars being 'strangled' by emissions equipment so that

the 528e was reasonably powerful, refined and unflustered, while being economical at the same time, came as a welcome surprise. Detroit did not make a comparable car, and the people at BMW awarded themselves a large corporate pat on the back for spotting a prime marketing opportunity.

E28 Owner's View

Kevin Evans from the Rhondda Valley in South Wales has worked in the catering and licensed industries for many years. The nature of his job requires him to be wide awake when the majority of folks are asleep, sober when his customers are indulging and performing administration duties when he should be asleep. Holidays are rare and, therefore, precious, and days away from work are spent on the golf courses of Britain and Portugal.

He is a latecomer to BMW ownership having purchased an E28 520i, of 1986 vintage, in 2000. Previously, he was the proud custodian of a 2-litre twin-cam Toyota Celica, a front-driver with a 'cammy' engine, 'buzzy' performance with superb acceleration, and one of the slickest gearboxes to be found in modern automotive manufacturing. The BMW, however, is an altogether different proposition, as Kevin explains:

> I had fancied a 5 Series BMW for many years, but somehow never got around to buying one. As a younger chap I was always attracted to more sporting cars like the Celica. It was economical, fast, comfortable and easy to drive but, the older I get, I've found, as I always assumed, that my motoring tastes would change.
>
> Originally, I was attracted to the 5 series for its looks alone. They are, without doubt, most elegant and exciting looking cars, but not in the sense of being garish or ostentatious. It's handsome, elegantly poised and confident. Naturally, I tended to notice everyone I saw being driven on the roads, but had little idea of what they were really like to drive. Friends who own BMWs had often related stories to me about their cars' comfort, reliability and so on, but I had for so long taken the view that most modern cars were in the same mould.

Kevin spotted his 520i on the forecourt of a tyre dealer close to his home, happened to be driving past and fancied it. 'The asking price seemed to be quite low, and the car looked superb; I just had to buy it,' he says.

Despite having covered over 180,000 miles in 15 years, the 520i's paintwork was generally in excellent condition, the interior unmarked, and the 2-litre engine ran superbly.

Kevin's BMW has made a huge and unequivocal impression on him.

> No other car comes close for smoothness, performance or ride quality,' he reckons. 'It does exactly what you want it to do; the handling and roadholding are first class – I can't see how it could be improved – and I just can't find anything to criticise about it. Even the dashboard is a pleasure to look at and, as a bonus all the instruments are exactly where they need to be.
>
> Working such long and anti-social hours, I always look forward to getting into the car, because it has a marvellous, relaxing effect and, from a practical point of view, the boot is big enough to take everything I need for a day on the local golf course. By comparison with the Toyota Celica, the BMW is clearly a better built car. It's most noticeable just closing and opening the driver's door; the BMW's is just so effortless and operates as if it were made from a solid piece of rock.

533i (1983–85) US-spec

Identical to 525e except for the following

Engine

Cylinders	6
Bore × stroke	89 × 86mm
Capacity	3210cc
Compression ratio	8.8:1
Fuel injection	Bosch L-Jetronic
Max power	181bhp at 6,000rpm
Max torque	195lb ft at 4,000rpm

Transmission

Final drive	2.63 with manual
Wheels	TR alloys
Tyres	200/60VR 390

The central console, angled towards driver for convenience and safety, was emulated by other manufacturers. Stylish and comfortable, the leather-covered three-spoke sports steering wheel was a worthwhile extra-cost option.

Kevin's son owns a Ford Sierra which Kevin describes, with 90,000 miles on the clock, as 'so obviously nearing the end of its useful life.' 'Frankly,' he laughs, 'the Sierra is an awful car, especially when you compare it to my old BMW.'

If he can find a black mark against the German car anywhere in its make-up, it is if anything on occasions, 'too smooth'. He explains:

Sometimes, I have been driving on an ordinary road, feeling totally relaxed, and under the impression that I'm ambling along at a nice, sedate 50mph. Glancing at the speedometer, I find that I'm actually doing 80, and quickly have to correct my speed. And, it's for this reason that my wife doesn't like driving it. She finds it too powerful.

Given limitless funds and time to acquire his all-time 'dream car', Kevin cites his 520i as perfect.

It really gives me everything I want from a motor car; I've never driven anything better, and I want for nothing else. A friend of mine has a new 3

Series, which is certainly a lot faster, and in some ways it's a lot nimbler through corners, but it hasn't the comfort of my 520i and I value comfort above almost all other considerations.

Resplendent in the winter sunshine, this E28 520i is an excellent example of a car built to typically German standards. Durable, dependable and reliable, it certainly bears signs of the ageing process (the BMW badges in the centres of the cross-spoke alloy wheels, for example, have faded and look a little tatty) but after covering such a huge mileage it is entitled to look a little weary around the gills.

Power Corrupts

The 2-litre 520i proved to be the most popular of the 5 Series range, for it more or less combined the economy of the 4-cylinder car with the performance of the 525i. Beyond these there was the exotic 528i, a powerful machine that served as the basis of the 3.5-litre cars, of which there were three types. In 'everyday' guise there was one with catalytic converter and special emissions equipment (designed to meet the requirements of future German legislation), developing a comparatively paltry 184bhp, and the more exciting M535i 218bhp version without a catalytic converter.

The latter was, as previously, prepared by the company's Motorsport Division, and to distinguish it from the less powerful car, it was fitted with sports seats, uprated suspension springs, sports seats, a plastic bodykit and colourful M logos. Both 3.5-litre versions were well-honed, fast, comfortable and came with the usual BMW hallmarks.

Although the cat-equipped car was no faster ultimately than the standard 528i, its superior torque gave better acceleration, especially in the lower rev ranges, and more relaxed travel at high speeds. With a top speed of around 134mph, it was deemed to be 'adequate' for the circumstances in which BMW found itself, while the 140mph M535i gave a taste of what BMW's Motorsport development engineers were really capable of.

In 1984, the company launched the M5, which many journalists across the world quickly dubbed as a 'wolf in sheep's clothing'. This old cliché was only partially correct, for the car was actually a wolf in the clothing of a killer whale, the ultimate expression on the BMW factory-inspired E28 theme.

By any standards the M5 was an expensive proposition, and BMW Motorsport initially planned on limiting production to just 250 examples. Pessimism of this kind had been

similarly exercised by Porsche in days of old. At the beginning of the 1950s, Ferry Porsche had anticipated producing no more than 500 examples of the 356, having taken the view that there would not be sufficient demand for more. In the event the company produced around 80,000 examples before production ended in 1965.

In 1972, the Stuttgart company launched the expensive 2.7-litre 'lightweight' Carrera version of the 911. The brainchild of Dr Ernst Fuhrmann, who had designed Porsche's famous 4-cam racing engine in the 1950s, it was planned to build just 500 examples. The marketing department went into panic and voiced the opinion that they would never be

---

535i and M535i (1985–87)

Identical to 518 except for the following:

Engine

Cylinders	6
Bore × stroke	92 × 86mm
Capacity	3,430cc
Compression ratio	8:1
Fuel injection	Bosch ME Motronic
Max power	218bhp at 6,500rpm
Max torque	229lb ft at 4,000rpm
Max power	185bhp at 5,400rpm
Max torque	209lb ft at 4,000rpm (cat model)
Max power	182bhp at 5,400rpm
Max torque	214lb ft at 4,000rpm (US-spec)

Transmission

Gearbox	5-speed manual with ratios from 518, optional 4-speed overdrive automatic
Ratios	First 2.48
	Second 1.48
	Third 1.00
	Fourth 0.73
	Final drive 3.25 (manual), 3.45 (auto), 2.63 (US-spec)

Suspension and steering

Suspension	Standard rear anti-roll bar
Steering	Servo-assisted ZF worm and roller

Brakes

	Vented front discs, ABS fitted as standard

Dimensions

Overall height	1,397mm/55in
Rear track	1,470mm/57.6in

---

able to sell them. Within a fortnight of the car's launch at the Paris Salon, the car proved so popular that the company quickly had to build a further batch of 500 merely to keep pace with demand.

It was much the same story with the M5 version of the 5 Series. Despite having been built largely by hand, BMW made 2,241 M5s between the beginning in 1984 and end of production at Christmas, 1987.

Although the M5 outwardly resembled a 'souped-up' E28 (a 'Q-car' with an external appearance that belied its performance and specification) it was representative of serious development work behind the scenes. At the heart of the machine was a wholly revised engine, which was close in specification to the contemporary mid-engined M1, some examples of which were being campaigned in international sports car racing. With 24 valves (four per cylinder) and twin-overhead camshafts, it developed 286bhp at 6,500rpm and 250lb ft of torque at 4,500rpm.

In terms of performance it was just about the quickest four-door saloon the world had ever seen, and even made the turbocharged Audi quattro look a little dated by comparison. With a top speed of 153mph, and 0–60mph capability of 6secs, this was a sporting Grand Tourer in the best traditions.

'Q' and Queue

Understated with a hint of motor sport breeding, the M5's appearance was subtly dramatic. The bumpers, deep chin spoiler, side skirts, door mirrors and shallow boot spoiler were all painted in body colour (an attractive and desirable contemporary trend) and there was a choice of attractive alloy wheels. Cross-spoke wheels from BBS were widely used on sports racing and Touring cars at this time, and they proved popular on the M5, but there was the alternative of a flatter disc alloy wheel with small vents and more conservative styling to fit in with the car's 'Q' image.

Attractive external badging was confined to an M5 logo, and BMW's Motorsport colours on the bootlid and radiator grille. A handful of owners removed these badges, so as not to give the 'game' away, a trend that

Owned by catering manager, Kevin Evans, this remarkable 520i drives as well and smoothly as ever, despite having led an active life for the best part of two decades.

spread among the owners of powerful Audis in the Ingolstadt range. As an aside, the owners of standard BMWs acquired BMW Motorsport logos, to make their more mundane cars resemble the M5, a style trend that continues among enthusiasts to this day, and a sure sign that BMW's heavy involvement in motor racing was having the desired influence.

In Britain these cars were listed at approximately £27,000, which led some journalists to note that this appeared to be a vast sum for such an ordinary looking car, but this was, of course, exactly what BMW had set out to achieve. And there were well-heeled customers who joined a long queue for the privilege of owning a tarmac scorcher that bore a passing resemblance to a common or garden 518i.

Although extremely powerful, the M5 was also very civilised. Power delivery was instant, and the 5-speed Getrag 'box about as smooth and precise a unit ever used in a BMW. To keep everything together on the road there were stiffer suspension springs and dampers and ventilated brake discs up front with ABS for the benefit of those who occasionally pushed their luck too far.

Tracking Out

The arrival of the M5 in Britain went unnoticed, by and large, except by a small minority who understood what it was supposed to represent. Up and down the country, local newspapers dutifully published brief extracts from BMW's publicity material, along with a photograph of the M5 which, in the good old days when all newspaper pictures were in black and white, left little impression on those who quickly thumbed through the pages in search of the obituary columns.

BMW's press-release material for this model was typically inhibited by the unwritten rules of good taste, superlatives being largely absent from a body text that simply stuck to the facts. Their approach at this time was like a breath of fresh literary air, particularly as so many manufacturers were spending lavishly on publicity material, that made extravagant, and in some cases laughable, claims about all sorts of dreary, mundane machinery. Inevitably, journalists had become weary of all this hype, and by the mid-1980s competition between manufacturers had become so intense that they began to spend more and more on entertaining journalists in the hope of making the 'right' impression. The constant round of car launches, where testing and photographing was almost secondary to indulging in the pleasures of the table, became a grinding bind.

In addition, many journalists and professional car commentators became blasé. Japanese manufacturers, in particular, were producing one car after another, with increasingly impressive specifications. Honda's CRX and Toyota's mid-engined MR2, both with fabulous handling and ground-breaking drivability, were available at a fraction of the cost of Italian exotica, and were almost capable of doing the same job.

In the upper echelons of the car world, several manufacturers were competing in a race to produce the ultimate road machine. The Ferrari F40, Porsche 959, Bugatti EB110, Jaguar XJ220 would all emerge as a new generation of supercars. Capable of over 200mph, and accelerating from 0–100mph in almost no time at all, such luminaries made it increasingly difficult to impress journalists and members of the car-buying public.

My introduction to the M5 BMW was at Thruxton, a tricky racing circuit with three corners in particular (Campbell, Cobb and Segrave) designed to catch out the unwary. Liveried in red with contrasting matt black trim, the test car sat resplendent in the paddock among a sea of brand new BMWs.

As I sat in the leather-clad comfort of the interior, the sunlit landscape, punctuated by

Among the last of the E28 Series built in 1988, the powerful 2.8-litre cars can now be purchased for 'peanuts'.

advertising hoardings, pit buildings and chatty motor racing folk, appeared to be a peaceful, pleasant and civilised place. Such was the comfort and apparent build quality of the M5, that I already felt cosseted from the outside world. It was like sitting in a cross between an S-class Mercedes and a works-prepared racing BMW, a car that massaged aches and pains away on the one hand, but inspired the possibility of exhilaration on the other.

With the 'six' switched on and idling, it was difficult to hear the engine, particularly as my passenger, a fellow journalist, was vociferously proffering his opinion that Niki Lauda was the best racing driver the world had ever seen. Quickly considering that he had no thoughts between his ears for Bernd Rosemeyer, Juan Fangio, Jimmy Clark and the greatest of all, Jacky Ickx, it seemed more appropriate to select bottom gear and venture out onto the track.

As we left the paddock it naturally occurred to me that, if the M5 had been compromised, it would show very quickly on a tight, twisting circuit at high speed. However, after an exploratory lap to warm up the engine and transmission oils, this 'wolf in sheep's clothing' demonstrated the litheness and agility, and sheer tractability, of a giant octopus with a long memory for the most nutritious prey.

Acceleration out of corners was unequivocal, anchor power equally certain, and the gearchange so slick that the lever 'swished' through the gate in the manner of five Formula One cars fighting for supremacy into the first corner of a Grand Prix. Floor the throttle in any gear, and the engine delivers power across the rev range, and with a fair shove in the back. There is none of the 'camminess' of a pure racing unit, just turbine-smooth torque, accompanied by the unmistakable roar of an in-line six, all the way.

Bang the car into top gear down the back straight at Thruxton and it pulls cleanly to 135mph before the brakes, and third, are needed once again. With this much power, the next corner is never very far away, and concentration is of the essence at all times. On this particular outing the weather was dry, and the grip from the big, meaty TRX Michelins proved most tenacious. In collaboration with precise, well-weighted power-steering, the M5 showed itself to be superbly balanced through both tight and sweeping corners.

At normal speeds, in other words those to which we are limited to on public roads by law, it is a simple matter of turning the steering wheel in the correct direction. The car does the rest for you, and there is never any drama. On an unrestricted track, it is a different story. Begin to push it deep into corners, and there's a hint of initial understeer, which diminishes instantly when throttle is applied. Bang the hammer hard to the floor, and the tail begins to dig deeply into the road surface; in lower gears there is a distinctive chirping from the rubber – a sure sign that the tyres are beginning to fight hard.

Losing the tail is almost wholly dependent upon throwing the car sideways intentionally, and balancing directional stability with opposite lock. It is at this stage that the BMW illustrates just how very well balanced the chassis is. For racing purposes the suspension needs to be considerably stiffer, of course, but the standard set-up takes into account the demands of ride quality. Harsh suspension is fine on a race track, but not so clever crashing over the potholes and bumps of public roads.

After several laps the M5 is clearly an addictive piece of machinery and, despite working the brakes up into a lather at one stage (smouldering brake dust is about as pleasant as a disco specialising in 1980s pop music) it behaved perfectly throughout.

Once parked back in the paddock, its magnificent engine silenced and 'pinging' as it cooled down, it was interesting to reflect on the nature of the car. Sitting on my old camera box in order to gaze at the car, it was easy to see the Fünfer in a wholly different light. Knowing, by this time, its full capabilities, it no longer looked like the ultimate in roadgoing 'Q' cars, or a wolf in sheep's clothing, but a purpose-built sports machine, with subtle body styling that shrieked: 'think again, dear boy, and open your eyes'.

That a car of this performance was capable of carrying four or five adults, and propelling them safely to 153mph, was a demonstration in real progress having been made in the motor industry. It showed perfectly that the lessons learnt from BMW's involvement in Touring Car racing ten years previously was being fed directly back into the road cars.

More than this, it also illustrated that rival manufacturers had a lot of catching up to do if they were going to remain on even terms.

That the M5 was capable of so much, though, was partially wasted because of the age in which it was conceived and delivered.

M5 (1985–87)

Identical to 535i and M535i except for the following:

Engine

Cylinders	6
Bore × stroke	93.4 × 84mm
Capacity	3,453cc
Compression ratio	10.5:1
Timing	Double-overhead camshafts, Bosch Motronic fuel injection
Max power	286bhp at 6,500rpm
Max torque	245lb ft at 4,500rpm
Max power	256bhp at 6,500rpm (US-spec)
Max torque	243lb ft at 4,500rpm (US-spec)

Transmission

Gearbox	5-speed manual only
Ratios	First 3.51
	Second 2.08
	Third 1.35
	Fourth 1.00
	Fifth 0.81
	Final drive 3.73 (Europe), 3.91 (US)

After a day at Thruxton, I climbed into the passenger seat of a friend's standard 525i. A group of friends jumped aboard their M5 and, prior to leaving the circuit, we arranged to meet up for supper in Gloucestershire. We trundled along at a steady 50mph and, as was to be expected, the M5 disappeared into the distance.

Arriving at our designated restaurant one hour later, I imagined that the party in the M5 had probably finished eating, and were ready for the home journey. Interestingly, they had beaten us by no more than a few minutes. Such is congestion on British roads that it seems to make little difference to journey times whether you have a 'screamer', like the M5, or a moped.

Nose on End

Depending upon your point of view the E28 was, by the mid-1980s, either the last of the classic Fünfers, predominantly determined by the familiar, sloping 'shark-nose' radiator grille, or an aged, venerable friend. Either way, it had enjoyed an extremely fruitful, and profitable, existence. Conservative in styling to some, but elegant and handsome, nevertheless, it also brought luxury and performance motoring to a much wider audience.

These cars were never cheap to buy, but no manufacturer provided so much in a motor car for what customers were expected to pay. A wholly competent engineering package, which impressed all who drove it, the E28 belonged to an era of great change. In some respects it was a period in which automotive designers pushed conventional boundaries. As more and more speed limits were imposed on roads, on both sides of the Atlantic, cars became faster and faster. However, as a bonus cars were also becoming more fuel-efficient; high performance and good fuel mileage began to walk hand in hand.

BMW's marketing strategy was also beginning to work especially well; a new tide of automotive social change began to sweep across Europe. Whereas the well-heeled had once expressed their social standing, and fulfilled their motoring aspirations, by driving a Rolls-Royce, the Crewe company's products were perceived in many quarters as anti-social dinosaurs. Many were reduced to the role of providing transport for brides on their wedding day, an ignominious end in which casting the 'Best Car in the World' would largely spend the dying days of the twentieth century. As an aside, it is ironical that Rolls-Royce's fortunes of the twenty-first century will be under the control of BMW, who own the right to produce these once revered cars.

Rolls-Royce's loss during the 1980s, and beyond, was largely BMW's gain, particularly as the luxury 7 Series gained in popularity. However, it had become clear that the Munich concern still had a long way to go before it could topple arch-rival Daimler-Benz.

Jaguar had a certain standing in Britain, North America and, surprisingly, in Germany during the 1980s but, despite sentiment for the luxury cats, many despaired of British build quality which, frankly, was awful, and lived in hope that their cars would one day become reliable.

By 1988, production of BMW's good old E25 5 Series ended to make way for a new kind of car that took BMW into a new era in which improved, sound aerodynamics would play a great part in creating one of the world's finest ever cars. The car-buying public and several outspoken journalists had sent signal after signal to manufacturers, that the ugly creations of the past would not suffice for the future. The message eventually filtered through and even Volvo, who for years had specialised in making the automotive equivalent of apartment blocks, began to dial style into their designs.

CHAPTER SEVEN

BMW 5 Series:
The Third Generation

Grown Up at Five: the E34

At the beginning of 1988 the E28 was super-seded by the third generation Fünfers. Codenamed E34, the new range of cars made its public debut initially in North America, BMW's most important and lucrative export market. At this time Audi, in particular, were making huge inroads into the America market, with new, more modern sporting cars, sales of which were undoubtedly aided by Audi's successful racing programme.

While BMW had spent some 30 years attempting, with varying degrees of success, to become a viable alternative to Mercedes-Benz, Audi were on a mission to challenge BMW's increasingly dominant role in the European sports saloon market.

During the first six years of the 1980s, Dr Ferdinand Piëch had overseen Audi's onslaught with the quattro in the world of international rallying. Piëch had also demon-strated the benefits of permanent four-wheel drive in track racing with various versions of the quattro range. Quattros won the famous Pike's Peak Hillclimb in Colorado three years in a row, comprehensively beating the indige-nous competition on each occasion.

In 1987, Audi attacked the American TransAm NASCAR series with a team of 200 quattros, employing Hans-Joachim Stuck, Walter Röhrl and American, Hurley Haywood, as works drivers. Audi cleaned up with the Constructors' and Drivers' Championship, Haywood taking the latter title. It was a mas-terstroke by the Ingolstadt company.

In 1989, Audi entered quattro 90s for the IMSA GTO series in North America, Haywood and Stuck once again as principal pilots. Although Audi finished second in the Championship to Mercury, the German cars scored a number of important victories and, needless to say, the company was richly rewarded with huge tracts of free publicity.

Audi had chipped away in America for sev-eral years; it had cost the company vast sums, as all racing programmes are apt to do, but it paid off, and BMW's board took notice. It was no coincidence that Audi had a luxury V8 saloon in the offing which, with permanent four-wheel drive, held a sales advantage over conventional two-wheel drive cars.

The most stylish of all BMW saloons to emerge for many years, the E34 debuted in 1988 to universal acclaim.

A much larger car than its predecessor, the E34 had virtually perfect 50:50 front-to-rear weight distribution, which made for class-leading handling and roadholding.

The third generation E34 5 Series had, therefore, to be better than good; it needed to be exceptional – a car that stood head and shoulders above its predecessor and comparable cars from Jaguar, Mercedes-Benz and the dark horse from Ingolstadt, Audi.

During one launch after another, at international, national and local levels, the revised Fünfer was received with 'oohs and aahs', as journalists and customers alike drew breath. The car was gaspingly beautiful, with a new style clearly aping the format of the larger, contemporary 7 Series. But, despite its larger body (the new car had grown considerably in size) it retained the elegance and chic more normally associated with much smaller passenger saloons.

As this shot illustrates the E34's flanks were more rounded; note that 'Special Equipment' models had cross-spoke alloy wheels and a bootlid spoiler as standard.

Generally, it was perceived as having the 'cute' good looks of a 3 Series but, with the practical advantages of a 7 Series.

Body Building Exercise

Although the E34 was 2in wider and 4in longer than the car it replaced, the use of curved shapes, particularly along the 'shoulders' of the flanks, gave it the appearance of being 'softer', more welcoming and less masculine. To use an oft-used phrase of the 1960s it had 'sex' appeal, but styled to court the attentions of both sexes.

In the fashion of the day the profile of the body was roughly wedge-shaped, which went a long way towards improving aerodynamic drag. Despite the increased width of the body, the 'snubbier' nose, narrower radiator grille, smoothly profiled door mirrors and flush glass and door handles brought the drag coefficient down to 0.30, a respectable enough figure, and a great improvement on the E28, but a long way from ground-breaking.

Although the design was substantially different from the cars that had gone before it, the usual BMW hallmarks (twin headlamps, 'kidney' grille, 'dogleg' pieces in the 'ears' of the rear side windows, and prominent swage lines on the bonnet and flanks) were all cleverly integrated into a package that was unmistakably from Munich.

Aerodynamic aids, which also enhanced the styling, included a deep chin spoiler with a leading blade in the manner of the racing 3 Series cars, shaped 'skirts' along the sill panels, and a rear bumper designed to dispense with 'spent' air as cleanly as possible. A curved boot spoiler was offered as an extra-cost option, but its effect on increasing greater stability was barely measurable at normal road speeds. Many considered, however, that the spoiler enhanced the car's sporting appearance, but conveniently ignored the difficulty it created. As I discovered myself, it is difficult to wash and polish the area of bootlid below the aerofoil; a small point, but one that probably causes those obsessed with concours d'elegance a few headaches.

Below the surface of the beautiful bodywork, BMW had also been hard at work. A much stiffer shell than previously, with improved crash protection, tests demon-

---

518i (1989–96), Touring (1993–96)

Body style   Four-door saloon and five-door estate

Engine
Cylinders	4
Bore × stroke	84 × 81mm
Capacity	1,796cc
Compression ratio	8.8:1
Fuel injection	Bosch Motronic, Lambda probe and catalytic converter
Max power	113bhp
Max torque	117lb ft at 4,250rpm

Transmission

Gearbox   5-speed manual, 5-speed close-ratio and optional 4-speed automatic

Ratios	5-speed manual	Close ratio	4-speed automatic
First	3.72	5.10	2.40
Second	2.04	2.77	1.47
Third	1.34	1.72	1.00
Fourth	1.00	1.22	0.72
Fifth	0.80	1.00	
Final drive	4.27	3.46	4.45

(Automatic box not made available on Touring model)

Suspension and steering
Susupension	(front) MacPherson struts, anti-roll bar
	(rear) Semi-trailing arms, struts and coil springs
Steering	Servo-assisted ZF worm and roller
Wheels	Pressed steel 6J×15, 7J×15 (Touring), alloys optional
Tyres	205/65HR 15

Brakes   Servo-assisted discs/discs, ABS standard from 1993

Dimensions
Overall length	4,720mm/185.8in
Overall width	1,751mm/68.9in
Overall height	1,412mm/55.6in saloon
	1,417mm/55.8in Touring
Wheelbase	2,761mm/108.7in
Track	(front) 1,470mm/57.9in
	(rear) 1,495mm/58.8in

Although the styling of the 5 Series had changed quite radically, the revised car was still instantly recognisable as a BMW. Boot space was huge and the tail-lamps, which 'ate' into the rear lid, were much more stylish than the E28's.

German owners in particular personalised their cars with 'after-market' wheels, performance exhausts and lowered suspension.

strated that the new Fünfer was among the safest passengers saloons ever built. Front and rear there were the usual 'crumple' zones, and a rigid central passenger cell, with reinforcements between all the major seam welds. Coupled with an increase in size, such attention to detail added weight, despite the extensive use of lightweight materials for items such as the bumpers, but performance was up to, and beyond, BMW's normal standards.

Having created a very good-looking bodyshell, engineered for safety and durability, BMW's computerised build techniques had also resulted in exemplary panel fit and paint finish, which were second to none. In conclusion, the new 5 Series was a state of the art expression of intelligent people, perfecting a complex combination of automotive culture, mass-production techniques and science in a machine representative of a zenith in twentieth century car manufacturing.

Fünfer plus Five

With a relatively large increase in wheelbase of more than 5in, cabin space was vastly improved, and particularly the available legroom in the rear. Due to the increased width of the body, there was also more elbow room, and a general aura of spaciousness. BMW's attention to detail also meant that there was added luxury, which was clearly aimed at catapulting the car into the upper echelons of the market. The 7 Series boasted more room, and greater prestige, but the 5 Series hit something of a chord with those in search of 'top-notch' motoring. Many began to wonder whether a range-topping 7 was worth the extra money, and they had a point, of course.

Perfectly shaped seats front and rear were covered in soft cloth materials, and tastefully matched, or contrasted, with body colour. Leather was an extra-cost option, but came as standard on some, though not all, SE (Special Equipment) models. Head restraints were fitted as standard to the front seats, and also in the rear on SE models, a feature that just a few years earlier had only been associated with expensive limousine-type vehicles. Rear passengers were also treated to an oddments tray between the two front seats, and recessed ashtrays in the door panels. Incidentally, the ashtray in the front, which includes a neatly built-in cigar lighter, is the only evidence that BMW's designers might have been a little more thoughtful. It opens perfectly adequately for cigarettes, but cannot accommodate this author's Peterson pipe!

No radical departures were made for the switchgear and instrumentation, and the dashboard, apart from the use of softer plastics,

520i saloon (1988–96), Touring (1991–96)

Identical to 518i except for the following:

Engine

Cylinders	6
Bore × stroke	80 × 66mm
Capacity	1,991cc
Timing	Single-overhead camshaft, VANOS variable valve timing from September 1992
Compression ratio	8.8:1
Fuel injection	Bosch Motronic, Lambda probe and catalytic converter
Max power	150bhp at 5,900rpm
Max torque	137lb ft at 4,300rpm

Transmission

Gearbox	5-speed manual, optional 4-speed automatic
Ratios	4-speed overdrive auto
	First 2.48
	Second 1.48
	Third 1.00
	Fourth 0.73
	Final drive 4.45 (1988–90)
5-speed overdrive manual (May to July 1990)	
	First 3.83
	Second 2.20
	Third 1.40
	Fourth 1.00
	Fifth 0.81
	Final drive 4.27
Optional 4-speed overdrive auto	
	First 2.40
	Second 1.47
	Third 1.00
	Fourth 0.72
	Final drive 4.55
From August 1990	
5-speed close-ratio manual	
Ratios	First 4.23
	Second 2.52
	Third 1.66
	Fourth 1.22
	Fifth 1.00
	Final drive 3.46
Optional 5-speed overdrive automatic	
Ratios	First 1.366
	Second 2.00
	Third 1.41
	Fourth 1.00
	Fifth 0.74
	Final drive 3.64

Wheels and tyres

Wheels	Pressed steel 6J×15 (saloon), 7J×15 (Touring), alloys optional
Tyres	205/65HR 15

Brakes

	Servo-assisted discs/discs, ABS standard from September 1991

As the E34's wheelbase was more than 5in longer than the E28's, legroom in the rear was vastly improved. Leather upholstery was standard on some models.

adhered to BMW's normal practice. The gauges were circular with white characters on black backgrounds, and there was the familiar orange illumination with the lights switched on, but the 'hood' shrouding the instrument panel was more rounded than previously and in keeping with the similarly curved parts of the bodyshell.

At the base of the instrument panel, there was an ECC (Electronic Check Control) system to warn of various malfunctions, and impending service intervals. Curiously, BMW also built in an audible 'bleep' to warn of a door being opened while the engine was switched on, which was useful for those with children, but more evidence of something approaching paranoia about safety.

Improved interior ventilation was provided through adjustable apertures in the doors.

The centre console, containing the particularly uninspiring analogue clock, optional radio and revised ventilation/heating controls and vents, was angled towards the driver (a long-standing BMW tradition) and there were new, adjustable ventilation outlets in the door cappings. The latter were not only eminently practical, but also emphasised the luxury nature of the car and BMW's determination to give customers the sort of features that were not fitted to vehicles from rival manufacturers. That Volkswagen had introduced air vents into the door cappings of the Type 2 Transporter some years previously largely went unnoticed, of course.

Power steering was standard and the stock steering wheel was a stylish, if tastefully conservative-looking, four-spoke design and a great improvement over the one fitted to the previous E28 models. Despite this, many owners plumped for the leather-clad three-spoke sports wheel, discreetly emblazoned with the M-tech logo, which BMW were only too pleased to provide at extra cost – in fact, a lot of extra cost!

Apart from the obvious comforts and high quality of the appointments, the new 5 was commendably quiet, the cabin having been extremely well insulated against engine and transmission noise, and vibration from the road surface. The sound insulation fitted to the underside of the body performed its role so effectively, that at tick-over it was actually difficult to hear that the engine was running, a blip of the throttle pedal and glance at the tachometer needle often being necessary to prevent stalling on take-off.

Estate Worker

Inspired by the success of the 3 Series Touring, BMW launched an estate version of the 5 Series in 1991, also dubbed as a Touring. Although the company had built an estate version of the 2002 in the early 1970s, it was not hugely successful, as motoring folk did not automatically think of BMWs as being in the nature of load-luggers.

Throughout the 1970s and 1980s, 'estate car' had become almost synonymous with Volvo, the Swedish workhorse that provided reliable, dependable, but far from exciting, transport for far from exciting people, many of whom built up a reputation for driving as if they had a grudge against common road sense. However, Volvo had demonstrated that there was a growing market for large load-carriers, and BMW, and others, spread their wings to include one in their line up.

Remarkably, the 5 Series Touring appeared as an estate version of the saloon. By contrast, so many other manufacturers who had taken a similar route had taken a base saloon and simply added an awkward piece on the pillion with aesthetically disastrous results. Japanese carmakers were among the worst offenders in this respect, and just one reason for the huge success of the BMW.

Although not cavernous in the manner of the contemporary 7 Series Volvo estate, the BMW Touring's load area was more than adequate for most and had the benefit of a 'split' and folding rear seat to increase luggage space as and when it was needed. Typical attention to detail included, for speed and convenience of loading, a rear window that could be opened without having to lift the tailgate.

During the 1990s, Tom Walkinshaw's racing outfit demonstrated with a team of Volvos entered for the British Touring Car Championship, that the estate versions of the Swedish cars were better suited to track work

than their saloon counterparts. Aerodynamic tests showed that the estate's long roof panel, in collaboration with a spoiler fitted to its trailing edge, enhanced the airflow over the body and allowed for a higher top speed and improved stability. BMW did not, however, pursue the same route with the 5 or 3 Series Tourings; these were not intended as sports cars, and would have done little for the company's image or illustrious racing past, but it is an intriguing idea just the same.

Fore, Six, Four Formation

Initially, the E34 was only available with a choice of 6-cylinder engines, including the 524td diesel version. In the interests of reducing exhaust emissions, and in anticipation of forthcoming legislation, all petrol engines were fitted with catalytic converters.

As previously, the model range comprised the 2-litre 520i with 129bhp, 2.5-litre 525i with 170bhp, 188bhp 3-litre 530i and 3.4-

Left: **Rear passengers got their own smoker's companion, controls for the electrically-operated windows and a rest for both arms, but not in all models.**

'Special Equipment' Fünfers were also fitted with armrests in the front. The leather seats are comfortable and easy to clean.

With a top speed of close to 140mph and 0–60mph potential of 8.6secs, the 525i was by far the pick of the range. Journalists and professional test drivers heaped huge praise on the car, and customers obviously agreed, because this model quickly became a best-seller in the Fünfer range. Surprisingly, the model's success was at the expense of the 530i which, despite a higher purchase price didn't offer a great deal more than the 2.5-litre car. By May 1990, this had resulted in the 530i being dropped from the range, leaving power-hungry Fünfer fanciers with the 146mph 535i as the top autobahn 'blaster'.

However, there were further developments: shortly after the 530i disappeared, the 520i and 525i were treated to more power by the relatively simple expedient of twin-cam cylinder heads and four valves per cylinder. This resulted in 150bhp for the 2-litre car and an impressive 192bhp for the 525i. With improved 'top-end breathing' the revised power units were 'cammier', more responsive and gave higher top speeds, and enthusiasts naturally revelled in them, despite a slight fuel-consumption penalty.

Dashboard layout is a shining example of BMW's no-nonsense approach, combining style with functionalism – an ideal driving environment for sports enthusiasts and sybarites alike.

litre 535i with 211bhp. The much-loved 528i was dropped from the range altogether, and the 4-cylinder 518i with 113bhp, which shared the same engine as the contemporary 3 Series, was launched in 1989. As before, an M5 version was delayed, and not part of the original line-up because, apart from BMW's natural desire to ensure that it was absolutely spot on, the waiting added something of an air of excitement and anticipation.

Twin-overhead camshafts and multi-valve heads were inevitable developments for BMW in the 'everyday' production cars, another example of racecar technology filtering through to daily drivers. However, there is little doubt that BMW's hand had been forced by Japanese manufacturers, like Toyota and Honda, who 're-invented' these engine 'tweaks' some years earlier with both small and large capacity engines. Their smoothness and enhanced performance had a tangible effect on sales, and European manufacturers had little option but to follow suit. That twin camshafts and four valve per cylinder technology had been introduced during the pioneering days of the motor car, most notably by Swiss Engineer Ernst Henry for the Peugeot Grand Prix cars of 1912, had largely been forgotten, except in racing applications. That it took so long for its revival is one of the unsolved mysteries of European motor manufacturing.

The 5 Series Touring model (left) was almost as popular as its smaller 3 Series sister (right). A spacious load-carrier, the estate version was an unlikely BMW, but quickly proved its worth.

Another significant break from BMW tradition in 1992 saw the introduction of V8 engines being made available in the E34. The Munich company's 'Baroque Angels' and gorgeous 507 two-seater sports car of the 1950s had been powered by V8s, but the revival of this configuration for the 5 Series (and 7 and 8 Series cars) was probably inspired by the use of 8-cylinder engines in sundry Mercedes, and by the popularity of V8s in North America.

Both power units (a 3-litre in the revived 530i and 4-litre in the 540i) were jewels of engineering and, being constructed with alloy cylinder blocks and heads, were also astonishingly light in weight. Both engines had chain-driven twin-overhead camshafts per bank of cylinders, and although maintenance and servicing was a necessarily lengthy, and therefore expensive undertaking, both engines were hailed as being among the smoothest and best of their type to be found anywhere in the industry. With the 3-litre car capable of well above 140mph and the 4-litre deploying a potential for 155mph, these cars were inter-city expresses par excellence. The dash to 60mph was possible in under 7secs in the more powerful of the two cars but, in customary BMW fashion, such antics were usually accomplished without drama. And, in both manual and automatic guises, power and torque were available in abundance right through the rev range.

Business as Unusual

The use of the ubiquitous MacPherson struts, wishbones and anti-roll bar up front, and semi-trailing arms for the rear suspension was inevitable. Despite predictions from some commentators at this time, that a young genius, somewhere in the motor industry, would hit on new and radical ideas for improving suspension systems, it was not to be. Citroën kept faith with their

unique 'doughnuts' and hydraulic system for certain models but, by and large, there seemed little point in trying to 're-invent' the coil spring.

Braking was by all-round discs (ventilated at the front on all models above the 520i) which were almost 12in in diameter, and powered by a vacuum servo. As an aside, attempting to operate the brakes with the engine switched off is not to be recommended.

Power-assisted steering was standard across the entire range, and both automatic and manual gearboxes were virtually to the same specification as the ones used in the E25 5 Series. When the twin-cam 5s were launched, however, there was a new 5-speed

The optional three-spoke steering wheel was one of the best ever devised, and proved that there's more to designing a wheel than 'meets the fingers'.

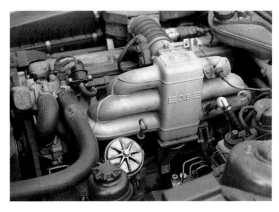

The 211bhp 3.5-litre engine makes for an impressive sight with its cast-alloy injection pipework.

automatic with closer ratios, and a revised 5-speed manual with new ratios and direct fifth instead overdrive top.

In standard guise the E34s were fitted with black-painted 15in vented steel wheels closed with silver-coloured plastic hubcaps. Despite BMW roundels to brighten the centres of the hubcaps, these wheels presented an uninspiring picture, and although a common enough sight in Britain, a majority of

---

525i saloon (1988–96), 525i Touring (1990–96), 525ix saloon Touring (1991–96)

Identical to 518i except for the following:

Engine

Cylinders	6
Bore × stroke	84 × 75mm
Capacity	2,494cc
Compression ratio	8.8:1
Fuel injection	Bosch Motronic, Lambda probe and catalytic converter
Max power	170bhp at 5,800rpm
Max torque	160lb ft at 4,300rpm

Modifications from May 1990
Double-overhead camshafts with 4 valves per cylinder

Max power	192bhp at 5,900rpm
Max torque	180lb ft at 4,500rpm

VANOS variable valve timing from September 1992

Transmission

Gearbox   5-speed manual or optional 4-speed automatic

Ratios	5-speed manual	4-speed automatic
First	3.83	2.48
Second	2.20	1.48
Third	1.40	1.00
Fourth	1.00	0.73
Fifth	0.80	
Final drive	3.73	3.91

From August 1990
5-speed close-ratio manual

Ratios	
	First 4.23
	Second 2.49
	Third 1.66
	Fourth 1.24
	Fifth 1.00
	Final drive 3.23

525ix with permanent four-wheel drive: ratios as for 525i made after August 1990, except for 3.38 final-drive ratio

Wheels and tyres

Wheels	Pressed steel 6.5J×15
Tyres	195/65VR 15

From May 1990

Wheels	6J or 6.5J
525i Touring	7J×15 wheels with 225/60VR 15 tyres
525ix	7.5J×16 wheels with 225/55HR 16 tyres
525ix Touring	225/55VR 16 tyres

Brakes   Servo-assisted discs/discs with ABS standard from September 1991

---

owners fitted alloys which were available at extra cost. Alloys reduced unsprung weight, naturally, but their greatest advantage was in improving, and doing full justice to the exquisite body styling. Among the wheels available from main dealers, the most popular were the cross-spoke items made by BBS of Schiltach in southern Germany.

This specialist company, based in idyllic countryside, held close links with motor racing, worked to the highest standards, and employed designers at the cutting edge of their art. Alloy wheels with the cross-spoke design had served racing BMWs, Porsches and Audis, and looked absolutely right on the 5 Series, and other cars in the BMW line up. A classic piece of design, although difficult to keep clean, it is arguable that their aesthetic appeal has yet to be bettered.

Owners' Views

I hope readers will, at this juncture, forgive a personal indulgence. A more objective view of the E34 follows this discourse, but the car featured here is my own personal transport, and my opinion is naturally inclined towards bias. And before going any further, I need to make it quite clear that, of the many hundreds of cars I have had the pleasure of driving, this E34 525i ranks as the second best.

A Special Equipment version finished in black, and fitted with BBS cross-spoke alloys, it replaced my beloved Saab 900, a wonderful old car with a robust body, predictable handling (including all the drawbacks of front-wheel drive), superb reliability, quite dreadful fuel consumption and dependable engineering that wouldn't look too out-of-place in an average farmyard (circa 1967). Having stumbled into Saab ownership by accident, and tired of it after a couple of years, I despatched it to my little brother who, in his customary manner, destroyed its clutch in less than a week.

After 1990, the under-bonnet picture changed, as BMW placed a black plastic shroud over the top of the engine.

By comparison with the Saab, and almost everything else, the BMW is a true sophisticate that really does live up to BMW's 'ultimate driving experience' slogan. In one piece of the company's official publicity literature a headline proclaims: 'Technology that follows the driver's thoughts makes motoring an even greater pleasure'. Such ostensibly meaningless 'drivel' turns out, more or less, to be completely accurate. The car might not be perfect – no car is – but it comes pretty close.

Effortless at legal speeds, fun at fun-speed, and both demanding and rewarding on the limit, no car comes close in terms of 'chuckability'. Audi's turbocharged ur-quattro ultimately has more grip from permanent four-wheel drive but, for purists there is no real substitute for a perfectly balanced rear-driver. Incidentally, BMW also produced a four-wheel drive version of the 525i (dubbed 525iX) which held obvious advantages for folks living in the hillier regions of the

A much wider kidney grille debuted in 1994, but arguably made no visual improvement to the front end.

A 520i 2-litre car fitted with standard steel wheels and painted hubcaps looks dull by comparison with those with the optional alloys.

Germanic countries, particularly during the snowy winters, but it was not especially popular. Audi had spent millions promoting the four-wheel drive message, whereas BMW had not. Ultimately, this was Audi's gain and BMW's loss, but inevitable in view of the Ingolstadt company's dominant quattro rallying programme during the 1980s.

Loss of poise and balance is almost wholly dependent on foolish, or skilled, driving. Enter a tight bend at high speed and there is a hint of understeer, especially if braking is left late, but wide throttle applications naturally brings the chassis back to heel. Full throttle in mid

corner is apt to bring the tail out but, with so much available power, the car's attitude is wholly predictable and controllable even in wet weather. Only under extreme circumstances of panic braking, when the ABS system kicks in, does the car begin to lose its composure, but drivers who conduct a car in such a manner that ABS needs frequent use should, in the interests of other road users, take several lessons in driving tuition.

Like all other Fünfer owners, I revel in the car's comfort, smoothness and the unequivocal feeling of safety you get simply sitting behind the leather-covered sports steering wheel. The

530i (1988–90)		
Identical to 518i except for the following:		
Engine		
Cylinders	6	
Bore × stroke	89 × 80mm	
Capacity	2,986cc	
Compression ratio	9:1	
Fuel injection	Bosch Motronic, Lambda probe and catalytic converter	
Max power	188bhp at 5,800rpm	
Max torque	188lb ft at 4,000rpm	
Transmission		
Gearbox	5-speed manual or 4-speed automatic	
Ratios	**5-speed manual**	**4-speed automatic**
First	3.83	2.48
Second	2.20	1.48
Third	1.40	1.00
Fourth	1.00	0.73
Fifth	0.81	
Final drive	3.64	3.73
Wheels and tyres		
Wheels	Pressed steel 6.5J×15 (alloys optional)	
Tyres	205/65VR 15	
Brakes	ABS fitted as standard	

cabin is simply a relaxing place to be and so well designed and made that it almost becomes part of your personality. Being cosseted in this way inevitably leads to a sense of complacency, until you are lucky enough to climb behind the wheel of a 'lesser' machine from 'mainstream' manufacturers. By comparison, many feel rough, unrefined, noisy, ill-mannered and, burdened with pedestrian performance, downright horrible. This, of course, is all relative, but makes for a greater appreciation of BMW motoring when the opportunity arises.

The 525i's natural composure recently hit home to me one bright evening in the otherwise dreary spring weather of 2001 when I was driving on a familiar road in my native Herefordshire to visit an old friend, John Day. Collectors of model cars will remember John Day as the father of modern 1:43rd die-casts – the man who pioneered manufacturing techniques, and a range of models made during the 1970s that stand as masterpieces of detail and quality.

Feeling tired after a long day's work, I pulled up at a set of traffic lights. Although feeling contented and at peace with the world, there was a Rover 216i sitting in front of me, nothing remarkable about that, but my peace was vaguely disturbed when the lights changed to green. The driver of the Rover appeared to be in something of a hurry to hasten the life of his clutch, and accelerated away in the manner of someone with an interest in making an early arrival in the next world.

For the next four or five miles, on a twisty road I have been travelling for several decades, it was with great interest that I observed the Rover being driven flat-out, the limit of its suspension travel being reached on every corner. While the man was so obviously driving as hard as he could (and, I hoped, enjoying it) I was listening to the evening concert on the radio, steering with one hand and looking forward to seeing my old friend.

After a couple more miles, the Rover had become rather tiresome and so, with a prod on the throttle pedal, I overtook and disappeared. Above all, this episode demonstrated the difference between Euroboxes and Grand Tourers. Many would interpret my attitude as one of crass arrogance, and they are entitled to their view, of course, but I cannot agree.

On arrival at John Day's house, I related this story to the venerable motoring sage who, in his customary manner castigated me for droning on and on about the pleasures of BMW motoring, before going on to relate the great days of Hans-Joachim Stuck's time at BMW when the talented German drove the 'Batmobiles' in the European Touring Car Championship. John's business, John Day Model Cars, sponsored 'Stuckey' and his Swedish team-mate, the late and very great Ronnie Peterson, when they drove for the March Grand Prix team in the mid 1970s, and has fond memories watching both maestros hard at work.

Sitting in John's summer house, enjoying several cups of strong coffee and the delights of equally strong tobacco, we chatted about days of old – good and bad. During the 1970s racing cars were a good deal safer than the machines of the previous decade, but safety considerations never held any fears for true racers. John recalled watching Hans-Joachim Stuck and Derek Bell in the works BMW coupés – fearsome machines – and reckoned that he always had to go and lie down afterwards.

The BMW coupés of the 1970s were not only fast and spectacular, but always painted to look like real racing cars. They were colourful and sounded magnificent, and when Stuckey took to the wheel, you knew you were always in for a real treat. That man's car control was inhuman – utterly breathtaking – and tiring to watch. 'Dinger' Bell, by comparison, was always fast, smooth and relatively unspectacular – a man who drove with motoring poetry in every artery – but Stuckey – heavens above! – he was something else.

530i saloon, 530i Touring (1992–96)

Identical to earlier 530i except for the following:

Engine

Cylinders	8
Bore × stroke	84 × 67.6mm
Capacity	2,997cc
Timing	Single-overhead camshaft per bank of cylinders, with 4 valves per cylinder
Compression ratio	10.5:1
Fuel injection	Bosch Motronic, Lambda probe and catalytic converter
Max power	218bhp at 5,800rpm
Max torque	209lb ft at 4,500rpm

Transmission

Gearbox	5-speed close ratio manual, or optional 5-speed auto	
Ratios	**5-speed manual**	**4-speed automatic**
First	4.20	3.67
Second	2.49	2.00
Third	1.66	1.14
Fourth	1.24	1.00
Fifth	1.00	0.74
Final drive	3.08	3.15
Touring final-drive ratio	3.23	

Suspension and steering

Suspension	Self-levelling rear on Touring

John Day took a thoughtful puff on one of his king-size cigarettes, stared at my Fünfer on the driveway and commented: 'Well, it looks nice – the styling's the same as it was in the good, old days – but it's not quite right.' I wondered what he meant. 'Looks too smooth and slinky to me, as if someone had tried to make a silk purse from a dog's tail and succeeded. What's it like to drive?' he asked.

I replied that he was welcome to take the keys and find out for himself, but he declined my invitation. He replied:

No thanks, I'd rather sit here, finish my coffee, and remember the days when BMW were struggling to succeed, rather than keep up with modern developments. BMW have obviously accomplished what they set out to do all those years ago, and now they've got young Ralf Schumacher in one of Frank's (Sir Frank Williams) single-seaters, I suppose Gerhard (Berger) will be itching to resume his Grand Prix career.

Chuckling wildly he added, 'but, like me, he's too old to mess about with fast cars.'

Coffee, smokes and philosophising ended for the evening, I climbed back into my car, and drove off wondering what it was really like for people like Stuckey, Dinger and Ronnie Peterson to have experienced the big racing coupés that trounced everything in their wake some 25 years earlier. My Fünfer provided a mere glimpse, I'm sure, and a glimpse from the viewpoint of a mollycoddled sybarite, and probably no more.

The 525i does virtually everything anyone might expect in a beautifully designed and executed motor car. It goes, stops and handles with perfection, and is also able to return in excess of 30mpg. My other car (a 1965 1,200cc Volkswagen Beetle) which is equally rewarding to drive, gives the same fuel mileage but, with only 34bhp from the air-cooled flat-four, is lacking the BMW's performance.

It's always interesting to compare the two cars for, as unlikely as it might seem, they share many similarities. Both are obviously the products of engineers working to the highest standards. Both are endowed with the highest standards of build quality, and engineering integrity. Both are reliable, dependable and durable, and stylish, controversial (few are wholly indifferent to Beetles and BMWs) and characteristically Germanic, despite six decades of development sitting between them. They also have enduring appeal, endowing the two cars with a rare, classic status with 'cult-like' features which are likely to leave a long legacy well into the twenty-first century.

I need to rest my biased case, but no-one need take my word for it alone. . .

Off His Tolley

Whether on two, four, or many more, wheels, Colin Tolley's everyday life is mostly about going forwards, but at very different speeds. A truck driver for HP Bulmer,

the world's largest cider makers, he is restricted to 40mph in the 'day job', but frequently suffers bouts of being delayed by a certain breed of motorist who seem determined to travel everywhere, in one gear, at 39mph. They are a source of frustration and gross irritation, which is why Colin keeps a very powerful Japanese motorcycle in his garage. The bike provides the ultimate antidote to the everyday difficulties of driving on the badly-maintained roads of Britain.

However, as a compromise between his Volvo truck and Suzuki motorcycle, Colin also enjoys his 525i, an automatic to SE specification, and recently acquired to replace his much-loved ur-quattro. He'd owned the quattro for some 17 years, and considered it to be the last word in performance family motoring. Colin commented:

The Audi did everything I wanted of a car. It was quick, had shattering roadholding – traction was formidable in all conditions – and had plenty of room for passengers. I also thought it was a good-looking car.

535i (1988–91)

Identical to 518i except for the following:

Engine

Cylinders	6
Bore × stroke	92 × 86mm
Capacity	3,430cc
Compression ratio	9:1
Fuel injection	Bosch Motronic, Lambda probe and catalytic converter
Max power	211bhp at 5,700rpm
Max torque	220lb ft at 4,000rpm

Transmission

Gearbox	5-speed manual, or optional 4-speed auto with identical ratios to 530i
Final-drive ratios	3.45 (manual to July 1990)
	3.64 (manual from August 1990)
	3.46 (auto to July 1990)
	3.91 (auto from August 1990)

Wheels and tyres

Wheels	7J×15 alloys as standard
Tyres	225/60VR 15, or 225/60ZR 15

After recent refurbishment of the Audi's paintwork in a local workshop, the Audi sat on Colin's drive and gleamed as brilliantly as the day it emerged from the Ingolstadt assembly lines. It was also in fine mechanical fettle, but things were not the same.

I lived with the Audi for many years, and enjoyed it. The car is truly great – possibly the finest machine of the 1980s – but I felt it was time for a change. Because driving forms the biggest part of my job, I find that my attitude to motoring has changed as I get older. Whereas 10 years ago I enjoyed performance and seat-of-the-pants cornering, I now yearn for comfort.

The fabulous M535i 6-cylinder car pushed out 315bhp at 6,900rpm, and gave superlative all-round performance, but...

Having sold the quattro to a young enthusiast, Colin naturally looked around for a more modern Audi as a replacement. Model designation was not important, provided it came equipped with an automatic gearbox and comfortable seats. 'When you have to change gear as many times a day as I do in my truck, the novelty

wears off after several years,' laughs Colin.

A test drive in an A4, however, suddenly saw a reversal in his opinion about further Audi ownership. Harbouring a preference for rear-wheel drive he quickly switched his attentions to a 5 Series, and bought a pristine example with leather upholstery and the 'obligatory' automatic gearbox. Colin readily admits that the car has changed his motoring life, as he explains:

I could hardly believe that the engine is so smooth and silent, and the driving so absolutely effortless. There was a time when I considered the quattro's 5-cylinder engine to be about the most vibration-free and refined engine there was. By comparison with the 6-cylinder BMW, though, the Audi feels distinctly agricultural, and although I love listening to a performance engine on song, I prefer the sweetness of the BMW these days rather than the raucous growl of the Audi.

Finished in metallic burgundy and fitted with

BBS cross-spoke alloy wheels, this Special Equipment model, without a boot spoiler, appears as an understated and 'superior' conveyance – a car that knows that it is good and great. With 100,000 miles under its belt (nicely 'run in' by BMW standards) it is almost indistinguishable from a sparkling new example, a great testament to its build quality. The engine runs perfectly, as it will for many more thousands of miles in the future, and the auto gearbox performs its role in changing up and down with almost imperceptible 'flicks'.

Colin continued:

The 525i is a great asset. Frankly, it's beyond criticism and one of the few cars that will almost drive itself if you want it to. I seriously considered a 7 Series as an alternative to the Five; elegant, luxurious and fast as the 735i undoubtedly is, I don't need a car of that size – it's just too big for narrow roads.

Now a committed fan of BMW, Colin Tolley is likely to keep his 525i for as long as he owned his Audi quattro. As he says, 'things that are built to last aren't meant to be discarded because of the implausible demands of fashionable whim.'

The M5

By the end of the 1980s exciting things were happening in the European motor industry. Volkswagen had launched the sporting Corrado, to great acclaim, and Audi had a new range of V8 saloons and 5- and 6-cylinder coupés clearly intended to take a big punch at Mercedes-Benz and BMW. South African designer Gordon Murray was under way with the Mclaren F1 supercar project (the Sultan of Brunei was reported to have bought three of these £600,000 road missiles) and the Rover Group launched a pretty cabriolet version of the much-loved Mini. At roughly the same time Rover also revived its historic association with John Cooper by making available a mod-

ern version of the venerable Mini-Cooper, complete with authentic bonnet stripes in the style of the 1960s track-racing versions.

In Formula One, Ayrton Senna, Nigel Mansell and Alain Prost were slugging it out in one exciting, furious and often controversial battle after another. Grand Prix fans around the world were gripped, and television viewing figures rose to around three-quarters of a billion for each round.

Conversely, international sports car racing took a tumble. The works Porsche team had long since packed up its bags and returned to Zuffenhausen. As the international series became more and more expensive, more and more famous names dropped by the wayside and, within a short time the whole shooting match fell into something approaching a shambles. Politics dictated in favour of Formula One but, for fans of fast saloons, which are the cars with which ordinary folk can identify, the various British and European Saloon Car Championships and DTM in Germany gave reason for great optimism.

BMW's fortunes began to rise throughout the 1990s, partially as a result of the performance and success of the 3 Series racing saloons, despite problems in western economies associated with the inevitable 'boom-and-bust' phenomenon resulting from monetarism policies.

The chips might have been down in the capricious world of financial investment, but BMW pressed ahead with the scorchingly hot and reassuringly expensive M5 version of the E34 just the same. Publicly debuted in the late

...journalists hailed the 525i, all things considered, as the best four-door saloon in the world. This immaculate automatic example belongs to lorry driver, Colin Tolley, and provides its owner with the automotive antithesis of his everyday truck.

One of the most dynamic production cars ever, Colin Tolley's 525i provides him with a quiet and comfortable environment in which to relax after a day at the wheel of his articulated Volvo but...

summer of 1988, a little time after the regular range was well into production, the new car was a different ballgame from its E28 predecessor.

Utilising a 3,535cc version of the twin-cam, 4-valve, 6-cylinder engine fitted to the mid-engined M1 supercar, it developed 315bhp at 6,900rpm. Acceleration from 0–60mph, for those who wanted to seriously reduce the life of their 17in diameter Michelins, was a whisker under 6secs. Top speed was a wholly theoretical 170mph, but entirely academic outside the confines of a racing circuit.

Externally, the M5 was distinguished from the stock 535i by a lower ride height, deeper chin spoiler, deeper rear bumper and sill skirts. Although bright trim was almost minimal on these cars, fashionable matt black was available as an extra-cost option, a styling touch that gave the M5 something of a more sporting, or more sinister, appearance depending upon your point of view.

Naturally, the suspension was beefed up to cope with the additional engine power; stiffer dampers and anti-roll bars were parts of the standard package, and there was the self-levelling system at the rear to keep the car on an even keel, irrespective of the presence of rear passengers and their luggage.

The cabin was in typical BMW Motorsport style, with half- or full-leather upholstery (leather was extended to the headlining), sports steering wheel, M-Technic gear knob and speedometer calibrated to 300kph. Naturally, the cabin was loaded with all the usual toys to be found in a car of this nature, although performance and fuel consumption would have been improved without them.

As a product of the Motorsport Division the M5 was largely handbuilt to customer specification, and became instant collectors' pieces on both sides of the Atlantic. A huge extravagance on the one hand, the M5 was in some sense the ultimate roadgoing saloon car of the 1990s. Some machines (two-seater supercars, for example) were ultimately faster, but there was nothing capable of carrying four adults in such comfort and safety that came close. As a bonus the car was just as competent on a race track. A lovely thing to drive and own.

535i: Owner Found the Right Clew

Among the very first 535i E34s built at the beginning of production in 1988, Graham Cleworth's standard metallic grey chariot is his second BMW and much cherished. The supermarket retail manager bought his car secondhand, having previously owned a 320i.

Graham laughs:

> My old 3 Series was completely falling to pieces with body rust, but this didn't detract from its performance, which was always exciting. I had a friend who owned a 518i; I loved the look of it – the body shape of the E34 is perfect to my way of thinking – but it was horribly underpowered. At first I wanted a 525i because it combines performance with economy but, when the opportunity came along to buy the 535i, I snapped it up and have never looked back.

Having once owned a 3-litre V6 Ford Capri, he was well used to the Bee-em's powerful engine, but he reckons that that's where the similarity between the two cars comes to an abrupt end. Simply closing the BMW's doors and bonnet, in Graham's words, is like 'banging cell doors shut', whereas the Capri's counterparts make the familiar 'twanging noise' of all the Dagenham products. He also owns a Toyota: 'alright for a banger, and an ideal slogger for lugging my three kids around, but nothing to get excited about.'

540i (1992–96)

Identical to 530i V8 except for the following:

Engine

Cylinders	8
Bore × stroke	89 × 80mm
Capacity	3,982cc
Timing	Single-overhead camshaft per bank of cylinders, 4 valves per cylinder
Compression ratio	10:1
Max power	286bhp at 5,800rpm
Max torque	289lb ft at 4,500rpm

Transmission

Gearbox	5-speed overdrive automatic
Ratios	First 3.55
	Second 2.24
	Third 1.54
	Fourth 1.00
	Fifth 0.79
	Final drive 2.93

To Graham, the 535i is the symbol of motoring at its roadgoing best. He claims:

The car is just 'sex on rubber', a gorgeous piece of Munich sculpture in steel, aluminium and leather. In all the years these cars were made, they just never aged, and still don't look dated, despite having been replaced by a more modern car. Personally, I don't think that the current 5 Series is anything like as good looking, which is why, in the absence of someone offering silly quantities of money for mine, I intend to hang on to it for as long as possible.

With such tall gearing and 'long-legged' cruising ability, the 535i returns a perfectly acceptable 30mpg, dipping in Graham Cleworth's experience to around 18mpg during the

Fünfer owners closely identify with motor sport, which is exactly what BMW had hoped and envisaged during the 1970s when the company invested heavily in the European, and other, Touring Car Championships.

Graham Cleworth's 535i, a hugely competent car with braking, balance and sheer grunt to allow it through virtually any corner, safely, at almost any speed.

tedious stop-go-stutter-go process of town driving.

> Although I enjoy my job I'm no different from anyone else in suffering from the stress that commercial pressures bring. At the end of the week there is nothing quite like enjoying the comfort of my BMW and putting your foot down. The car provides me with the same effect that some people might get from, for example, going to the gym for a workout. I'd love to own a Z3 sports car but, with three children a two-seater is not a practical proposition.

While interviewing people for this book, I sought to discover the identity of each subject's all-time favourite, or 'dream', car. It's a question that I've put to hundreds of people down many years, and have obtained many interesting answers. The sales manager of a Renault dealer, for example, once cited the Renault 21 estate as the finest car he'd ever driven, which I took with several pinches of salt. Many have spoken of sundry Ferraris, Porsches, Bentleys and others of similar ilk, but generally BMW owners remain loyal to Munich in this respect.

Like so many BMW people, though, Graham Cleworth remains happy with his Fünfer, although he confesses to harbouring desires to own a 3 Series cabriolet: 'one of the finest-looking two-door ragtops ever made,' he says. The idea that BMW owners are unofficial members of an exclusive international club has certainly played a part in maintaining loyalty to Munich.

But it's not the whole picture. A final comment from Graham Cleworth:

> A BMW has the build quality of a Merc, comfort of a Rolls, performance approaching Porsche, roadholding of a Lotus and unique looks, that I regard as being the equal of anything else. It's impossible to tire of the 535i's shape because it's in BMW's classic mould – a true 'gent' in every sense.

But it Had to End

From the earliest days of production, both journalists and owners regarded the E34 as the finest all-round saloon. It was hailed as a masterpiece of automotive engineering, and a monument to the challenging task of crafting high-performance, mass-produced vehicles that tower peerlessly above the efforts of others. By the mid 1990s, though, E34 production had ceased to make way for its successor.

Like all manufacturers, BMW have a policy of creating cars with a 'shelf-life', that are replaced, as a matter of course, every seven years or so, whether they need to be or not. Improvements in the products of competitors, technological progress, the onslaught of boredom among customers and designers, and the simple desire for change will ensure that this will always be the case. There was a time when replacement cars were not always worthy of their predecessors, and in some cases are not representative of improvement, but this is rarely the case in the modern era. Motorists, in other words the car-buying public, have become ever more discerning, and will not be fobbed off with the 'facelift mentality' in which the purpose of a revised radiator grille is to extract more money from the gullible.

A new car today, if it is to stand up to the close scrutiny exercised by journalists and car buyers, has to be genuinely new and better than the outgoing model. Many owners of the classic E34 do not agree, but it many respects the E39 5 Series was genuinely representative of progress in the hallowed, quiet corners of BMW's design offices.

Twisty country road, or smooth straight autobahn at high speed, the E34 Fünfer is difficult to beat – from any point of view. A peerless saloon of the 1980s and 1990s.

CHAPTER EIGHT

BMW 5 Series:
The Fourth Generation

Introducing the E39

The fourth generation 5 Series debuted in the autumn of 1995 during a period of increasing economic affluence throughout the western world. Many of the recessionary difficulties of just a few years earlier had largely disappeared in Britain, mainland Europe and the United States, but it had become apparent that the Japanese economy was teetering on the brink of nervous uncertainty. Japanese motor manufacturers in particular were suffering the effects of over-production and unsustainable expansion, despite healthy global sales of cars. In 2001, this uncertainty continued with some commentators expressing fears that a complete collapse of the Japanese economy could lead to a 'domino' effect in markets around the world.

Despite several claims to the contrary by certain journals, the German economy, and more particularly this extraordinary country's manufacturing base, remained healthy. By the mid-1990s, Daimler-Benz, Volkswagen, and BMW were all selling more cars than at any time in their history. Germany's 'big three' had become global concerns with international interests extending beyond the car industry. Their influence in world economic affairs was not to be underestimated.

The current E39 Fünfer originally debuted in 1995. Illustrated in mid-range 525i SE guise, it was faster, safer, more economical and boasted superior handling, but not everyone warmed to the styling at first.

A large car, many considered that the rear styling was awkward and 'flabby'...

There was increasing evidence that several carmakers would not survive alone. The cost of developing new models had risen astronomically. The great Swedish manufacturer, Saab, would be swallowed by General Motors, future models being based on the Vauxhall/Opel range. Daimler-Benz would team up with Chrysler, and eventually take over Mitsubishi, while BMW, under Bernd Pitschetsrieder's helsmanship, bought the ailing Rover Group – a move that the German giant would come to regret.

By the time of the E34's launch, competition for this medium-size saloon was even greater. Daimler-Benz had launched the E-class Mercedes-Benz, but the threat from the senior Stuttgart manufacturer was expected and never likely to go away. However, Toyota's luxury brand, Lexus, had also become a new force to be reckoned with. The Japanese 'pretender' was clearly aimed at niggling both Mercedes and BMW but, good as this machine is thought to be by some, the Lexus badge means little to established Merc and Bee-em clientele, and its styling leaves acres to be desired.

BMW's E39 was predictably well received, for it was most handsome and dashing at a time of great change in automotive styling. Twelve months previously, Volkswagen had unveiled the Concept 1 which, four years later would go into production as the New Beetle. The Lotus Elise, Porsche Boxster, BMW Z3 and Mercedes SLK (all with exciting 'grass-roots' bodyshapes) were all either available or in the pipeline.

The revised BMW, therefore, arrived at an interesting time. Although similar in appearance and dimensions to the outgoing E34, the fourth generation was more aerodynamically efficient, safer, lighter in weight and torsionally more rigid. From a styling viewpoint, the car held tight to BMW's long-standing tenets, and was seen as a scaled down 7 Series, which it closely resembled. By the same token, the current 3 Series resembled a scaled-down Fünfer. Corporate image had become more important than ever, and this manifested itself particularly strongly in BMW's styling package across the entire range.

At the front of the car the headlamps were enclosed with polycarbonate covers and the kidney grille was incorporated into the front of the deeply fluted bonnet, giving a 'snouty', and not altogether pleasant, appearance. The bonnet, like the windscreen, was more steeply raked than previously and, in conjunction with other small revisions, was responsible for improving the drag coefficient. In contemporary fashion, there was a deep chin spoiler, aerodynamically shaped sills, and a deep rear bumper designed in the style of a 'splitter', prevalent on contemporary racing machinery.

As previously, the 'shoulders' of the flanks were nicely rounded and contoured – no-one at BMW was tempted to revert to the angular muscularity of the 1970s – and 'broken' by a shapely swage line. Flush with the sheet metal, the door handles were in contemporary style and elliptical, a modern fashion that Porsche in particular would use to good effect in the interiors of both the Boxster and 996.

At the rear the lights were made to wrap around the wings, and were very much in keeping with the style of similar units used on the 7 and 3 Series. The rear surface of the bootlid was slightly concave, which gave the new car a most distinctive, sporting look very much in the mould of 1960s sports racing machinery.

On the face of it the E39 could have been mistaken for a 're-shelling' exercise, a car that was representative of change for its own sake. However, some of the biggest improvements lay below the surface. The bodyshell gave improved crash protection, was torsionally stiffer, and was responsible for all the usual gains to be had from greater aerodynamic efficiency. The biggest departure from tradition, however, lay in the suspension components which, instead of being made from steel, were fashioned from aluminium-alloy.

This was yet another example of a supremely confident manufacturer feeding racing technology through to a road car, and innovation that was virtually unique in the industry. The use of aluminium certainly increased BMW's costs and the purchase price of these cars in dealers' showrooms, but the advantages were huge and many-fold.

That weight is the natural 'enemy of speed' is an inevitability that has been known since pioneering days. Indeed, Ettore Bugatti famously used this adage as a basis, or excuse, for reducing the weight of all his cars, making extensive use of aluminium-alloys for his engine components, wheels, dashboards, floor panels and bodywork.

The greatest advantage of using aluminium for suspension, though, lies in the reduction of unsprung, or 'dead', weight. From the early 1950s onwards, many amateur motor racing enthusiasts, who raced their ordinary saloons and sports cars in club events at weekends, quickly cottoned on to the idea that stripping their steeds of superfluous bits and pieces gave appreciable gains in performance. Many removed seats, bumpers, hubcaps and even glovebox lids in some cases. Window glass was changed for Perspex panels, and heavy steel doors and front and rear lids were changed for items fashioned from either aluminium or fibreglass. In this way, a car's weight could be decreased in some cases by many scores, if not hundreds, of pounds.

Appreciable gains in acceleration were made in this way, but there was a penalty to pay; roadholding and handling suffered in high-speed corners, because weight had been shed from the 'wrong' parts of the car. It was discovered from an early stage that shaving body weight was desirable, but only if it was achieved in conjunction with a corresponding reduction in unsprung weight. Using lightweight materials for brakes, axles, wishbones and the rest was the way to go, but extremely expensive and prohibitive for everyday 'clubbie' racers. Exotic purpose-built sports racing cars like Porsches have used titanium suspension components since the 1960s but such materials are well out of the financial reach of most individuals.

...whilst the aerodynamically superior front was 'snouty', giving the appearance of a disgruntled rat.

The later 'facelifted' model, with revised headlamps, was an improvement.

That BMW should use aluminium-alloy for the suspension (and road wheels) in a production road car was truly startling. The result, of course, was an appreciable improvement in drivability and, in conjunction with the optional sports suspension dampers and shorter springs, dynamic handling and roadholding. The car was by far the best handler in its class, and ride quality was approaching that of a range-topping S-class Mercedes. Theoretical rivals from Alfa-Romeo, Jaguar, Saab and Volvo were not in the same street.

Changing Rooms

The interior was redesigned, but not everyone agreed that the changes were in the nature of improvements. The seats, in cloth or leather, were as comfortable as ever, and beautifully shaped, but so were those of the previous E34. Electrical adjustment for the front seats was a standard feature across the range, but something of a contradiction. Along with so many others, BMW had worked hard at improving engine efficiency, aerodynamics and saving weight but, to comply with the sybaritic demands of customers, added unnecessary 'flab' which partially negated the hard work of clever engineers.

Instrumentation was in BMW's classic style and as perfectly positioned as ever; the hood of the binnacle being curved in the modern vogue. As previously there was a standard four-spoke steering wheel, with an airbag in the central pad, and a three-spoke sports item at extra cost. There was also the option of a four-spoke wheel with integral switchgear to operate the radio, heating system and cruise control. It is surely just a matter of time before a BMW becomes available with a clutch paddle and gearchange button on the steering wheel.

Apart from the usual electrically-powered 'toys', one especially clever device, situated in the front passenger footwell, was a 'gizmo' that collected heat from the engine to feed warm air into the cabin before the engine reached its optimum operating temperature. This was a modern innovation, and ingenious, but heated seats such as those of Volvo and Saab (and BMW), would have been a simpler solution.

Although generally accepted as extremely comfortable and ergonomically perfect, the revised Fünfer's moulded plastic dashboard did not meet with universal approval. On the one hand it was commendable that plastic was being used with a view to being recycled, but this was achieved at the expense of aesthetic compromise. Some considered that the wood veneer trim on some models gave the cabin a traditional, crafted appearance but, in view of the state-of-the-art nature of these cars, a more modern material (carbon composites, for example) would have been more appropriate. Polished wood has no place in modern cars, but its use is one area of car design in which the British, and not the Germans, excel.

A Staggered Start

The E39 range was introduced in a piecemeal fashion, with the Touring, for example, appearing some 12 months after the four-door saloon.

First models to appear were the oddly badged 523i, with the 170bhp 2.5-litre engine, and a 2.8-litre 528i developing 193bhp. Both were in-line 6-cylinder units with double-overhead camshafts and four valves per cylinder, tuned to give improved acceleration in low gears and better fuel mileage. In addition there was the 525tds, a turbo diesel with 143bhp.

In 1996, the entry-level 520i debuted with an unchanged 2-litre 150bhp from the outgoing model. A 4-cylinder 518i was never on the cards, as appealing as this model might have been to some. Down many years the 1.8-litre 4-cylinder Fünfer had been criticised for being grossly underpowered, despite the healthy number of devotees it attracted, but it didn't fit in with BMW's intentions for, and image of, the range. As it would have been almost possible to build a bungalow on either

---

520i saloon, Touring (1996–)

Engine

Cylinders	6
Bore × stroke	80 × 66mm
Capacity	1,991cc
Compression ratio	11:1
Timing	Double-overhead camshafts and 4 valves per cylinder
Fuel injection	Bosch Motronic
Max power	150bhp at 5,900rpm
Max torque	140lb ft at 4,200rpm

Transmission

Gearbox: 5-speed close-ratio manual, or optional 5-speed automatic

Ratios	5-speed manual	5-speed automatic
First	5.10	1.366
Second	2.77	2.00
Third	1.72	1.41
Fourth	1.22	1.00
Fifth	1.00	0.74

Optional Steptronic from 1996

Ratios
First 3.72
Second 2.04
Third 1.34
Fourth 1.00
Fifth 0.80

Suspension and steering

Suspension	(front) Double-joint spring struts, aluminium-alloy control arms and anti-roll bar
	(rear) Multi-link with coil springs and anti-roll bar
Steering	Servo-assisted ZF rack and pinion
Wheels	6.5J×15, or 7J×15 alloys
Tyres	205/65R 15, or 225/60R 15

Brakes

Servo-assisted discs/discs, ABS standard

Dimensions

Ovberall length	4,775mm/188in
Overall width	1,800mm/70.8in
Overall height	1,435mm/56.5in
Wheelbase	2,830mm/111.4in
Track	(front) 1,512mm/59.5in
	(rear) 1,526mm/60in

side of the cylinder block, peering into the engine compartment of such a car alone would have been sufficient to convince the majority that a 518i wasn't an appropriate member of the line-up.

In addition, there were two new versions of the V8, with a 235bhp 3.5-litre in the 535i, and whopping 286bhp for the 4.4-litre 540i. Both units were improved to give greater flexibility across the rev range and better fuel economy.

Clearly designed to give broader appeal primarily in the North American market, where V8s had ruled the roost for many years, these power units were typically smooth and extremely quiet almost across the entire rev range. Purists remained unconvinced – the classic BMW 'six' was in a class of its own – but there is no denying the 'corrupting' influence of the more powerful 8-cylinder cars.

A Box of Slicks

A 5-speed manual gearbox with close ratios was the norm across the Fünfer range, with a 5-speed automatic being offered as an option fitted with Sport and Economy modes to be

chosen at will. From the middle of 1996, however, BMW also offered a new Steptronic gearbox as an extra-cost option. This technically advanced device, which was by no means unique in the motor industry, gave the driver the choice of using the gearbox in the usual automatic fashion, or as a manual by pushing the gear lever over to a second 'gate'. With the latter system, it was possible to use the lever in a normal manual fashion, but without having to use a clutch pedal.

The system was similar to those used in contemporary Grand Prix machinery, but came to particular prominence during the mid-1980s when Porsche developed their own PDK system for the Group C 962 sports racing car. A test mule was used extensively in racing, and although slower than its purely manual counterpart, it obviously held great promise in both road and racing applications. People like Hans-Joachim Stuck, who drove the PDK-equipped Porsches, held the system in high esteem. According to Stuck, it felt 'weird' to change up and down in mid-corner without a clutch pedal, and without having to lift off the accelerator, but once used to it, he and others reported that it was relaxing and saved energy.

Jam-packed with clever engineering innovations, the Touring, although large, is unequivocally Europe's best and most outstanding estate car.

Have I Got News . . .

Major developments from 1996 also included the introduction of a satellite navigation system, Xenon headlamps and airbags positioned in the doors. Although technologically advanced and a true manifestation of human endeavour and discovery, satellite navigation was an expensive option and largely unnecessary.

On the other hand the Xenon gas headlamps, which replaced the halogen units of yesteryear, and airbags, made a genuine contribution to enhancing the safety of these vehicles. The headlamps concentrated the beam more precisely, and were considerably more powerful, and although airbags are far from being the last word in crash survival, their role is proven and likely to be more significant in future years.

All Behind

With Touring versions accounting for roughly a quarter of E34 sales, it remained in production for some 12 months after the introduction of the E39 saloon range. Tooling up for the new model was a necessarily expensive and lengthy process (which was the principal reason for the E39 Touring arriving late in 1996) but the wait was worth it, for the replacement was genuinely improved.

A larger load area and 'flatter' floor, largely dictated by modifications to the rear suspension, gave Volvo-like accommodation in the loading bay. Self-levelling suspension, which was a standard fitment, ensured that the handling remained on an even keel irrespective of the load carried.

As with the previous model, the styling was extremely pleasing, the additional bodywork at the rear having been beautifully integrated into the overall smooth shape of the car. Some came to regard the contemporary estate version of the Volvo S40 saloon as the best looking of all estates but, for such a large model, BMW's Touring was in a class of its own. And, of course, it held the distinct advantage of rear-wheel drive, whereas Volvo had long since taken the front-wheel drive route.

The Touring's flanks closely follow the lines of the saloon's, although the former has slightly more overhang at the rear.

523i saloon (1995–), Touring (1996–)

Identical to 520i except for the following:

Engine

Cylinders	6
Bore × stroke	84 × 75mm
Capacity	2,494cc
Compression ratio	10.5:1
Max power	170bhp at 5,500rpm
Max torque	181lb ft at 3,950rpm

528i (1995–), Touring (1996–)

Identical to 520i except for the following:

Engine
Cylinders	6
Bore × stroke	84 × 84mm
Capacity	2,793cc
Compression ratio	10.2:1
Max power	193bhp at 5,300rpm
Max torque	206lb ft 3,950rpm

Wheels and tyres
Wheels	7J×15 alloys
Tyres	225/60R 15

By this time the 5 Series Touring had become an accepted, and even most welcome, part of the BMW scene. It did not quite fit in with the company's sports-racing image, despite sizzling performance across the range, but this was not especially relevant. Aimed at the sporting motorist who also happens to have children, pets and a lot of baggage, the Touring was ranked among the world's best estates and that's the way it is likely to stay.

The Most Five

With the potential to reach 60mph from rest in around 5secs and without drama thanks to electronic traction-control, the M5 stands as a technical tour de force: a state-of-the-art sports saloon, which in theory could only be improved by the use of the company's magnificent 5-litre V12 engine.

Range-topping M5 was late in joining the range, not being seen in public until September 1997. With a 4.9-litre V8 engine developing 408bhp at 65000rpm, it is capable of travelling rather rapidly.

525i (1996–)

Identical to 520i except for the following:

Engine

Cylinders	8
Bore × stroke	84 × 78.9mm
Capacity	3,498cc
Timing	Double-overhead camshafts per bank of cylinders, with 4 valves per cylinder
Compression ratio	10:1
Fuel injection	Bosch Motronic DME 5.2 system
Max power	235bhp at 5,700rpm
Max torque	236lb ft at 3,300rpm

Transmission

Gearbox: 5-speed close-ratio manual, 5-speed automatic

Ratios	5-speed manual	5-speed automatic
First	4.20	3.57
Second	2.49	2.20
Third	1.66	1.51
Fourth	1.24	1.00
Fifth	1.00	0.80
Final drive	2.93	2.93

Steering

Recirculating ball

Wheels and tyres

Wheels	7J×16 alloys, or optional 17in wheels
Tyres	225/55R 16

BMW are currently working on a replacement for this car.

Land Rover Discovery or BMW Fünfer Touring? BMW considered their own products to be a better bet – just one reason why they sold the Rover Group.

For young car enthusiasts today who pore over speed statistics, the M5's performance figures are probably plausible and exciting. The really interesting facet of this, and similar machinery from other manufacturers, is the sobering reality that, just 30 or so years ago, there was no roadgoing sports car capable of comparable performance, let alone capable of achieving such lofty velocities with four adults aboard. Even Ferrari's mighty 4.4-litre V12 365GTB4A Daytona was 'only' capable of 174mph. That a roadgoing saloon of the late 1990s was faster, quieter, safer and more comfortable made for admirable demonstration yet again, that real progress was being made in the industry. Those who took a contrary view, and there were several, clearly had their heads buried in the stagnant sands of the 1960s.

Outwardly distinguishable from the regular 5 Series cars by 18in diameter alloy wheels, lower ride height, revised front and rear spoiler and side skirts, and 'four-prong' exhaust system, the M5's aesthetics were dramatic without being in any way ostentatious.

The interior boasted close-fitting sports seats, every conceivable toy, leather upholstery and for those who could not live without them, there were planks of wood for parts of the dashboard, central console and door cappings at extra cost. Wood veneer trim appeared as incongruous in the M5 as a Kenwood CD player in a vintage Lagonda but, to traditionalists, wood is part and parcel of luxury motoring and they are, of course, welcome to it.

True M5 rivals were few and far between. Nothing in the form of a four-seater saloon had the guts, audacity, competence, fluidity, performance or presence. It was also typically and characteristically Germanic; it was also wholly representative of everything BMW stood for – a sporting performance car designed by people for whom second-best was a non-starter. Desirable and exclusive it was almost the antithesis of the antiquity and mediocrity to be found in certain tracts of the British motor industry. And I applaud BMW for producing it.

540i saloon and Touring (1996–)

Identical to 520i except for the following:

Engine
Cylinders	8
Bore × stroke	92 × 82.7mm
Capacity	4,398cc
Compression ratio	10:1
Max power	286bhp at 5,700rpm
Max torque	310lb ft at 3,900rpm

Transmission
Gearbox	6-speed manual
Ratios	First 4.23
	Second 2.52
	Third 1.66
	Fourth 1.22
	Fifth 1.00
	Sixth 0.83
	Final drive 2.81

Lexus, Jaguar, Mercedes, Bentley, Audi, Volvo and Saab and the like are all, without exception, competent and strong, but they are not BMWs and this, for the many devotees of Munich thinking, puts them on the second rung of the motoring ladder.

Fair Comment

When BMW launched the original Fünfer at the 1972 Olympic Games, the company that thirteen years earlier had been on the brink of extinction was a well-respected maker of cars that could be regarded as underdogs to Mercedes-Benz. Slowly, the engineers, designers and marketing men chipped away to forge a distinctive path that would result in production of some of the world's finest and most coveted cars. Through four generations of the

5 Series, the cars were markedly improved, each successive generation quickly becoming the benchmark mid-range saloon by which all others would be measured.

During my travels down many years among motoring people whose opinions I respect, I have never met anyone who has not got a 5 Series within his or her list of top 10 all-round cars. Naturally, one or two have a preference for Porsche's wonderful range of sports cars but, with just two seats, they are not practical for those with families.

As testament to BMW's standard of build, many early cars remain in regular use, and there is evidence that enthusiasts are restoring the more desirable examples to top-notch standards. Simply, each mark stands as a classic in its own right. Naturally, there are motorists who continue to loathe BMWs for all sorts of reasons, and it is just as well for Jaguar's fortunes that they do.

CHAPTER NINE

The Big Coupés:
The 6 Series

Meet the Ancestors

When *Motor Sport*'s editor Bill Boddy tested an early 633CSi in 1977, he described it as 'near perfect'. However, Boddy, like everyone else who had extensive experience of this model's predecessor (the 3.0CS Series) held reservations about the 6 Series. The majority of journalists, and owners to a certain extent, naturally viewed the new coupé as a successor to the outgoing model, whereas BMW had intended it as an entirely different car with a fundamentally different design basis and philosophy.

Modern BMW coupés owe their origins to the 4-cylinder 2000C and CS cars styled by Wilhelm Hofmeister. Publicly launched in 1965, these handsome two-door cars were elegant, exotic and because of their most unusual frontal aspect, extremely controversial; no-one was indifferent to the tall kidney grilles and unique shape of the headlamps, and this remains the case today.

In 1968 the company debuted the 6-cylinder 2800CS, followed by the 3-litre version a couple of years later, with styling heavily influenced by the earlier 2-litre model. However, BMW capitulated in the wake of

The 6 Series followed on the heels of the...

criticism, and restyled the front end of the larger-engined cars. With a longer bonnet, twin circular headlamps and a much narrower radiator grille, the 2800CS was hailed as one of the best-looking cars – an overnight classic – of all time.

Behind its beauty and its lithe, purposeful stance, however, was a Grand Tourer-cum-sports machine of state of the art competence. Crisp handling, precise steering and wholly predictable and safe roadholding were part and parcel of a new breed created by BMW. Naturally, it was not cheap to buy; the Dino Ferrari 246, also launched in 1968, was roughly the same price but, although the exotic Italian car was desirable to some, the BMW's trump card was German build quality, durability, reliability and the practicality of four seats and cavernous boot space. Regrettably, rust would take its toll on both the Italian and German supercars.

The BMW coupés also held great development potential, which the company's Motorsport division was quick to exploit from the early 1970s. For several years, the many different racing versions completely dominated in European Touring Car Championships, and provided spectators with some of the closest and fiercest battles in the history of the sport.

Naturally, the road cars created an enthusiastic following worldwide, the racing cars being responsible for enhancing BMW's image as a winner among the cream of European sporting manufacturers. Until the 1973 Middle East oil crisis, BMW were riding high on huge doses of commercial adrenaline. There appeared to be no limit to what could be done, with a massively powerful V12 engine under development and intended for production versions of the 3.0CS.

Works racing driver, Hans-Joachim Stuck, had a V12 test mule as everyday transport for development and assessment purposes, but, alas, the oil crisis laid to rest all plans that BMW had made to build a Grand Tourer in the tradition of Ferrari, Aston Martin and Lagonda. There was nothing wrong with the traditional in-line 'six', but a V12 would have projected BMW into the uppermost part of the automotive top drawer.

...classic 3.0CS coupés of the 1970s, and got a lukewarm reception in some quarters upon its launch in the mid-1970s.

By the mid-1970s the classic coupés had, regrettably, had their day. Not only had these superb models been in production for seven years, but they were also incapable of complying with forthcoming laws governing safety in the United States. The pillarless doors compromised the strength of the shell to resist deformation in the event of inversion, and a new coupé was therefore planned to amend this. A successor would have to be stronger all-round, and be able to meet the demands of crash-testing more successfully.

It needed to retain, or improve upon, its predecessor's lively performance and fine road manners. In the manner of a traditional Grand Tourer it also had to be luxurious, but without becoming a middle-aged heavyweight full of 'flab' and sloth.

6 Series – A Bit of This and That

From the outset it made good financial sense to rifle the BMW parts skip for the 6 Series. The company had an extensive range of cars; their mechanical components were well tested and proven. Producing wholly new components would not only have proved costly, but unnecessary. The 5 Series, launched in 1972, therefore, would amply provide as a basis for the new two-door coupé.

Styling was in BMW's classic and enduring mould, with much of Paul Bracq's influence present in several aspects. A mid-engined two-seater with 'gullwing' doors and 2-litre turbo engine designed by Bracq appeared as a 'concept' car in 1972. Paraded on the annual show circus it caused something approaching sensation on each occasion the wraps were removed from its bodyshell. Although this version did not go into production (the later M1 version did), many of its styling hallmarks were used on several production saloons, including the 6 Series.

The sloping radiator grille, finished in black, gave a frontal appearance of an aggressive shark. Twin headlamps and kidney grille are also similar to the contemporary 7 Series.

6 Series (1975–89) 630CS (1976–89)

Body style	2-door coupé	
Engine		
Cylinders	6	
Bore × stroke	89 × 86mm	
Capacity	2,986cc	
Compression ratio	8.1:1	
Fuel injection	Bosch L-Jetronic	
Max power	176bhp at 5,500rpm	
Max torque	185lb ft at 4,500rpm	
Transmission		
Gearbox	4-speed manual, or optional 3-speed automatic	
Ratios	**4-speed manual**	**3-speed automatic**
First	3.86	2.48
Second	2.20	1.48
Third	1.40	1.00
Fourth	1.00	
Final drive	3.64	3.64
Suspension and steering		
Suspension	(front) MacPherson struts, lower lateral links and drag struts, coil springs and anti-roll bar	
	(rear) Semi-trailing arms, coil springs and anti-roll bar	
Steering	Recirculating ball	
Wheels	Cast-alloy 6J×14	
Tyres	195/70VR 14	
Brakes	Servo-assisted discs/discs	
Dimensions		
Track	(front) 1,422mm/56in	
	(rear) 1,486mm/58.5in	
Wheelbase	2,624mm/103.3in	
Overall length	4,854mm/191.1in	
Overall width	1,725mm/67.9in	
Overall height	1,364mm/53.7in	

A famous BMW hallmark, the distinctive and attractive shape of the rear side window was carried through from the 3.0CS.

The sloping grille with two 'nostrils', or kidneys, in the centre, twin headlamps and 'Y-shaped' swage lines on the bonnet were similar to the 5 Series saloons, and gave a typically sporting, aggressive frontal appearance. Bright trim, although not excessive, was used for the leading edge of the nosecone and window surrounds. Italian manufacturers had favoured matt black trim for several years but, although BMW's customers were not as conservative as the typical Mercedes owner, BMW clung to the idea that a little bright-work was better, for the time being, than none. A similar front end, incidentally, was used for the Mk1 7 Series.

The cabin had a very large glass area, a long-held BMW safety tenet dating back to the early 1960s when the 1500 saloon was introduced. Naturally, the distinctive 'dogleg' rear side window piece was retained, and survives to this day in so many of the company's models. Interestingly, Japanese manufacturers

in particular appear to have copied, or at least been influenced by, this styling for many of their mundane saloons.

Impact-resistant bumpers were used front and rear, and projected prominently from the bodywork but, like the contemporary Porsche 911, these 'metal crunchers' were integrated with the body shape. Conversely, British Leyland fitted huge rubber bumpers to both the MGB and Triumph TR7, also for the sake of meeting stringent US rules on safety, and ruined the looks of both these cars in one fell swoop.

In traditional sporting fashion there were flared wheel arches, BMW's usual swage line along the shoulders of the slab-sided flanks, attractive alloy wheels as standard, and a short rump concealing a huge boot. Although the 5 Series saloon provided the basis for the chassis, and shared the same 2,626mm (8ft 5in) wheelbase, the 6's Karmann-built body was larger than that of its predecessor. That it looked so well, despite criticism in some quarters that it resembled a 7 Series with the middle chopped out, was a credit to the penmanship of BMW's designers.

While *Motor Sport's* Bill Boddy had described the original 4,750 mm (15ft 7in) car as 'unobtrusive', the later 635CSi tested for the same journal by Clive Richardson, was a very different kettle of fish. Richardson commented:

> The two-door, four-seater coupe takes on a much more aggressive demeanour from the addition of a deep front spoiler and a large rubber tail spoiler on the boot lid. These are not merely cosmetic appendages: they reduce lift at high speed by 15per cent, an essential consideration on a car capable of 140mph on the unrestricted autobahns of the homeland. The spoilers are neatly absorbed into the overall lines, unlike the strange growths that sprouted from that splendid 3.0CSL 'Batmobile'. 'Go-faster' stripes are tidily laid along the waistline and an increase in rim width to 6.5in from the 633's 6in enhances the squatter

look on the road . . . I liked the appearance of this surprisingly big coupe, but that might reveal a subconscious boy-racer streak within me!

Clive Richardson's comment about 'boy racers' hit the nail on the head. In its broadest sense, the 6 Series was a car for 'grown-ups', but grown-ups who had not forgotten the sports cars of their more youthful days!

Internal Dispute

There is little doubt that the original layout of the 1972 Fünfer's interior had broken new ground in functional design, and not only set a precedent for future BMW models, but had a marked influence among designers in the employ of other manufacturers. 'Ergonomics' had yet to become an everyday word at this time but, as this important branch of car design became better understood the efforts of those working in this specialised field became more and more impressive.

Although billed as a four-seater legroom in the rear of the 6 Series was restricted, and although this was adequate for children, adults forced to travel for any distance in the back seat rarely did so more than once. Fully adjustable sports seats were fitted in the front, and gave perfect support; upholstery was in cloth or leather. Of the seats, Motor Sport commented:

> The test car had dark grey, velour trim to the seats, which picked up fluff and dust worse than any trim I have experienced. That aside, the bucket seats were most comfortable, less unforgiving and better locating than other BMW seats, their back rests adjustable for rake, their squabs with height adjustment and a tilt facility.

In moulded plastic the dashboard and layout of switchgear and instruments was a masterpiece of pure function. A bold, large-diameter four-spoke steering wheel, with a horn button in each spoke, confronted the driver. Although the steering wheel could be adjusted for distance, it could not be tilted, which some considered to be inconvenient.

In contrast to contemporary Jaguars, the BMW had just three principal instruments which, like other models in the range, were illuminated at night in orange. *Motor Sport's* revered opinion was that the layout switchgear and instruments was 'hard to beat', and noted: 'What the facia panel lacks in quantity of instruments it makes up for in clarity.' Housed in a 'humped' binnacle, the Vdo dials and warning lights sat beneath a piece of glass angled to cut all reflections in the windscreen, an idea that was much copied and became an almost universal feature across the European car industry.

In what had become time-honoured BMW fashion, the central part of the dashboard was angled towards the driver, and contained the radio, clock, ashtray, cigar lighter and controls for the ventilation and heating system. Air outlets featured seemingly everywhere, in response to criticism of poor ventilation on

The 6's body styling was so well balanced that it disguises the true size of the astonishingly large boot.

past models. The large glass area had a tendency in warm weather to turn the cabin on early 5 Series cars into a greenhouse, while occupants of the 6 Series could treat themselves to large blasts of cold air at will.

This aside, *Motor Sport* continued to hold reservations; the magazine commented:

> Although the water valve controlled heater warmed up quickly on those cold mornings its heat delivery was badly inconsistent. I had no cause to use the ventilation system, but this is unchanged from that which Bill Boddy criticised on the 633 in the summer of 1977.

and, as an aside, added:

> On the right of the facia is the by-now familiar BMW check panel, which gives visual reassurance at a touch of a button that all the systems are working. The Porsche 928's automatic warning system is more sophisticated than this BMW arrangement, which I tended to forget.

Road & Track were generally very complimentary about the new car's interior, criticism being confined to 'the top of the dash which reflects into the windshield if the sun strikes the car at a certain angle', and the in-car-entertainment. The writer of this American magazine's June 1977 road test reported:

> Adding insult to injury, BMW has the audacity to charge extra for the radio. BMW believes a person who spends $24,000 would want to personalize the car with his own sound system. This might be true, but the least BMW could do would be to tell a 630CSi owner to install the system of his choice (up to a maximum of £500 seems fair) and send the factory the bill. Admittedly, the base price includes several items – air-conditioning, electric window lifts, fuel injection – not standard on the previous coupe, the 3.0CS, but still, charging extra for a radio on this type of car seems a bit much.

This kind of criticism had long been aimed at all sorts of products of the German motor industry. Year after year, journalists and owners moaned and groaned most vocally, but it seemed to make little difference until comparatively recently when several carmakers, under increasing threat from Japanese competition, began to respond more positively.

Very much in the mould of Porsche's mighty 928, also launched in the mid-1970s, the 6's cabin was a model of ergonomic design. All controls were within easy reach, the seats were comfortable and supportive, and there was ample feeling of spaciousness for the driver and front passenger. It was, however, from the no-nonsense school of traditional German thought, which led *Road & Track*, among others, to knock it for 'lacking warmth'. The same criticism was levelled against both the Porsche 911 and 928.

Wood trim, which had been much in evidence in the outgoing 3.0CS, was entirely lacking in the 6 Series, and in this respect the 6 was bang up to date.

Burly Chassis

As the 6 Series was planned as a 6-cylinder from the beginning (a 4-cylinder version was never on the cards) so the running gear and suspension not only had to be light in weight, but sufficiently robust to endure the loadings imposed by the large-capacity engines.

Naturally, the drivetrain was to BMW's normal front engine, rear-wheel drive set-up at a time when 'mainstream' manufacturers of 'lesser' cars were switching in droves to front-wheel drive. BMW-power, coupled with front-wheel drive, would have been courting disaster, of course, but four-wheel drive, such as that of the Spen King designed Range Rover, might have been considered as an alternative. With the exception of Ferry Porsche and his nephew, Ferdinand Piëch, few saw a market for passenger cars with four driven wheels. In later years Audi would capitalise on this omission, and BMW would miss the boat.

Similar to components used on the 6-cylinder 5 Series, the suspension was to a predictable pattern. Up front there were MacPherson struts with lateral links, coil springs, tube dampers and an anti-roll bar. Rear springing was by semi-trailing arms, coil springs tube dampers and anti-roll bar. Handling and roadholding were, therefore, entirely predictable, safe and to the standards that owners had come to expect.

Road behaviour was exemplary, the engineering of the suspension components providing one answer among many to the perennial question over the high purchase price of these cars. As *Road & Track* remarked:

To appreciate how BMW can even begin to justify charging $24,000 for this car, one must drive it . . . and drive it hard.

This was nearly double the cost of the 5 Series saloon but, as the American journal went on:

Out on a twisty road you discover the combination of ride, handling, braking and steering that make the coupe one of the world's best road-going GTs. On a skidpad the 630CSi generates 0.754g higher than all but a handful of all-out sports cars, and the way it hangs on during fast transitions as in our slalom test is confidence inspiring.

The chassis was so well balanced that handling was always of a neutral stance until the car was pushed to and beyond the limit, when initial understeer preceded inevitable quantities of oversteer. Despite superb handling, though, ride quality was both supple and compliant and, although typically firm, was sufficiently forgiving to appeal to both European and American tastes.

With its characteristically detailed analysis, *Motor Sport* tended to be more critical, especially of the earlier cars. In testing the 635, Clive Richardson commented:

The revised suspension settings have transformed the 635 compared with the 633. Gone is that floating feeling over some surfaces, gone is most of the diagonal pitching, roll and sogginess when cornered hard and in its place is new found tautness and obedience to the helm which make this a much more enjoyable car to drive quickly.

Communicative and forgiving ride improved with speed, the fat Michelin tyres transmitting harshness over bumps at low speeds, but this was to be expected. No road car has ever been built without compromise being dialled into its make-up, and although many recognised that the 6 Series was not in the Porsche 928 class where drivability was concerned, it shone above the majority of its peers. Incidentally, *Motor Sport* once compared a Porsche 928's running costs with those of the least expensive helicopters, and discovered that they were roughly the same!

During this period of development, there were also great improvements made in tyre technology. The ultra low-profile tyres that are the norm on performance cars today were in their infancy, and the many owners who 'updated' their cars with more modern rubber quickly discovered handling benefits, but often at the expense of ride quality.

Over several years, the 6's suspension was developed and adapted through successive models; the M635CSi, for example, being treated to special Bilstein gas-filled shock absorbers. However, despite the demands of increasing engine performance, the overall handling package remained virtually unaltered throughout.

Predictably, braking was to the same general specification as the anchor system used on the 5 Series, except that the big coupé got vented discs (11in at the front and 10.7in at the rear) all round from the beginning of production. Until 1977, when the Fünfer had ventilated front discs, the brakes were of the 'solid' variety, and perfectly adequate for the less powerful cars.

Of braking, *Road & Track* commented:

During panic stops there's a tendency for the fronts to lock but the ease of pedal modulation makes for straight and undramatic stops. In normal driving they're even better; pedal effort is just about ideal and the linear relationship between effort and deceleration rate makes for smooth comfortable stops, something your passengers will appreciate.

This complimentary view differed a little from *Motor Sport's* opinion. One tester complained bitterly about the car's braking ability, which would 'only withstand a handful of stops from high speed before fading.' Another tester using the same car remarked, however:

I suspect that new pads had been fitted before the car came to me, because I had no such complaints. Admittedly the bad weather I experienced may have helped their survival. Come to think of it, slight fade did show up after one particular long, downhill 'blind', but on the whole braking performance, feel and firmness of pedal was rather better than on the earlier BMW coupes which have passed through my hands.

Stylish fluting on the front-hinged bonnet extends to the narrow front panel. Note the continued use of brightwork around the top of the radiator grille.

The cars I have driven in more recent times have, inevitably, been fitted with modern brake pads, and have never failed to impress, initial bite being followed by powerful and progressive retardation. The only drawback to modern asbestos-free brake pads is that the dust they generate tends to spoil the appearance of alloy wheels, but this is a small price to pay for their superior stopping power.

Of the recirculating-ball variety similar to the system used on the 5 Series, the steering was power-assisted as standard and had a generous 3.6 turns from lock to lock. Where steering is concerned it is worth quoting *Road & Track's* views once again. The magazine commented:

Up to about 2000rpm the pump delivers full boost for easy parking and low-speed manoeuvres. From there up to redline the assist is reduced to 70 per cent of maximum, so that at high speeds the steering communicates a firmer feel to the driver. The coupe's steering is wonderfully exact and accurate, giving the driver a computer-like ability to instinctively crank in precisely the right amount of lock regardless of the speed or tightness of a turn. Even the impressive Mercedes steering, which we have considered the world's finest, can't top the BMW's in overall road feel, effort and response. Marvellous.

This latter comment was most interesting, for one of BMW's prime goals for so long was to challenge, and ultimately beat, Daimler-Benz. That *Road & Track* and others acknowledged this, albeit in a relatively minor manner, was ample illustration that BMW were slowly, but most surely, achieving what they had set out to do many years earlier.

Engines for Cars

As BMW originally ventured out as manufacturers of aero-engines, it is not at all surprising that the company has built up a tradition for excellence in this field which many regard as being second to none. One director of Daimler-Benz once admitted that BMW made the best car engines, while BMW engineers have often cited Daimler-Benz as the company that makes an awful lot of trucks – as well as lorries.

Among the difficulties in creating suitable engines for the 6 Series were increasingly stringent rules in the US governing exhaust emissions. Both Jaguar and Mercedes circumnavigated this problem to a certain extent by using large capacity engines which, although strangled by emissions equipment, continued to give good performance under the old rule of thumb of 'no substitute for cubic inches'.

BMW stuck to capacities of around 3 litres and, for the American market, largely relied on Bosch L-Jetronic fuel injection and a low compression ratio to meet Federal emissions laws. For North America the early cars were fitted with the 3-litre (2,985cc) engine developing 176bhp at 5,500rpm (630CSi) which, with a compression ratio of 8.1:1, was capable of running on low 87-octane fuel, and the 3,210cc (633CSi) unit developing 197bhp at

633CSi (1977–)	
Body style	Two-door coupé
Engine	
Cylinders	6
Bore × stroke	89 × 86.1mm
Capacity	3,210cc
Compression ratio	8.4:1
Fuel injection	Bosch L-Jetronic
Max power	177bhp at 5,500rpm
Max torque	196lb ft at 4,500rpm
Transmission	
Gearbox	4-speed manual
Ratios	First 3.86
	Second 2.20
	Third 1.40
	Fourth 1.00
	Final drive 3.45
Suspension and steering	
Suspension	(front) MacPherson struts, lower lateral links, coil springs and anti-roll bar
	(rear) Semi-trailing arms, coil springs and anti-roll bar
Steering	Power-assisted recirculating ball
Wheels	Cast alloy 6J×14
Tyres	195/70VR 14 Michelin XDX
Brakes	Servo-assisted discs/discs
Dimensions	
Track	(front) 1,422mm/56in
	(rear) 1,494mm/58.8in
Wheelbase	2,626mm/103.4in
Overall length	4,920mm/192.7in
Overall width	1,725mm/67.9in
Overall height	1,364mm/53.7in

BMWs, and particularly the 6 Series, became cultural motoring icons among ethnic groups in Britain. Jamaican cult hero, Bob Marley, owned a black 3 Series: his only concession to the world of materialism.

and exhaust-gas recirculation rob it of some its around-town response, when driven hard it frees up, smoothes out and goes nearly as well as the 3.0CS we tested in 1973. The 630CSi is quicker from 0–60mph, only a tick slower in the quarter mile and only begins to lose out to the less tightly controlled 1973 version in the illegal speed ranges.

The same magazine recorded an overall fuel consumption figure of 18mpg which, by the standards of the day, was felt to be quite acceptable, especially for a car weighing in at 1,592kg (3,510lb). Unlike Jaguar's contemporary 5.3-litre V12, which shifted along at high speed in almost complete silence, BMW enthusiasts revelled in the unmistakable sound from the exhaust of their cars. For many there is nothing to equal the cacophony from a BMW engine, particularly under hard acceleration, which makes it all the more surprising that some were apt to criticise the cars from Munich for being 'unrefined'.

In European specification the 3-litre car was capable of a 0–60mph time of 8.6secs, the 3.3-litre CSi performing the same sprint in 7.8secs. Top speeds were in the region of 130mph and 134mph respectively with fuel consumption for both cars working out at a realistic all-round figure of 20mpg.

Gearbox options included a 4-speed manual or 3-speed automatic, both with a final-drive ratio of 3.45:1. Although 5-speed gearboxes in production cars were by no means standard in the mid-1970s, many considered that the 6 should have had a 5-speed box from the off. BMW obviously considered that engine torque was sufficient for a fifth 'cog' to be unnecessary. Porsche took the same view with the early 930 (911 Turbo), although both companies would eventually relent and fit five speeds.

Road & Track decsribed the 6 Series' 4-speed manual box as a 'real delight' and added:

5,500rpm. All early power units, fitted at a slant to allow for a low bonnet line, were to BMW's normal configuration of an in-line 'six' with a single-overhead camshaft.

For Europe there were 2.8-, 3-litre, and 3.3-litre cars, with a 3-litre carburettor model for the home market, and the later 3.5-litre engine in range toppers. All were noted for their tractability, smoothness and performance. In US 3-litre guise, performance was strangled, almost beyond belief, the 60mph dash being achievable in around 9.5secs. Top speed was a paltry 124mph but, in a country where a national speed limit of 55mph prevailed, 'top-end' velocity was becoming increasingly insignificant.

Road & Track's view of the 3-litre version was much the same in 1977 as the one expressed about all past BMW engines. They remarked:

> This engine is without a doubt the most sophisticated production in-line six in the world. Although the effects of retarded ignition timing

The light clutch and crisp gear changes are perfectly matched to the sporty character of the car and really let the driver get a lot out of what is a relatively small displacement engine.

Small Fry

Although the 6 Series was not in the same league of elegance and beauty as its predecessor, customers accepted the revised coupé as a seriously grand Grand Tourer, but the car was not without niggling problems. Understandably, some American owners were not especially enamoured with the performance of their emissions-choked cars after experiencing the superior performance of the 3.0CS. So many American enthusiasts were well used to huge V8s, with torque by the bucketload, and the 3-litre BMW's performance, which was on a par with the European-spec 2-litre 4-cylinder Porsche 924, simply did not shape up, despite the contrary views of magazines such as *Road & Track*.

Despite the bespoke nature and low-volume production of these cars, there were initial question marks over the quality of the paintwork, and rainwater leaking at various points of the bodywork. BMW quickly addressed these problems, and from 1977 fitted the 3,210cc engine from the 7 Series in the American-spec 633CSi, which took output to 181bhp.

In the summer of 1978, the company publicly debuted the 635CSi, a model that helped to redress the charisma and power imbalance between the 3.0CS and 6 Series. Journalists and owners alike hailed the new car as an 'overnight classic', and as one of the most desirable ever BMWs. In view of the presence of Porsche's mighty 4.5-litre V8, and later 5-litre variant, the 3.5-litre BMW did not arrive a moment too soon.

The Three and a Half

When BMW introduced the 3.0CSL road car in 1972, it served as a basis for the successful racing coupés. With their lightweight aluminium body panels and superb engines, these cars were quick and, with development they would produce increasingly large horsepower figures. In 3.5-litre guise the racing cars were pushing out more than 450bhp, whereas one works turbocharged car, entered for the 1976 Le Mans 24 Hours, saw as much as 750bhp. That this example could not cope with such formidable engine power was neither here nor there; BMW's engineers had demonstrated exactly what they could produce when given a free hand.

When the 6 Series was launched in the mid-1970s, there was no true successor to the lightweight 3.0CSL. Understandably,

---

635CSi

Identical to 633CSi except for the following:

Engine

Cylinders	6
Bore × stroke	84 × 93.4mm
Capacity	3453cc
Fuel injection	Bosch L-Jetronic
Max power	218bhp at 5,500 rpm
Max torque	229lb ft at 4,000 rpm

Transmission	5-speed manual

Ratios the same as 633 except for final drive: 3.45 (US-spec), 3.25 (European-spec)

---

enthusiasts muttered words of discontent along the lines of 'BMW losing the plot'. The 635CSi was late in arriving but proved to be a worthy attempt to fill the gap.

Developed from the BMW racing engines used in the 1970s coupés, the 3,543cc 'six' used a stroke of 84mm, an unusually wide bore of 93.4mm and a relatively high compression ratio of 9.3:1. Small changes included the latest version of Bosch L-Jetronic fuel injection which, in conjunction with simaesed cylinders and wide-bore exhaust system, markedly increased engine efficiency. Maximum power of 218bhp was developed at a leisurely 5,200rpm, with torque weighing in a hefty 224lb ft at 4,000rpm.

Although the 635CSi did not have lightweight body panels, and had the regular, heavy impact-resistant bumpers, its performance was, more or less, on a par with the previous CSL model.

Drive was taken through a Getrag 5-speed manual gearbox with a tall 3.25:1 final-drive ratio. The suspension was both lowered and stiffened, and the wheels were widened from 6in to 6.5in, although the familiar 195/70VR-14 tyres were retained. Externally distinguishable by its deeper chin spoiler, rubber spoiler on the trailing edge of the boot lid, coachline striping along the flanks and lower ride height, the 3.5-litre car had remarkable presence, even though it created none of the drama of its illustrious predecessor. With such firm suspension and revised spoilers, there is little doubt that the car was more stable at high speed than the 3.0CS of yesteryear, even if some owners considered that they compromised the 6's looks. Manufactured by Mahle and designed by BBS, the cross-spoke alloy wheels undoubtedly enhanced the car's sporting stance, becoming a firm favourite for alloy wheels on BMWs during the many years ahead.

Inside the car there was a speedometer calibrated to 260kph, and Recaro sports seats with improved lateral support. Leather covers were available at extra cost. Depending upon specification, these cars were quoted at between £16,000 to 17,000 in Britain ($25,000 in the US), with equipment such as a sunroof being charged at more than £500 extra, and some continued to complain about BMW's high prices.

Naturally, driving impressions of the big coupé differed from one journalist to another. Writing in *Road & Track*, Ron Wakefield commented:

> In general driving feel it comes surprisingly close to big-bore exotics, such as the Maserati Kyalami I tested recently . . . Not until you're on an unlimited speed Autobahn does the 635's brilliant performance come into play. Despite two attempts, I didn't get to run it at maximum speed, thanks first to heavy vacation traffic and later to rain, but 200kph (125mph) came up effortlessly and all too rapidly. The factory figure (for top speed) is 225kph (140mph) and that seems about right.

Wakefield went on to criticise the gearbox for not being to the same standard as the engine, noted that the tyres were apt to squeal on twisty roads, and was not especially happy that his test car pulled slightly to the right under heavy braking from 125mph, but generally gave favourable impressions. He concluded:

> In the European market the 635CSi will compete directly with the Mercedes-Benz 450SLC 5.0. Its character expresses the basic difference between the two makes these days: BMW does essentially the same job in a smaller-displacement, sportier fashion. So it is that the BMW has 3.5 litres instead of 5.0 and a 5-speed manual gearbox instead of an automatic.

The comparison with Daimler-Benz's products was as inevitable as ever, the choice between the two at this stage being measured chiefly by personal preference. Those who liked neither plumped for a Porsche.

Also writing in *Road & Track*, the Belgian ex-racing driver, Paul Frere, was unequivocal in his praise for the 635CSi. He remarked:

> The new car is certainly what owners of the famous and late lamented 3.0CSi coupe (who had been disappointed by the marginally lower performance of the 633CSi) have been waiting for. The car is great fun to drive, is utterly safe and will easily see off any 3.0CSi around. The performance of the new BMW is just short of the considerably less roomy Porsche 928 which accelerates slightly faster and has a top speed advantage of only 7mph.

Frere discovered a slightly harsher ride than the standard 633CSi and, in contrast to Ron Wakefield's comments, considered the gearbox 'as nice to handle as BMW's 4-speed box'. Of its road behaviour, Paul Frere remarked:

> Handling is obviously first class, though the 70-series Michelin XDX tires don't grip as well as Pirelli P7s. As with all BMWs, the 635CSi oversteers at the limit, and though the car is beautifully controllable – thanks to the very accurate and progressive power steering in which the assistance is reduced as the engine speed increases – I have a feeling the oversteering tendency is a little overdone. The car would probably corner even faster if the behavior were slightly more neutral.

Paul Frere recorded a 0–60mph time of 7.2secs and a maximum speed of 139mph, which compared well with the times he had previously recorded for the 3.0CSi of 7.1secs for the 60mph sprint and a top speed of 135mph. The difference between the two was that the older car was stripped of superfluous weight, while the 635CSi came equipped with 'every item of luxury equipment imaginable'. The Belgian concluded his missive with an interesting question, and asked:

> I wonder if any company in Europe would still make such beautifully handling and wonderfully safe high-performance cars if Germany put a speed limit on its Autobahnen?

Owner's View

Motoring enthusiast Gary Bexton has owned hundreds of different cars, citing the Austin Mini Metro as the worst, and his 635CSi as among the very best. A 1986 example, acquired in 2000 for the laughable sum of £200, it stands as glowing testament to BMW build quality.

'I bought it with a broken gearbox, found a replacement unit for £120, fitted it myself, and wound up with one of the best sporting cars ever made for £320.' he says. Gary also owns a direct contemporary (a Porsche 928) and has the benefit of experiencing and comparing both on a weekly basis.

With 150,000 miles under its belt, the BMW is nicely bedded in and loosened up,

Germany's national racing colour, white, with a touch of black, gives Gary Bexton's 635CSi a most purposeful appearance. Vents at the trailing end of the bonnet are also typically Germanic.

Cast alloy wheels were standard wear and to a magnificent, if complex, design.

but remains remarkably taut and supple. An automatic, with sports and economy mode, the car is in original condition and has a few of the battle scars of everyday use. Inside, the black leather-clad Recaros are beautifully creased with age and, despite having been sat upon by previous owners for many years, retain their firmness and original moulding.

It's absolutely lovely to drive – one of the best – and the sort of car that you can't help playing with. It's firm, the power-assisted steering is most controllable and you always know where you are. You can feel where the road is in relation to your hands on the steering wheel, and the Avon Turbospeed tyres, which appear to have a soft compound, stick to the road as well as anything I've tried in the past.

Chromium plating for the door mirror contrasts sharply with the colour-coding or matt black of the majority of the car's contemporaries.

Interestingly, he compares the BMW to a Ford Escort RS2000 he owned, and rallied, many years previously. Gary laughs:

The differences between the two cars are rather obvious, but share a surprising number of similarities. Both cars lend themselves readily to being pushed, especially through corners. They have the same rear-drive handling characteristics. By contrast, I once owned a Range Rover, which was a real nightmare in corners. Apart from the commanding driving position, most of my time spent in the 'Rangey' was a nightmare. The novelty of the vehicle quickly wore off; running around at 12mpg – if I was lucky – led to long periods of driving slowly just to save fuel, which wasn't a lot of fun, so I 'ditched' the thing.

Gary Bexton cites BMW build quality as being on a par with that of his Porsche 928, but reckons that the two cars are very different in character.

For long runs, I take the BMW every time. The Porsche is a faster accelerating car, and ultimately has a higher top speed, but the Bee-em's Recaros are much more comfortable, and the 635CSi also has more room in the rear for the kids and a much bigger boot space. The BMW also uses less fuel – 20mpg is typical on the school run – but the Porsche shines in other areas. I'm not especially enamoured with the cost of spare parts for the 928 – a cambelt for instance is £1,000 – but there is little doubt in my mind that it is one of the great Grand Tourers of all time. The BMW for me, however, is the pick of them, because it's a much better looking car.

Although he never keeps a car for very long, Gary has become attached to his 6 Series, although ownership of a Jaguar XJS, and possibly a Mercedes-Benz, beckons.

I'm attracted to the XJS because of its styling. I also love the traditionally crafted leather and wood veneer of English classics, although in Jaguar's case – and I've owned several – their reliability record in my experience is quite dreadful. I've never owned a Merc of any kind, but I love their unique styling, build quality and reliability. The BMW is in much the same mould, but I've just got to own a Mercedes one of these days.

Gary's wife, Liz, who works in the motor trade, owns a fairly new Daewoo saloon which has covered just 38,000 miles. Gary remarks:

It's extraordinary that its driving seat is already showing serious signs of wear whereas the BMW, which is 15 years old and has covered 150,000 miles, sports an interior, including the carpets, which looks as good as new.

Although like many who continue to yearn for another motoring life beyond traffic jams, Gary Bexton insists on returning to the Escort rally days of his youth. He muses:

And maybe I'll get around to building a Westfield 7 as well. I've often thought that a Westfield would be the same as a 6 Series BMW with its bodywork removed – a sort of high-speed soap-box cart with rocket power. What could be better?

For Gary Bexton, and the many other people interviewed for this book, owning a BMW is primarily about the acquisition of a quality motor car with known tenets and parameters. The 6 Series in particular was the company's sporting flagship (notwithstanding the presence of the exotic mid-engined M1), a car that forged a unique path in the world of classic Grand Tourers.

Beautiful, firm and hip-hugging, Recaro sports seats are among the most comfortable, and expensive, ever devised.

There are those who hold the view that BMWs, Mercedes, Porsches and the like are little more than status symbols, but this is not an opinion that anyone with an interest in elite engineering could possibly share. During the late 1970s, these famous German manufacturers almost exclusively shared the 'top-drawer' market. Competition from Japanese manufacturers at this time was almost entirely absent in the sporting market; Datsun had made inroads to a certain extent with the

M6	
Engine	
Cylinders	6
Bore × stroke	84 × 93.4mm
Capacity	3453cc
Max power	286bhp at 6,500rpm
Max torque	251lb ft at 4,500rpm
Brakes	Vented front discs with 4-pot calipers, solid rears

The rear seats are also beautifully upholstered, but there is only limited legroom for adults.

240Z (a car now hailed in some quarters as a classic) but this 'pretender from the East', despite quite sizzling performance, was hardly a model of desirability and longevity.

Gary Bexton believes that for him the perfect car would be one that was built in Germany, with an interior styled in England, and bodywork designed in Italy.

For me personally, the best looking car ever built was the Ferrari Dino 246, and although I've never driven one, I believe that their reliability record makes even a 1970s Jag look like a long-term prospect. Which is why I'm perfectly happy with my BMW for the time being.

Into the Eighties

Development work on both the 7 and 6 Series ran on virtually parallel lines, both models being updated with similar equipment. From the summer of 1979, an on-board computer, with twelve different functions, was fitted along with a digital clock to replace the traditional analogue variety. Anti-dive front suspension, tailored for the 7 Series, came a little later on the 6 Series and improved stability, particularly under braking.

As the 633CSi was to be discontinued in some markets, including the UK, BMW introduced a new model, the 628CSi. Initially, this 2.8-litre car was only available in Germany, filtering its way into foreign markets roughly a year or so later. The engine, which had already seen service in both the 5 and 7 Series, developed an impressive 184bhp, and endowed the 628CSi with a top speed in the region of 130mph.

In concept the new model was entirely logical, and founded on common sense principles, but there were some in the BMW fraternity who saw it as pointless. Their argument was based on the fact that the 2.8-litre car's performance was vastly inferior to that of the 635CSi, yet both models returned roughly the same fuel mileage.

Changes across the range included a new front spoiler with integral foglamps, wider 205¥14 tyres on 6.5J alloy rims and a closing panel at the bottom of the engine bay which, in conjunction with redesigned chin spoiler, brought aerodynamic drag down to a Cd figure of 0.39. By this stage, BMW was heavily involved in the company's partnership with the Brabham Formula One team. As more and more information about aerodynamics was learnt by specialists in the Grand Prix world, lessons slowly, but surely, filtered through to production cars. Ironically, while BMW were making attempts to improve the wind-cheating ability of their cars, Audi's Martin Smith took the opposite route with his design for the quattro, which was angular and lean and possessed the aerodynamic properties of a grandfather clock.

Apart from being more aerodynamically sound, the cars from 1982 were also substantially lightened in weight. More than 58kg (130lb) was shed due to the employment of new body-building techniques. At the same time the front and rear suspension were revised, with double links at the front, and trailing arms at the rear placed at an angle of 13 degrees. The 5 Series had previously adopted this layout, which contributed in both models to much tidier road manners. To a certain extent, this move was aimed at dialling out oversteer from the cars, and it worked, but did not please everyone. Sliding the rear end, for many enthusiasts, had become part and parcel of the charm of owning a BMW, but the critics who labelled oversteer as 'dangerous' were beginning to have an effect.

With the march of time more and more folks began to view the 6 Series as a worthy successor to the 3.0CS coupés. Those who had not initially warmed to its looks also slowly changed their minds. As *Road & Track* pointed out:

Most members of our staff were impressed with the 630 when it made its debut, but scarcely a soul waxed enthusiastic about the styling. The handling, yes, the ergonomics too and the driving pleasure quotient – however, the appearance of the car from outside was appreciated for being lean and clean but not much more. It's interesting, therefore, that some 18 months later one of the most persistent comments of all staffers is, 'This design has really grown on me.' The subtlety of the styling has enabled the 633CSi (and its predecessor 630) to look fresh and contemporary as it moves toward the third year of its life, and a rework of the rear bumper's wraparound rubber has made it more harmonious in side view.

From 1982, the 635 received a revised engine, the original 3,453cc unit having proved to be troublesome. Although the 86mm stroke was retained a narrower bore of 92mm was adopted to give an overall capacity of 3,430cc. Power output at 218bhp, however, was unchanged.

The Champion

By the end of 1983, Brazilian ace Nelson Piquet had won the Formula One Championship in his BMW-powered Brabham. The slim single-seater, fitted with one of the most powerful 4-cylinder engines in the history of internal combustion, was painted in BMW's house colours of blue and white. Although the 1983 Championship winner's nosecone was not liveried to resemble the famous BMW 'kidney' radiator grille, as is the 2001 BMW-Williams, media coverage worldwide was, of course, immense; BMW had invested heavily in F1, and reaped rich rewards. Sales of the 6 Series increased healthily, and the company's Motorsport division was inspired to take the coupé concept further.

The M635CSi, launched in early 1984, was, and remains, among the world's best cars, a delight to drive, with almost electrifying performance contained within the civilised comforts of a sybaritic muscle machine. Its additional performance also helped BMW to convince a number of motorists, who might have otherwise plumped for a 5.3-litre V12 Jaguar, that the 6 Series was also a front-runner in terms of out-and-out performance.

The M-powered car was not cheap (around £24,000 would have been sufficient to acquire one in Britain) but the perceived benchmark sports GT from Porsche, the 928S, weighed in at 20 per cent more. At the heart of the

Expansive and made largely of plastic the dashboard was styled along the lines of the contemporary 5 Series, with a 'humped' instrument binnacle.

revised car was the 3,453cc 6-cylinder engine, with four valves per cylinder and double-overhead camshafts, similar in layout to that of the M1 supercar.

In conjunction with a high compression ratio of 10.5:1, the latest Bosch ML-Jetronic fuel injection and Motronic engine-management system, maximum power was rated at 286bhp, with 250lb ft of torque at 5,000rpm. Not only powerful, the engine was also astonishingly fuel efficient, and in theory was capable of returning between 30 to 40mpg.

With a top speed of around 155mph, and a 0–60mph potential of a little more than 6secs, the M635CSi was commendably quick, and on a par with the majority of its peers. Naturally, the gear ratios were altered, the suspension stiffened and brakes uprated to cope with this extra power. At the front, the discs were increased in diameter and thickness, and there were four-piston calipers to the same design as those fitted to the M1.

Driving a 6 Series is so rewarding that it matters little that the instruments are not works of art.

Having scored four outright victories in the 1983 European Touring Car Championship with Jaguar, Tom Walkinshaw's Oxforshire-based company,

TWR, announced a special version of the Jaguar XJS in 1984, a direct competitor for the 635CSi. With 330bhp from its 5.3-litre engine (the standard unit developed 30bhp less) and very much improved aerodynamics by the expedient of wind-tunnel-developed aerofoils, the big cat was faster than the BMW. Capable of a claimed 164mph and accelerating from standstill to 60mph in 5.8sec, the TWR XJS was an attractive proposition for some but, at £13,000 more than the standard Jaguar XJS, the purchase price of nearly £35,000 raised a few eyebrows even among committed Jaguar enthusiasts.

According to *Motor Sport*:

> The TWR Jaguar is aimed at a specific market occupied by the Mercedes 500 SEC, the BMW 635CSi, the Porsche 928S, even the Ferrari 400i and the Aston Martin V8, with prices as diverse as £24,000 and £44,000.

The magazine added:

> When people buy a car costing that much it isn't so much as the model they select as the image they wish to project, so value-for-money and levels of equipment hardly come into the equation; all creature comforts are assumed.

While sales of the 6 Series continued throughout the 1980s in the manner in which BMW had come to expect, the Munich company went from strength to strength. The motoring world was also beginning to change. Huge sums were being spent, on both sides of the Atlantic, on 'classic' cars. 'Mainstream' manufacturers were slow to react to criticism that their products were dull, grey and characterless. In an attempt to recreate the glories of the past, motoring enthusiasts of all persuasions revelled in nostalgia. Motor sporting events increased manyfold, particularly in Britain, and although the classic car 'bubble' comprehensively broke in 1989, its legacy would have lasting implications for manufacturers.

At the end of the 1980s, the 6 Series bowed out to make way for a new generation of BMWs, which would include the Z3 and Z8 sports cars, with 'retro' styling from the 1950s and early 1960s. Although the 635CSi and its closely related M-powered sister are correctly viewed as classic cars in their own right, not everyone in the BMW fold wholly accepted the 6 Series styling package. Some viewed it as awkward and 'bulky', while it obviously captured the imaginations of others. Whatever one's views there is little doubt that, with the benefit of hindsight, the

6 Series, along with the Audi quattro, Jaguar XJS, third generation Mercedes SL and Porsche 928, were products of 1970s thinking.

Today, many view them as 'dinosaurs', but the fact remains that many of these cars remain in the hands of real enthusiasts who use them on a daily basis. However, progress moves things on; the M635CSi was capable of 155mph but, just a few years later, Audi, Volvo and BMW would all make family estate cars with similar performance. In order to stay ahead, BMW would be forced to pull something really special out of its tool bag.

CHAPTER TEN

The Big Coupés: The 7 Series

The 7 Series: Munich's Merc 'basher'

By the mid-1970s the 2500/2800 and 3-litre saloons had been in production for nine years. During that time, these glorious, stylish machines had brought much of the prestige that BMW sought in their attempt to equal, and ultimately beat, the luxury saloons from arch-rivals, Daimler-Benz.

BMW's saloons were stylish, comfortable, quick and endowed with first-rate road manners but, despite enthusiasm from journalists such as Motor Sport's Bill Boddy, the motoring public at large continued to hold the

three-pointed star in the highest regard. Some even expressed the view that Rolls-Royce's Silver Shadow was among the elite saloons, but this archetypal British company, hit hard by financial crisis in the early 1970s, built cars for people who 'understood' the Rolls way, and as such were in a different motoring furrow.

As good as BMW's saloons undoubtedly were, new technology, changing customer taste and demands, and increasing competition from within the motor industry, had caught up with these models. By 1975, BMW had added the 7 Series to the range, and unofficially 'invited' Daimler-Benz to reply.

Although a little 'slab-sided' the new car, which shared several components with the 6 Series, was elegant, lean and unmistakably from BMW's stable. There were three models, namely the 728, 730 (both with carburettors initially) and fuel-injected 733i (3,210cc), each designation denoting engine capacity in the company's customary manner.

Predictably, the Seven was considerably larger than the outgoing range – 2in wider, 6in longer and 4in longer in wheelbase, and roughly priced between the Mercedes-Benz 280SE and 350SE. Jaguar also provided competition for the new BMW, of course, but the Coventry-based car maker's products in this era were heavily compromised by quality problems which would take many years to rectify.

When the 7 Series was launched in the US in 1977, *Road & Track*'s first road test was simply headed: 'Your move, Mercedes-Benz'.

Despite its increased size, the styling of the 7 Series was wholly in keeping with the other cars in the range. Twin headlamps, sloping 'kidney' grille, large glass area and neat proportions all collaborated to give the impression of a 3 Series on a large scale. Unlike Daimler-Benz's saloons, however, the 7 was intended as sporting limousine, and in this respect, there was nothing quite like it – anywhere.

In keeping with contemporary vogue, external brightwork was kept to an acceptable minimum, and in some markets attractive multi-spoke alloy wheels were fitted as standard. The standard steel wheels, closed with plastic hubcaps, were a common sight in Britain although they were out of character with the luxury nature of the car and looked frightful.

The bodyshell incorporated the latest thinking in passenger safety, with a rigid central cell and crumple zones fore and aft. Such was BMW's faith in their standard of build quality, each car came with a six-year warranty against body corrosion, a move that many other manufacturers would follow in the years ahead.

In the Driving Room

The 7's interior held no surprises for those familiar with BMWs, for it was similar in lay-out to all the other cars in the line-up. The most instantly obvious difference, however, was in the sheer scale of the big saloon, the increase in body size being responsible for additional leg, head and elbow room. A full 5-seater, notwithstanding the large folding cen-

A luxury 'limo' but, with sporting feel and performance, the big 7's 'slab-sided' appearance wasn't to everyone's taste, but there's no doubting its contemporary elegance.

That the 3, 5, 6 and 7 Series cars all bore a resemblance to each other was not coincidence. By the mid-1970s, car companies were striving for a new 'corporate image', and adhere to the same policy today.

tral armrest in the rear, the feeling of spaciousness was equalled by solid build quality and an overwhelming sense of safety. Incidentally, a first-aid kit was positioned behind the rear armrest.

Hard-wearing cloth upholstery was standard in most markets, with leather at extra cost. Naturally, the front seats were fully adjustable and capable of accommodating all shapes and sizes. In keeping with the sporting potential of the car, there was ample lateral support for legs and torso. With one of the front seats fully reclined, it was even possible to get a good night's sleep in a 7 Series.

The instrument layout and four-spoke steering wheel were similar to those of the 6 Series, and included the check-control panel and warning lights for all fluid levels and brakes. Electrically-powered toys were much in evidence, including central locking that also controlled the fuel filler cap. In the unfortunate event of a heavy accident, there was a special electrical sensor which unlocked the doors, allowing access to the interior for the emergency services.

On first acquaintance with the 7 Series, *Road & Track's* road tester commented:

> Looking out over the expanse of hood I said to myself, '. . . this is a big car,' but then I remembered that in America, where large cars are the norm, the 733i would be related to the status of a compact or midsize luxury sedan. The seats are as comfortable as they look and I especially appreciated the way the ribbed velour material gripped my body during spirited cornering . . .

> For the most part the interior design illustrates the Teutonic thinking in ergonomics and safety padding: eminently practical and efficient but lacking in warmth. Strips of wood along the top of the doors and surrounding the shift lever help break the monotony of the all-black dash.

Automatic transmission, electric windows, auto load-levelling, telephone and air-conditioning were all extra-cost options of which the majority of customers availed themselves. The telephone was of particular novelty in the mid-1970s, and something of a status symbol. Some 25 years on, a car *without* a telephone would become the ultimate in status symbols in some quarters.

Familiarity Breeds

Widely acknowledged as the smoothest in-line 6-cylinder engine, the single-overhead camshaft unit was certainly viewed by Americans as a 'tiddler' from a capacity point of view, but power output was as impressive as

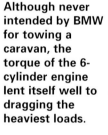

Although never intended by BMW for towing a caravan, the torque of the 6-cylinder engine lent itself well to dragging the heaviest loads.

ever. The 2.8-, 3.0- and 3.3-litre units pushed out 170, 184 and 197bhp respectively, sufficient for relaxed cruising at 115mph in all three models. Naturally, the 733i was the quickest with a top speed of 130mph, and a 0–60mph capability of 8.5secs which, in a car weighing 1,601kg (3,530lbs), was impressive to say the least.

Of the 733i, Road & Track remarked:

The injected 3.3-litre six provides the smooth, quiet and easy revving performance for which BMW's inline six has long been famous. A cold start is done without touching the throttle; simply

Distinctive Alpina body graphics are garish, but wholly in keeping with the times and BMW's motor racing activities.

733i (1975–85)

Body style	Four-door saloon
Engine	
Cylinders	6
Bore × stroke	89 × 86mm
Capacity	3,210cc
Compression ratio	9:1
Fuel Injection	Bosch L-Jetronic
Max power	197bhp at 5,500rpm
Max torque	206lb ft at 4,300rpm
Transmission	
Gearbox	4-speed manual
Ratios	First 3.86
	Second 2.20
	Third 1.40
	Fourth 1.00
	Final drive 3.45
Suspension and steering	
Suspension	(front) MacPherson struts, lower A-arms, coil springs and anti-roll bar
	(rear) Semi-trailing arms, coil springs and anti-roll bar
Steering	Power-assisted recirculating ball
Wheels	Cast alloy 6.5J×14
Tyres	205/70VR 14 Michelin XWX
Brakes	Servo-assisted discs/discs
Dimensions	
Track	(front) 1,501mm/59.1in
	(rear) 1,516mm/59.7in
Wheelbase	2,794mm/110in
Overall length	4,859mm/191.3in
Overall width	1,801mm/70.9in
Overall height	1,430mm/56.3in

Alpina's 3.5-litre B9 was an exciting alternative to the regular range. This rare example, belonging to vintage car enthusiast, David Lee, is tucked away from prying eyes.

The standard four-spoke steering wheel was of truck dimensions. Wood veneer was extended to parts of the dashboard, gear lever console and door cappings, but was not to the same standards as English contemporaries.

turn the key and the engine lights instantly. It idles roughly for the first few seconds but the car can be driven away immediately without stumbling or stalling. With 197bhp DIN and 206lb ft of torque on tap, it's easy to break the rear wheels loose when starting from rest or around tight corners negotiated in second gear. The 733i is a relaxed Autobahn cruiser and the brakes and chassis are more than capable of coping with these speeds, as I discovered more than once when the inevitable VW Beetle pulled out to pass the inevitable Citroen 2CV while woefully misjudging the BMW's closing speed.

One of the most extraordinary parts of the character of the 7 Series was the encouragement it naturally gave spirited drivers to get a move on. Whereas the equivalent Mercedes washed away aches and pains, and was refined to a degree that travelling quickly became almost irrelevant, the BMW's sporting nature shone through. Some considered it to be considerably less 'raw' and 'seat-of-the-pants' by comparison with the old 2500/2800 cars, but suspension changes to the 7 made it considerably more civilised.

For the 7 Series, BMW adhered to their traditional MacPhesron struts up front, and semi-trailing arm fully independent rear. However, there were changes, aimed at reducing pitch and yaw, that saw the adoption of double-pivot struts at the front. This comprised an upper pivot point and two lower ones, one at the outside ends of the lower links, and the other where each link attaches to the MacPherson strut. In conjunction with positive scrub dialled into the geometry, the car's road behaviour was considerably improved, particularly in relation to stability under braking.

With revised suspension, there were bigger and more powerful brakes and softer springs for improved ride quality. Caster action was also doubled and gave better high-speed stability, improved steering return and handling. At the rear there was a tubular subframe, which was torsionally stiffer and, in conjunction with solidly pivoted trailing arms, camber changes under braking were almost entirely negated.

Inevitably, with a car of this weight and performance, disc brakes were fitted all-round, and were similar to the system used for the 6 Series. Both the brakes and steering were power-assisted from a crankshaft-driven pump. Steering was by ZF's recirculating ball, which replaced the worm-and-roller design of the outgoing model. A rack-and-pinion system, which had been broadly adopted across the motor industry by this time, might have been a better bet from the point of view of improving the precision of the steering, but it is assumed that BMW's people knew best. The steering system was weighted to allow for more road 'feel' with increased speed, and as such was as near perfection as possible.

On the Loose

The metallic blue example I tested (a later 735i) in the early 1980s left a lasting impression. Sliding onto the smart black leather driving seats, and idly looking around the cabin, the car gave the appearance of an enormous limousine.

In the manner of all BMWs, the instruments and controls of my test car were perfectly laid out and, in the manner of all German cars since the beginnings of internal combustion, the switchgear felt as if it had been hewn from solid. This aside, the gear knobs of manual cars did have a tendency in old age to snap off, as happened in my own car at an inopportune moment.

With the engine at tickover little noise entered the cabin, although a blip of the throttle would leave you in no doubt as to the power harnessed under the right foot. An automatic, I selected 'drive', glided away and enjoyed a trip around my native Herefordshire.

Magnificent 6-cylinder 'lump' was offered in 2.8-, 3.0, 3.2- and 3.5-litre guises. Illustrated is the 3.5-litre fuel-injected unit.

Up through the villages of Trumpet, Ashperton and Stretton Grandison, a mixture of tight corners, and long straights, the BMW showed itself to be perfectly nimble and capable of behaving like a well-honed, if heavyweight sports car. Entering a bend at high speed produces initial understeer, but application of the throttle quickly turns to oversteer in the traditional manner. Apart from being safe and predictable, this manner of driving is fun, and, with such a taut chassis, a most comfortable means of exploiting the lusty 6-cylinder engine.

With a 'kickdown' facility for overtaking, whizzing past other motorists is unequivocal; the car simply picks its feet up and goes. Acceleration is not explosive in the manner

The Alpina's steering wheel and appointments are much more stylish by comparison.

of, for example, a Porsche Turbo, but there is a shove in the back that certainly tells you that this car means business.

On up the A49 to Leominster, and the BMW was well and truly into its stride. Having seen highly illegal speeds registered on the speedometer on several occasions, I stopped at the late Bill Bengry's fuel station for a fill-up. Bengry was, of course, the man who won the International RAC Rally Championship in both 1960 and 1961 in his famous old Tomato Red Volkswagen Beetle.

Never short of conversation (Bill was one of the greatest talkers on motoring subjects I've ever known) Bill came out to look the 7 over.

'I'm glad you've called in that thing,' he shouted in his local lilt, 'because it's always a great pleasure to take petrol money off people, especially when it's as much as you've just spent.' His view of the car was favourable but, typical of the man, he pronounced it unsuitable for use on the East African Safari Rally without extensive modifications. I protested that BMW had never intended it as a rally

735i (1976–86)	
Body style	4-door saloon
Engine	
Cylinders	6
Bore x stroke	86 x 92mm
Capacity	3,430 cc
Compression ratio	10:1
Fuel injection	Bosch Motronic
Max power	218bhp at 5,200 rpm
Max torque	228lb ft at 4,000 rpm
Transmission	
Gearbox	5-speed manual
Ratios	
	First 3.82
	Second 2.20
	Third 1.40
	Fourth 1.00
	Fifth 0.81
	Final drive 3.25
Suspension and steering	
Suspension	(front) Double joint spring strut, coil springs, rubber auxiliary springs and anti-roll bar
	(rear) Semi-trailing arms, coil springs, and additional semi-trailing arms to reduce drive
Steering	Power-assisted with varying assistance
Wheels	6.5Jx14
Tyres	195/70 VR 14
Brakes	Servo-assisted discs
Dimensions	
Track	(front) 1,508mm
	(rear) 1,522mm
Wheelbase	2,795mm
Overall length	4,860mm
Overall width	1,800mm
Overall height	1,430mm

Good old sloggers that they undoubtedly were, the first generation 7 Series is largely neglected and forgotten today. Examples in first class condition are rare, as many have been consumed by rust.

car, but it was no use. Bill had made his mind up; he clearly saw it in the same mould as the Rolls-Royce he drove on the 1970 London-to-Mexico World Cup Rally, and Bill had views about the Silver Shadow which, if repeated here, would probably result in an attempt to stave off a libel suit.

As I bade Bengry good-bye and sped off in the direction of Pembridge and Shobdon, where Innes Ireland and Peter Walker once lived, it occurred to me that Bengry was right. The 7 Series wouldn't have made a good rally car, for much the same reason that a Land Rover would-

n't have been entirely at home at speed on a German autobahn. The 7 Series was so obviously built for high-speed travel in complete safety and comfort, which it does exceedingly well.

Shaping Up

In 1978 *Road & Track* published an interesting piece in which their staffers had made a comparison between the 733i, Jaguar's XJ12 and the Mercedes-Benz 450 SEL. They posed the question: 'If the BMW is delightful and the Mercedes is serious, what is the Jaguar?' And added by way of answer, 'Elegant, of course, but is that what it needs to be the best of the three?'

For *Road & Track*, the best car of the three, in conclusion, was the BMW. The magazine commented:

> The 733i won on the Cumulative Rating Sheet by a narrow margin over the Mercedes (554 total points versus 542) and by about 10 per cent over the Jaguar. The BMW was the winner in 12 of the 22 categories, the Mercedes followed with 10 Category wins and the Jaguar notched only 2 (the numbers don't agree with the total number of categories because of ties). But that's not the total yard stick. Each evaluator is also asked to choose, independently of his rating sheet, his favorite among the three cars and here the BMW was the unanimous choice.
>
> The new 733i and the 450SEL are very comparable in so many ways, their differences often being less than a matter of better or worse than just two different approaches to the same end. There is, however, one difference we feel is quite important: price. As much as we like the 450SEL, we don't feel it's $6360 better than the BMW. With that difference you could buy a Honda Accord LX or Toyota Celica or . . .
>
> As for the Jaguar, we still love her but despite her beauty and grace, she is aging. We hope British Leyland will soon put the quality, style and Jaguar tradition, along with the V12 engine, into a new model.

Interestingly, most people who took an interest in these cars were agreed that the Jaguar was the prettiest, and the Mercedes the least well styled, with the BMW sitting somewhere in the middle. The Jaguar's interior styling was also without the aesthetic compromises made by the two great German companies, but in all other respects the Mercedes and BMW were streets ahead.

Above all the 7 Series showed that the great tenets of a sports saloon could be combined with the refinement and grace of a 'top-notch' limousine. However, there was another economic spectre on the horizon in 1979.

Oh Heck, OPEC

The expensive 7 Series sold comparatively well, but OPEC (Organisation of Petroleum Exporting Countries) increased the price of fuel around the world. By 1982, they had cut oil production by 2.5million barrels, and pump prices rocketed upwards. Oil crises come and go and usually cast gloom across the world, and always have an effect on the people whose job it is to plan for the future well-being of car manufacturers. BMW increased production of diesel-engined cars – a wise and popular move – but the future looked pretty grim for top performers such as the 6 and 7 Series cars. BMW had had a V12 on the stocks since before the 1973 oil crisis, and were once again working on the development of a new V12 in the 1980s. Such investment is extremely expensive and, with such a lack of stability among oil producers, it took a very brave decision to press ahead with work on luxury cars against such an economic background.

During the 1970s, BMW were among the world's most rapidly expanding and successful car manufacturers. The success continued through the 1980s, and no-one at Munich was going to wittingly return the company to the dark days of the late 1950s. An expensive, exclusive flagship had to be maintained, irrespective of rising oil prices.

BMW's marketing department, part and parcel of all car companies in the modern era, knew a great deal about their customers. They figured, quite correctly, that there were still many successful, well-heeled individuals who could afford the best. Fuel consumption, however, had become a pressing issue, and BMW went all out to discover ways and means of making their power units more efficient. Fuel injection became standard across the 7 Series range from 1979, and engine management systems became more sophisticated.

Beyond this, BMW led the world in the fields of experimentation with hydrogen-fuelled cars. Prototypes were produced and ran successfully. Today, BMW's hydrogen-powered cars are still running, and undoubtedly point to hydrogen becoming the fuel of the future. As this gas only produces steam and nitrogen oxide when it is burnt, it is almost certain to replace fossil fuels, the only difficulty, now overcome, being the safe containment of the gas within the confines of a motor car.

Despite fluctuating oil prices, and increased prices at the pumps, BMW's board remained resolute in its long-held aim of providing elite carriages at all levels. For volume sales, the company relied on its amazingly successful 3 Series. It was extremely profitable, and so was the 5 Series, but inevitably the 7 Series accounted for only 10 per cent of total sales. The car was seen on both sides of the Atlantic

as the only true alternative to a Mercedes-Benz. Preference largely came down to marque loyalty and perceptions of image.

BMW knew this, of course, and surged ahead plans to launch the second generation 7 Series in 1986, a car that was light years ahead of almost every other four-wheeled machine in the world. By the mid-1980s, Daimler-Benz could ignore nothing that BMW did. The Stuttgart company was being equalled, if not beaten, at its own game. BMW's production increased year on year, annual turnover exceeded DM20 billion by the early 1990s and, because of the sheer quality of the cars, 'everyone' aspired to BMW ownership.

A Second Seven

When the 7 Series was dropped in the mid-1980s to make way for the second generation, the original car suddenly appeared to be very

Launched in 1986 the second generation 7s were much more attractive cars. With similar styling to the E34 5 Series (debuted in 1988), the 7 still looks fresh today.

dated. The revised car was not only bigger in all directions but it was also better looking. It was so well engineered that many viewed it as the definitive luxury sporting saloon and became the benchmark by which the mighty S-class Mercedes would ultimately be measured.

Codenamed E32, it was styled along the lines of the contemporary 3 Series and would influence the looks of the forthcoming E34 5 Series. With a view to reducing fuel consumption, the bodywork was more aerodynamically efficient, detail changes having been made across the board. A narrower radiator grille, deep chin spoiler, flush glass and door handles, low side skirts and an upturned boot spoiler all contributed to reducing drag. The body was also more rounded, less aggressive – even feminine in the eyes of some – and because of its slender shape, this gargantuan heavyweight did not need deep swage lines along the flanks to disguise the 'endless' nature of the sheet metal.

From every angle and view the 7 looked right, well balanced and integrated, irrespective of body colour. All the usual BMW styling hallmarks were present and, because of the car's size, they emphasised the distinctive and distinguished nature of BMW's in-house design philosophy.

Smart alloy wheels were standard across the range, with various styles available but, as is the case with the E34, the BBS cross-spoke variety were the most stylish and enhanced the 7's sporting image.

With new laser welding techniques, the body was torsionally more rigid than the original 7, and safer from a passenger's viewpoint. As was to be expected crash-testing exceeded all requirements under US Federal laws by a healthy margin.

Stateroom

The E32's interior held no surprises, for it was the most sumptuous of all cabins yet to be devised by BMW. Interestingly, it was in some ways reminiscent of the 'Baroque Angels' of the 1950s. These expensive and beautifully executed cars were largely responsible for BMW's financial problems of the period. Built on a 'no expense spared' basis, they were expensive to buy and run, and came at a time when Germany was clearly still attempting to recover from the ravages of war. Their interiors were to state of the art 1950s 'limo' philosophy, and much the same mentality would prevail in the creation of the E32, the difference being that

Neat rear styling, with discreet 'in-built' boot spoiler, finally showed to the world that high-speed luxury cruisers didn't necessarily have to look, or drive, like barges.

730i (1986–95)	
Body style	4-door saloon
Engine	
Cylinders	6
Bore x stroke	80 x 89mm
Capacity	2,986cc
Compression ratio	9.2:1
Fuel injection	Bosch Motronic
Max power	197 bhp at 5,800 rpm
Max torque	203ft lb at 4,000 rpm
Transmission	
Gearbox	5-speed manual
Ratios	
	First 3.83
	Second 2.20
	Third 1.40
	Fourth 1.0
	Fifth 0.81
	Final drive 3.64
Suspension and steering	
Suspension	(front) Double-joint spring strut front axle
	(rear) Semi-trailing arm, twin-tube dampers and anti-roll bar
Steering	Engine-speed related, power-assisted
Brakes	Servo-assisted discs, ABS
Wheels	6.5J x 15
Tyres	205/65 VR 15

this time there were customers in sufficient numbers for BMW not to have to worry about its fiscal future.

Tailored as much for the pleasure of driving as it so obviously was for stress-ridden executive passengers, the layout of the E32 was a model of comfort and luxury. As a bonus it was also a pleasant, spacious place to be – somewhere as inviting as a remote alpine hotel, where it is possible to revel in total escapism. Well insulated against sound, even with the engine at peak revs, the 7 could be as sporting or as 'limo-like' as its owner wanted.

Cloth upholstery was standard, with leather available if preferred. The seats, front and rear, were with head restraints, and perfectly contoured for body comfort and lateral support. Seating was provided for up to five adults, although the large armrest between the rear seats lent weight to the idea that it

was a four-seater in reality. Some models had individual rear seats which, like those in the front, were electrically adjustable and had a 'memory' facility.

Instrumentation and switchgear also held no surprises, for they were entirely in keeping with contemporary BMW thinking. The gauges were minimal, circular and crystal clear, ventilation and heating were supremely efficient, and the leather-covered steering wheel was a four-spoke design with the familiar roundel at its centre.

Where equipment was concerned, it was very much the case that, 'if it had been invented it was available'. At that time it seemed almost ridiculous that a car should become overburdened with electrical 'condiments'. The electric motors and attendant wiring increased the weight of the 7, and other cars, to an unnecessary degree. After

The long-wheel-base 750i V12 illustrates that size really does matter, but so does performance and drivability, which these cars had in abundance.

road testing a 735i in 1986, it occurred to me that the only thing missing from the big Mercs and BMWs was double-glazing. It came as quite a surprise when a little while later, Daimler-Benz announced their range-topping S-class was actually fitted with double-glazed windows!

Mechanically Speaking

Much of the 7 Series was to the same specification as the 5 and 6 Series cars, with the usual badging of 730i and 735i denoting engine capacity. These power units, along with the V8 (740i from 1992), were discussed in previous chapters, and they need not detain us here.

The suspension, brakes and steering were also to BMW's tried and tested formulae. As a result, the car handled and stopped in the same manner as a 3 or 5 Series, except that it felt like the larger machine that it so obviously was. Ride comfort, of course, was outstanding – as good as anything from Jaguar or Mercedes – but there was always an underlying feeling of a sports car wanting to be unleashed. Floor the throttle of a 735i and it would bellow forward in the manner of a herd of stampeding elephant but, with a lot less dust and noise.

Beyond the regular models, though, BMW had a final ace up its sleeve that would finally project the company's products into, and

beyond, the upper echelons of automotive excellence. In 1987, BMW launched the 750i, a 5-litre (4,988cc) V12 that eclipsed all that had gone before it.

The Victor That Vanquished

The 750i V12 was the most expensive and technically advanced production car built by BMW, and the first German car to have a V12 engine since pre-War days. During the 1920s and 1930s, V12 and V16 power units were not uncommon among luxury carmakers, particularly in America, where petrol was cheap and the rich seemingly had money to burn. The economic depression of the early 1930s changed this situation to a certain extent. After the War engines of more modest proportions, and fewer cylinders, predominated, except in Italy where Enzo Ferrari's machines were not even considered as 'proper' Ferraris if they did not have a powerful V12 in front of the driver.

The advantages of a V12 are, of course, smoothness, refinement and extra horsepower for a given capacity. Disadvantages generally include relatively poor fuel consumption, complexity and time-consuming and expensive maintenance. BMW had mooted and built a V12 engine during the zenith of the 1973 oil crisis, the political turmoil in the Middle East being responsible for the car failing to enter production.

The idea of V12 power could not be resurrected by German manufacturers for many years. Germany has one of the strongest environmental lobbies in western Europe; their political clout is never to be underestimated, which is why BMW shied away from entering this elite market until 1987. In Britain, Jaguar had had a V12 version of the Jaguar XJ from the mid-1970s but, of course, the political environment in Britain has always been very different from that in Germany.

In one sense, BMW's decision to produce a V12 was a brave one, but there was no going back this time. Once the board had given the final nod to the engineers to pull the stops out, there was feverish and excited activity at the hallowed desks of Munich's design studios.

As the company's 2.5-litre in-line 'six' had been hailed in most quarters as the best power unit of its type, it was almost a foregone conclusion that the specification of the 'ultimate' power unit would be a brace of sixes 'welded' together on a common crankshaft. This is what BMW broadly did, of course, and the result was a 5-litre V12. With a bore and stroke of 84mm × 75mm cubic capacity totalled 4,998cc to produce a maximum of 300bhp at 5,200rpm, and maximum torque of 332lb ft at 4,100rpm. Top speed was artificially limited to 155mph, of course, but acceleration was electrifying, with 62mph arriving from rest in less than 7secs for those who could not resist playing with the throttle pedal.

BMW also built a long-wheelbase version which was 4.5in longer than the standard car and, despite the extra weight, the performance differential was minimal. The 750iL, incidentally, was lengthened to allow additional legroom in the rear, the extra sheet metal being integrated into the rear doors. Unlike so many 'stretched limos' the V12's styling was not upset or unbalanced in any way, which some regard as sufficient testament to the car's quite astounding styling.

Formula One ace, Austrian Niki Lauda, was enlisted to drive one of these sumptuous cars through the streets of Vienna upon its launch in 1987. Lauda, who is also a great fan of the Volkswagen Golf GTi, declared that the big BMW was an extremely 'nice car', and it is difficult to argue with his point of view. While Lauda would 'retire' from Grand Prix

735i (1986–95)	
Body style	4-door saloon
Engine	
Cylinders	6
Bore x stroke	86 x 92mm
Capacity	3,430cc
Compression ratio	9:0
Fuel injection	Bosch Motronic
Max power	211bhp at 5,700 rpm
Max torque	225lb ft at 4,000 rpm
Transmission	
Gearbox	5-speed manual
Ratios	
	First 3.83
	Second 2.20
	Third 1.40
	Fourth 1.00
	Fifth 0.81
	Final drive 3.91

Selwyn Eagle's 1988 750i, fitted with 18in Alpina alloy wheels, has proved reliable and faultless for more than 180,000 miles. Despite hard everyday use the body and paintwork remain in perfect condition.

racing to become a consultant to Ferrari, and more latterly, Jaguar, his fellow countryman, Gerhard Berger, would become the driving force behind BMW's initiative in Formula One from 2000.

A Bird of Prey

Engineer, Selwyn Eagle, is a dyed-in-the-wool BMW man, the owner of a superb 1988 750iL in metallic blue. His march towards V12 ownership began in the mid-1990s with a 325i. 'A friend owned one, allowed to me to drive it, and I became instantly hooked,' he says. At the time, Selwyn owned a Golf GTi, 'a good little car', but it was not in the same league as the 325i and he swapped his allegiance to BMW in an instant. Selwyn explained:

728i (1999–)	
Body style	Four-door saloon
Engine	
Cylinders	6
Bore x stroke	84 x 84mm
Capacity	2,793cc
Compression ratio	10.2:1
Max power	193bhp at 5,500rpm
Max torque	206lb ft at 3,500rpm
Transmission	
Gearbox	5-speed automatic/Steptronic
Ratios	First 3.67
	Second 2.00
	Third 1.41
	Fourth 1.00
	Fifth 0.74
	Final drive 3.23
Suspension and steering	
Suspension	(front) MacPherson struts, multi-link, coil springs and anti-roll bar
	(rear) Semi-trailing arms, multi-link, coil springs and anti-roll bar
Steering	Power-assisted rack and pinion
Wheels	Cast alloy 7.5Jx16
Tyres	215/65 R16
Brakes	Power-assisted discs/discs, ABS standard

735i (1995–)

Identical to 728i except for the following:

Engine

Cylinders	8
Bore x stroke	78.9 x 84mm
Capacity	3,498cc
Compression ratio	10:1
Max power	238bhp at 5,800rpm
Max torque	254lb ft at 3,800rpm

Transmission

Gearbox	5-speed automatic/Steptronic
Ratios	First 3.57
	Second 2.20
	Third 1.51
	Fourth 1.00
	Fifth 0.80
	Final drive 3.15

The 325i was the only seriously quick member of the 3 Series breed, but beyond performance I liked the fact that there were many on the roads in those days – Golfs are two a penny – and the BMW's reliability, build quality and superb roadholding obviously held great appeal.

A motoring programme on British television, however, convinced him that a secondhand 7 Series was the car he really wanted.

> I could hardly believe that used 7s were so cheap to buy, so I swapped the 325i for a 735i and went touring in a big way.

He was attracted to the 7 by its styling, power and spaciousness and, despite a blown head gasket during an early stage of his custodianship, it proved to be exceptionally reliable.

> For a car weighing 2 tons the 735i was astonishingly agile and quick. It also went like anything, but never felt flustered, never lost its composure and was always smooth even when I gave it a hard time.

One thing the second generation 7 cannot do, however, is look inconspicuous. It has huge presence and great beauty but, regrettably, that can make it a target for vandals, as happened to Selwyn's car.

Selwyn kept the 735i for an enjoyable two years, before completely falling for the magnificent V12 long-wheelbase model featured here. Now with close to 200,000 miles under its belt, it has a couple of insignificant engine oil leaks, but has otherwise proved entirely reliable. A niggling brake problem

Leather-clad comfort and every conceivable piece of luxury equipment, the long-wheelbase V12's additional length allows for generous rear legroom.

As he admits, though, the painful bit of V12 ownership is the expense of running such a machine. Petrol consumption fluctuates between 16mpg 'around town', and between 25-27mpg on a long run, the latter being perfectly acceptable, the former dipping into the realms of being anti-social. As he carries out maintenance and servicing himself, Selwyn does not especially revel in the inescapable fact that the V12 has 'two of everything', except the sparking plugs, of which there are twelve. As Selwyn says

Servicing takes twice as long as a 6-cylinder car but, on the plus side it's pretty straightforward for the most part. I wouldn't like to have to tackle a complete rebuild, though. There is no getting away from the V12's complexity, and the sheer size of the thing. The engine bay is completely filled with pipes, electrical bits and pieces and one hell of a lump of engine.

The magnificent 5-litre V12 engine is smooth, powerful and complex. It is also reliable and long-lived, but drinks plenty around town. A version of this power unit propelled McLaren to victory at Le Mans, 1995.

apparently cured itself, and the electrics occasionally play up, but this is a small price to pay for the privilege and pleasure of driving one of the world's most magnificent motor cars on a daily basis.

Selwyn claims:

'By comparison with the V12, the 735i appears tame and slow. When I post my foot to the floor in the 750i, motoring assumes a different meaning. It's difficult to describe; everything seems so natural, so powerful and together. On one occasion I had to catch a flight from Cardiff Airport; we were late and I was trying to make up time by getting a move on. At one point I saw the speedo needle hit 145mph, which was the only indication that we were really motoring. In the V12 you just have no idea that you're travelling so quickly, because it's so very smooth and quiet.

Sitting at the wheel of the V12 it is impossible not to be impressed with the cabin. Trimmed in leather and the usual planks of polished timber, you are incarcerated in a perfect motoring environment. 'Everything' is electrically powered, and there is cruise-control, air-conditioning, CD player, an on-board computer and a host of other gadgets to amuse those for whom such things are important.

Of all special equipment the adjustable suspension – for comfort or sport – is arguably the most useful. At the flick of a switch to the right of a gear lever, you can cruise like a Mercedes or fly like a V12 BMW, and the system works well. However, this car is fitted with 17in diameter Alpina wheels (10in wide at the rear and 8in up front) and, with tyres in the nature of elastic bands, ride quality inevitably varies.

Bowling along Herefordshire roads, the car takes unkindly to irregularities, particularly in the wet, and great care has to be exercised with the accelerator. There is such an abundance of raw power, that it is not difficult to

With such huge engine torque, automatic V12s were more popular than manuals. The quality of the leather and wood veneer is exquisite.

imagine that it would be comparatively easy to provoke a complete spin. Conversely, dry-weather roadholding is almost beyond belief. Steering is pin-sharp, the tyres bite as hard as any tyres can and, with hard throttle, the car leaps from corners as if launched.

The 4-speed ZF automatic gearbox can similarly be flicked to manual mode, but playing around with the stick for long periods, although completely exhilarating, of course, inevitably results in loud applause from those holding large shares in oil companies.

As we rowed the big car along through the villages of Hampton Bishop and Mordiford, it occurred to me that, in many respects, the 750i is a 1980s successor to cars like the Speed 6 Bentley: a Grand Touring car in the old tradition that would come into its own in a 24-hour race around the old Nürburgring, preferably with a riding mechanic to light the driver's finest cigars as and when required.

After a splendid blast in the V12 we parked the car, and in the manner of all civilised motoring folks, retired to drink large quantities of strong tea. Selwyn remains enthusiastic about his car – 'the best I've ever owned' – but in the fashion of all young people, he is beginning to hanker after a new challenge.

I no longer need the space I have in the 750i, and am now looking for an 840i. With the possible exception of the Ferrari Boxer and Aston Martin Virage, the 8 Series BMW is the best looking sports car I've ever seen. The 840i, for me, also has the advantage of being less complicated than the V12. I feel that fettling a V8 engine after the 750i would be a piece of puddin', but it's the shape of the 8 Series that really draws me.

Tea over, I climbed back into my 525i, drove home and reflected on Selwyn's view that his 735i felt tame by comparison with the V12. He was right. But it is inevitable that while the big car's power virtually eclipses all, such refinement and superiority has to be paid for. I am relieved that I am not the one picking up the bills for running Selwyn's V12, but it is an amazing car that must surely be among the top ten on anyone's shopping list – real or imaginary.

Confirmed BMW devotee, Selwyn Eagle, loves his 750i but would not have another. Acquisition of an 8 Series is a high priority.

Not the End

The second generation 7 Series enjoyed a long production run, and was not replaced until 1995, when the third generation got into full swing. Fans of these models are generally agreed that the E32 'Mk2' was the pick of the lot. Better looking and better engineered than the original car, it has everything to commend it. Although it only accounted for some 10 per cent of total BMW sales, it not only paid for itself, but brought handsome profits.

Considering its size and weight the 7 Series handles remarkably well. With V12 power there are not many quicker cars on the open road.

Despite 155mph potential these cars never lose their composure, even through tight bends, although the low-profile tyres on this example tend to compromise ride quality.

Third generation 7 Series is among the most advanced machines ever made, but some regard the styling as undistinguished.

It came as no surprise to anyone that the range-topping V12 version inspired a new Mercedes-Benz flagship, also fitted with a V12 engine. Clearly, BMW had raised the stakes to the point where a successor would have to be something a little more special.

By the late 1990s, BMW had more to contend with in the way of competition. Like Porsche, they had to fend off fierce marketing by rivals, but there was more. Luxury boats, second homes abroad and light aircraft were all viable alternatives to expensive cars for the well-heeled with cash to spend. In addition, spiralling fuel costs continue to be a real problem for many motorists.

740i (1995–)	
Body style	4-door saloon, plus long-wheelbase bodyshell
Engine	
Cylinders	8
Bore x stroke	82.7 x 92mm
Capacity	4,398cc
Compression ratio	10:1
Max power	286bhp at 5,400rpm
Max torque	324lb ft at 3,600rpm
Transmission	
Gearbox	5-speed automatic/Steptronic
Ratios	First 3.57
	Second 2.20
	Third 1.51
	Fourth 1.00
	Fifth 0.80
	Final drive 2.93

Car manufacturers are constantly aware of these problems, and have to juggle a fine balancing act when pitching new models into an uncertain marketplace. In launching the third generation 7 Series, BMW were certain that they had done their homework thoroughly and carefully. As it turns out the company got their sums right – once again.

Riding High – the Third Generation Seven

By the late 1990s BMW had little, or nothing, left to prove to the motoring world. The company, which could have so easily become extinct in 1959, produced the finest range of cars bar none. Virtually all Series models stood as benchmarks by which others would be measured. Not everyone agreed, of course, and a handful of journalists loathed the cars from BMW, but BMW's sales continued to increase, despite, or even because of, the views of dissenters.

At the top of the motoring scale, the second generation 7 Series stood as pillar and pinnacle of luxury sports motoring. The days when heads of state almost exclusively travelled in S-class Mercedes, were coming to an

end. The 7 Series had become the 'smart' alternative to Daimler-Benz's splendid machines, and the preferred transport of both those who were driven and enjoyed driving.

It goes without saying that the revised car, the E38, had to be superior in every way, although not all have taken to its unremarkable styling. Sophisticated and complex, the latest 7 Series models do everything that a motor car is supposed to and more. Beyond the usual comforts, hallmarks and inevitable performance, some of the real engineering genius of these cars lies well below the surface. One small example is the 'occupation detector' fitted in the front seat which

Like other models in the range the current 7 has its twin headlamps concealed by plastic covers.

A refined, safe, economical and quick machine, BMW's 7 is representative of state of the art executive motoring in the early twenty-first century.

The current 7 Series, with revised tail-lamp clusters, also has an integral spoiler built into to the trailing edge of the bootlid.

propelling the car to a top speed of 140mph. Acceleration is equally impressive, with 0–62mph being possible in 9.6secs, and overall fuel consumption floating in the region of an acceptable 25mpg.

Past criticism that BMW, along with other German carmakers, provided a 'base' car and charged high prices for luxury equipment was completely absent with all models in the 7 Series range. The list of standard equipment includes air-conditioning, leather upholstery, electrically-adjustable front seats (with memory), alloy wheels, ABS brakes, remote-control anti-theft system, radio/cassette with six-speaker system, six airbags, seat-belt tensioners, side-impact beams in the doors, automatic traction control and AGS Steptronic gearbox.

Beyond these advanced features is a steering wheel with integrated controls for the telephone, cruise control, radio and air circulation.

In a market vigorously contested by Lexus, Toyota's luxury brand, a new breed of Jaguars, the ever-present Mercedes-Benz and Audi's big guns, in 2001 the war among these manufacturers is largely one of purchase price. In Britain, the 728i was listed at £37,545, a hefty sum, but something of a snip in this exclusive market.

For those for whom the 728i won't suffice, there are the 3.5- or 4.4-litre V8s, or 5-litre V12, which are made with the same degree of comfort, refinement and engineering input, but inevitably have a vast amount of additional engine power. With 238bhp at 5,800rpm from the 3.5-litre car and a top speed of 151mph, and 286bhp at 5,400rpm with the 4.4-litre machine (limited to a top speed of 155mph) the 7 Series is the master of high-speed express travel.

automatically determines, through pressure sensors, whether the seat is occupied. If the seat is empty during a collision, the airbag on the passenger's side will remain inactive. This obviously has practical implications, but more importantly it is typical of BMW's remarkable attention to detail.

Out on the Range

At 'entry level' the 2.8-litre 728i is the only 6-cylinder model in the 7 Series line-up, the 735i, 740i being fitted with the V8 engines, and the 750i with the mighty V12. Although the 'baby' of the range, the 728i develops 193bhp at 5,500rpm, and is capable of

Blue and White Silver Lady

For the future, however, one of the most interesting directions for the company, in terms of luxury motoring, will be its acquisition of the right to build cars with Rolls-Royce badges. To be built in Britain, at a new plant in Sussex,

The big V12 version is distinguished externally by a chromed badge on the roof 'C' pillar.

The paddock at Donington, May 2001; a new V12 pulls up and is instantly swamped by 'head-turners'. These cars command a presence, even among the massed ranks of the Vintage Sports Car Club, who don't usually admit to taking interest in cars made after 1930.

many of the components for the Rolls will inevitably be sourced from Munich. To this end, it is highly likely that the car will be propelled by a version of the V12 BMW power unit, arguably the finest of its type made in the history of internal combustion.

Industry analysts who have argued that the Rolls will step on the toes of the prestigious 7 Series have a point, of course, but it is difficult to appreciate their reasoning. The Rolls-Royce brand has been universally famous since before the Great War, and has occupied an almost unique market ever since. Ironically, competition for the BMW-produced Rolls, provisionally scheduled for launch in 2004, will arrive from Volkswagen, who hold the right to make cars under the Bentley flag.

Although BMW has published artists' impressions of their British flagship, the final specification of the car remains well-guarded, for obvious reasons, but it is likely to be tailored to cater for expensive tastes on both sides of the Atlantic.

CHAPTER ELEVEN

The Special Tourers

Recapturing the Magic

As is well known, BMW's first production car was made in 1928. An Austin 7 built under licence from the British manufacturer and badged as a Dixi, it was entirely undistinguished. After a couple of years BMW dropped it, and began manufacturing cars to its own designs. Despite producing a number of perfectly good saloon models throughout the 1930s, the company's sporting two-seaters, most notably the quite superb 328, gave BMW its enduring reputation as a manufacturer of exciting sporting machinery.

Although the 1950s saw a downturn in BMW's fortunes, mainly as a result of its stolid, expensive luxury saloons, the two-seater V8-engined 507 sports car maintained the company's reputation for producing top-flight roadsters. The 507, hailed as being one of the world's most beautiful ever cars, was the only alternative in Germany during the 1950s to the wickedly expensive Mercedes-Benz 300SL. Porsche were also producing fine two-

seaters, of course, but the Zuffenhausen company's machines had yet to reach the 'dizzy' heights of supercar status.

At the beginning of the 1960s, however, BMW had no choice but to return to earth. The company had to become involved in the serious business of making cars for profit, and turned exclusively to the production of saloons. During the following years the saloons inevitably gained an envied reputation for their sporting prowess. Success in European Touring Car Championships, mixed fortunes in Formula Two, and the supply of engines to Chevron for sports racers like the Chevron B8 all conspired to keep BMW's name in the sporting arena. But the idea of producing a thoroughbred sports car was not even on the agenda.

Indeed, during the 1970s the very idea of a roadgoing sports car was under threat. It appeared at one stage that the car-buying public had simply lost interest in two-seaters, particularly at the 'budget end' of the market. As cars like the MGB and Triumph TR7 faded away there was virtually nothing in the

BMW's long history of building sports cars began in the 1930s. The 328 (illustrated) was the company's finest pre-War car, and continues to attract interest among small boys.

'affordable' bracket until the advent of Toyota's' mid-engined MR2, debuted in the mid-1980s. Porsche enjoyed a degree of success with the 2-litre 924 from the mid-1970s, but for the most part, the sports car industry tended to fluctuate between short-lived highlights and long periods in the doldrums.

Naturally, the exotic end of the market, occupied by Ferrari, Aston Martin and Porsche and the like continued in its normal way, with good years and bad, as had always been the case. BMW had attempted to gain a foothold in this market, first with the mid-1970s 'Batmobiles', and later with the mid-engined M1 but neither were financially viable.

For all its performance, poise and drivability, the 6 Series BMW was more of a Grand Touring car than an out-and-out sports machine. By the end of the 1980s, however, BMW's outlook was slowly beginning to change. The 8 Series, launched in 1989, although a direct replacement for the 6 Series, combined the best features of its predecessor with the sporting nature of the two-seater 'Z' cars.

Beyond producing fabulous sports cars for the 1990s, though, BMW, along with Porsche, Mercedes-Benz, Volkswagen and others, sought to capitalise on the growing interest in classic cars. Classics, particularly from the 1950s and 1960s, were held in great esteem by a growing band of enthusiasts worldwide. Modern cars were failing to capture the imagination of those whose happiest motoring memories were firmly back in the heady days of previous decades.

To this end Porsche released the Boxster, styled on the late 1950s RSK Spyder, Mercedes produced its SLK with overtones from its cars of the 1950s, Volkswagen debuted the Concept 1, which would go into production as the New Beetle, and BMW joined the fray with its sporting machinery that also 'borrowed' from past styling exercises. This resulted in the birth of the 'retro-look', which so many manufacturers would adopt to a lesser or greater extent from the mid-1990s onwards.

Above: **Handsome, high-speed coupés were also among BMW's armoury in the late 1930s, this example having been entered for the company's victorious assault on the 1940 Mille Miglia.**

Left: **With advanced road manners and superb performance, BMWs were marketed in Britain by AFN Ltd as Frazer Nash BMWs, the BMW engine design also being used by Bristol until the early 1960s.**

Although a successor to the 6 Series, the 8 Series combined the dynamics of a Grand Tourer with the excitement of a true sports car, and went a long way towards recapturing BMW's sporting past and present.

Although the 8 Series was not strictly built to this formula, its frontal resemblance to the M1 supercar was not to be denied, while the Z cars unashamedly fell into the retro style. That BMW were so obviously correct to drive down this particular alley was quickly demonstrated by encouraging sales. At one end of the scale the 8 Series was representative of everything a really top quality sporting machine should have been, which, inevitably, was reflected in its high purchase price, while the Z cars were designed and priced to appeal to a younger motoring audience.

By the beginning of the 1990s, when the 8 Series was in full swing, BMW were employing more than 60,000 people, and had increased its annual turnover tenfold by comparison with figures from the close of the 1960s. The company had brought pressure to bear on all its competitors, and was clearly spreading its wings into fresh territories.

The Z1 sports car was the first creation of BMW's 'new thinking', and it was shown as a concept in 1986. In some respects it recaptured the spirit of the pre-War 328 in that it was traditional in layout, but very much to an advanced design. A 6-cylinder engine was used up front driving the rear wheels, but there was a fully galvanised, 'self-supporting' chassis, to which detachable plastic body panels were attached. Light in weight and aerodynamically sound the Z1 two-seater was capable of topping 140mph, and accelerating

from 0–60mph in around 7.8secs. Potential customers reacted favourably to the prototype, and production began in 1988 at a rate of around six units per day.

The car was not especially cheap to buy, but was built to BMW's traditional high standards. Some regarded the car as faultless, and it was certainly among the best-handling sports cars, but the important point for BMW was its standing. BMW had returned to making true sports cars after many years' absence. The success of the Z1 (all production examples were snapped up as quickly as they were made) would pave the way for future models.

Pieces of Eight

After the demise of the 6 Series, BMW changed its approach, and produced the 8 Series as a symbol of the company's technical know-how. The first 850i appeared in the autumn of 1989. Fitted with the 5-litre V12, the car was the result of an initiative by BMW's Motorsport division to create the world's most practical and competent high-speed express. Variants on the 8 Series theme appearing from 1993 included the 5.4-litre 850CSi with 326bhp (or 380bhp), and V8 4.4-litre 840Ci with 286bhp.

As Grand Tourers and out-and-out sports cars they excelled themselves. Technically sophisticated and built to hitherto unknown levels of safety, these fabulous two-door coupés also looked wonderful. Unlike contemporary Ferraris the 8 Series did not appear brash, but was instead understated– quietly introspective and confident.

The narrow radiator grille naturally incorporated the 'kidneys', the bonnet was fluted and the headlamps were of the pop-up variety to give a smooth, low aspect when they were tucked away. Both the windscreen and rear window were steeply raked and of typically generous proportions

The 8's unusual nosecone, with 'pop-up' head-lamps, bore more than a passing resemblance to BMW's mid-engined M1 supercar.

8 Series 840Ci	
Body style	2-door coupé
Engine	
Cylinders	8
Bore x stroke	75 x 84 mm
Capacity	3,982cc
Compression ratio	10:0
Fuel injection	Bosch electronic
Max power	286bhp at 5,800rpm
Max torque	295lb ft at 4,500rpm
Transmission	
Gearbox	5-speed manual
Ratios	
	First 4.23
	Second 2.51
	Third 1.67
	Fourth 1.23
	Fifth 1.1
	Final drive 3.08
Suspension and steering	
Suspension	(front) Multi-link, coil springs, telescopic dampers and anti-roll bar
	(rear) Multi-link, coil springs, telescopic dampers and anti-roll bar
Steering	Power-assisted rack and pinion
Wheels	Light alloy 7.5J x 16
Tyres	235/50R 16
Brakes	Power-assisted all-round discs with ABS
Dimensions	
Track	(front) 1,554mm
	(rear) 1,562mm
Wheelbase	2,684mm
Overall length	4,780mm
Overall width	2,037mm
Overall height	1,340mm

A splendid looking car by any standards, with subtle, graceful lines, the 8 held the advantage of not standing out in a crowd.

Abandon All Hope . . .

The 8's interior stood as a model of comfort, a driving environment of perfection. Sports seats, covered in soft Napa leather, had full electrically-powered adjustment, and the seat belts automatically adjusted to the driver's height. BMW's usual attention to detail included door windows that automatically dropped a little way when the doors were opened and closed when the doors were pulled shut. Drivers of Volkswagen Beetles will fully understand the reasons for this facility. Cars like the Beetle – and there are not many – were built to such high standards that the cabin was often said to be 'air-tight', necessitating the opening of a window before the doors could be closed properly. The 8 Series was very much in the same mould; that BMW thought to include an automatic facility to negate the effects of air-tight build quality was yet another example of state of the art technology hailing from one of Germany's leading manufacturers.

for safety reasons, and the rear was neatly finished with a 'Kamm' tail. In short, the car was to classic coupé dimensions, the front, rear and cabin section sitting in perfect balance. With fat alloy wheels the overall aesthetics were of a type that will endure for many decades. This was not a product of fashion, to be discarded at whim, but a car that bred long-term enthusiasm – a true classic.

Along the same theme, the steering wheel was made to tilt automatically when the handbrake was engaged, thus allowing easier access for the driver from the cabin. This latter idea was, of course, first incorporated in a 'production' car on the 'Gullwing' Mercedes-Benz, launched in 1954. The Mercedes' system was operated manually, while the BMW's worked as if by 'magic'. However, these advanced systems seem less attractive if they malfunction, resulting in substantial repair bills.

Confronting the driver was the usual clutch of crystal clear instrumentation. BMW's on-board computer, check-control and service-interval indicators gave information about the normal travel and service functions. For those more interested in the stereo system, no fewer than 12 speakers were provided. This was presented under a new banner: ICE, or In-Car Entertainment.

Handsome cross-spoke alloys enhanced styling appeal; a set of steel wheels with hubcaps would not have been 'quite the ticket'.

It goes without saying that practically everything fitted to the interior which was capable of being moved was powered by electricity, including the windows, sunroof, central locking and the rest.

All Systems Are Go

Advances in computer technology during the 1980s and 1990s inevitably led to the greater use of microchips in motor cars. BMW's contribution to this complex modern world resulted in Digital Motor Electronics (DME), one of the most complicated engine management systems ever devised.

Apart from controlling and monitoring fuel consumption with pin-point accuracy, it included a self-diagnosis system and fail-safe programme, which constantly monitored engine performance, faults in the system and was able to make corrections to 'abnormalities'. From a practical point of view it helped to reduce maintenance, and because of its complexity, also discouraged do-it-yourself amateur mechanics from tinkering.

The 8's suspension system (EDC) was similarly controlled by electronics, a computer adjusting the shock-absorber settings to suit changes in the road surface and loading under acceleration and deceleration. A switch on the central console also allowed the driver to select Sport or Comfort mode. In conjunction with a new rear suspension system, with five guiding elements per wheel (an upper transverse link, two lower transverse links, a longitudinal link and an integral link) the ride quality, handling and roadholding were all of a new standard.

Such revisions were not only aimed at providing superior dynamics, but had every bit as much to do with safety issues. BMW's FIRST philosophy, an acronym for 'Fully Integrated Road Safety Technology', resulted in a car that stood as a model of safety for drivers, passengers and other road users.

Body crumple zones, a rigid passenger cell designed to absorb serious impacts, ABS brakes, driver and passenger airbags and smooth body contours with rounded edges all contributed to greater automotive safety. Just as important in this respect was an excess of engine performance which allowed for drivers to power their way out of trouble. The 8 Series is capable of accelerating from 0–60mph in roughly 6secs and has a top speed of 155mph (electronically governed).

With the exception of the world's 1990s supercars, such as the BMW-powered McLaren F1, Jaguar XJ220 and Bugatti EB110, the 8 Series was representative of state-of-the-art motoring know-how. Only Porsche's 928 could be considered as a serious rival, for Jaguar's venerable XJS was beginning to show its age by this time.

Owner's View

A down-to-earth person, David Craddock has an entirely practical approach to motoring. His needs are for a comfortable, reliable and quick machine capable of travelling in the shortest possible time between points A and B on a daily basis. He has owned various BMWs (and a couple of Mercedes'),

Originally available with the V12 engine (this is the later 4.4-litre V8) the 8 Series issued power with the force of a killer whale, but in a most civilised manner.

The stark, clean interior of David Craddock's 840i.

including assorted 3, 5 and 7 Series cars over many years, but his current car, an 840i, is probably the pick of the crop.

After many years he has concluded, in his words, that the only alternative to an 8 Series, for his purposes, is a Toyota Land Cruiser. He says:

They have very different uses, but the German and Japanese products are equally dependable, and just never let you down. For me, though, the critical thing in any car is comfort, and in this respect, I've never found anything as good as my 840i. It's also smooth, quiet, quick and has absolutely wonderful roadholding.
[end quote]

As a successful businessman, David Craddock also believes in getting good value for money from his cars.

The 840i was expensive to buy but, as it never goes wrong, it actually provides for very inexpensive motoring. A Ford Fiesta at £10,000 is, to my way of thinking, a complete joke. The things rust away in no time, and just lose heaps of money. Pointless.

8 Series 850Ci	
Body style	2-door coupé
Engine	
Cylinders	12
Bore x stroke	80 x 89mm
Capacity	4,988cc
Compression ratio	8.8:1
Fuel injection	Bosch electronic
Max power	300bhp at 5,200rpm
Max torque	295lb ft at 4,500rpm
Transmission	
Gearbox	5-speed manual
Ratios	
	First 2.48
	Second 1.48
	Third 1.00
	Fourth 0.73
	Fifth 0.25
	Final drive 3.15

His only dislikes of the 840i are its lack of space in the rear (the car could never have been appreciated as a full four-seater) and tendency to momentarily 'steam-up' in cold weather. Other than that David says it is just about perfect.

> Frankly, I haven't any ambitions to own Ferraris, Porsches and other similar cars; the BMW is all I want, although I might consider swapping the 8 for a 7 Series. The new 7s are good-looking, practical cars with plenty of room for rear-seat passengers, and the only alternative, I suppose, is a Mercedes.

David reckons that the two Mercedes he owned were comfortable, well built motorway cruisers, at which they excelled but, as he says: 'They're just too big for country lanes, and just don't seem to handle as well as BMWs.'

Like so many BMW owners I interviewed for this book, David Craddock has little to say on the subject of his BMW, for the simplest of reasons. 'BMW have got everything just about right' he comments, 'and when you've got perfection, there isn't much else to say.'

Long Since Gone

Production of the 8 Series ended in 1999 after 10 years. Expensive and beautifully crafted, the big sporting coupé certainly had its place, but was not quite as successful as BMW had

once hoped. Like the Porsche 928, it fell into something of an odd category, and, perhaps, became a victim of image. Was it a sports car, or a GT? In fact it was both, but not everyone saw it that way. Like the two-seater 500SL Mercedes-Benz the BMW was, in the eyes of some, just a little too perfect, too clinical and so easy to drive that it required little driver input.

At the time of writing (early summer 2001) BMW have not replaced the 8 Series. After so many years in the wilderness, it appears that the pure sports car has undergone something of a renaissance. From the mid-1990s onwards, there has been a plethora of two-seaters ranging from the MGF at the 'budget' end of the scale through to Porsche's quite astounding GT1 at the other. Porsche's Boxster, the Mercedes SLK, Lotus Elise and BMW Z cars, Z3 and Z8, have all, in their way, helped to redefine the concept of two-seater motoring. BMW's contribution to this rejuvenated concept has, naturally, captured the imagination of all aficionados and followers of Munich's philosophy.

The Z3

Unlike the Porsche Boxster, BMW's Z3 followed Z1 practice in that its engine was placed in front of the driver. Inevitably, and thankfully, it put power onto the road through

David Craddock at the wheel of his 840i, a car that continues to serve his every motoring need better than anything else.

Arrow-sharp, the 8 Series no longer features in BMW's range; used examples represent good value.

In place of the original 1.8-litre car, much criticised for its lacklustre performance, the latest incarnation has been upgraded to 1.9 litres.

In Britain, prices range from £19,000 to almost £28,000, which the majority of commentators believe to be cheap, considering the car's outstanding build quality, comfort and performance. Like the Boxster and Mercedes-Benz SLK, the BMW's interior fits driver and passenger like a well-crafted leather glove – a perfect place for enjoying the delights, and experiencing the many miseries, of open-top motoring.

In contemporary vogue, the Z3's interior is stylish, understated and to BMW's usual ergonomic standards. Steering, stopping and handling are of the highest possible order, and, frankly, it is difficult to appreciate that a car of this nature could be improved upon in any significant way. Roadholding and handling could be improved by placing the engine amidships, but possibly at the expense of limiting luggage space. In any case, BMW's aim in producing the Z3 was to provide for a seriously fun but also practical sports car. Not surprisingly, the Z3 has proved popular on both sides of the Atlantic, the choice among the current crop of European sports cars largely boiling down to marque loyalty and aesthetic preference.

However, there is no getting away from the fact that the Z3 is not entirely intended as a 'raw' sports car in the Healey 3000 sense. Extra-cost options, for example, include air-conditioning and heated sports seats – questionable accoutrements in any car that purports to be a true sporting roadster. However, as a 'boulevardier', object of automotive art, and dynamic road performer, the Z3 works well. Its classic looks will also secure it a small place in motoring history, for its 'retro' features were bold and brave touches that worked most strongly in BMW's favour.

the rear wheels. The front-drive route would have been quite unforgivable.

Body styling was unique – stumpy, short and chic – but incorporated long-standing BMW features, including distinctive, vertically-slatted grilles behind the wheel arches that harked back to the 507 sports car of the 1950s and early 1960s. Designed to have a broad appeal across the board, the frontal appearance was typically aggressive, but retained BMW's classic twin headlamps concealed behind Perspex covers. A deep chin spoiler and side skirts helped to create smooth, clean airflow over and around the body, but a bootlid spoiler was conspicuous by its absence.

The short rear was in the nature of a neat 'rump', a feminine touch that endeared itself to many. For some, however, the Z3 was the archetypal 'hairdresser's car', a spiritual successor to the much-loved MGB. Since the Z3's introduction, however, the range was updated in 2000 with a series of powerful engines. At the top of the range the 3.0i Sport (a replacement for the 2.8-litre) develops 231bhp at 5,900rpm, and has the capacity to sprint from 0–62mph in 6secs.

The 2.2-litre version has replaced the 2-litre original, and with a top speed of 139mph is clearly aimed at the specialist market occupied by Audi's sensational TT.

Z3	
Body style	Two-seater sports coupé
Engine	
Cylinders	6
Bore × stroke	84 × 75mm
Capacity	2,494cc
Max power	171bhp at 5,800rpm
Max torque	160lb ft 4,300rpm
Wheels	Cast alloy 7.5J×16
Tyres	225/45ZR 16

Up at Eight

A modern interpretation of the 1950s BMW 507 sports car, of which there were just 252 examples built from 1955, the Z8 combines classic styling with state-of-the-art engineering know-how. Styled by Albrecht Graf von Goertz the original 507 was hailed as a masterpiece – a thing of sheer beauty – and the Z8 no less so. Paying a handsome compliment to Christopher Bangle and his team at Munich, in charge of the Z8 project, von Goertz commented: 'If I were to design the 507 today, it would look like the Z8'.

Although a supercar by 1950s standards, and exclusively owned by wealthy people, the 3.2-litre V8 507 was no match for the con-temporary 300SL 'Gullwing' from Daimler-Benz. The BMW's top speed of 125mph, although impressive, was a long way from the Gullwing's 155mph and, unlike the car from Stuttgart, the BMW had little in the way of truly innovatory engineering.

By any measures, though, the 507 was a classic in its own right, and in producing the Z8, BMW claim that they are merely reinforcing and reinstating the concept of the original car. BMW's view of the Z8 is that it is:

> breathtakingly beautiful, classic in proportions and offering the very best technology available in modern automobile production . . . a dream car far beyond the constraints of fashion and fleeting

Designed to attract a younger audience, the Z3 sports car encompasses traditional BMW values with...

...a hint of the fashionable 'retro' look. Vents similar to these were featured on the BMW 507 of the 1950s.

Unmistakably a modern BMW from the front but, with air outlets behind the front wheel arches as in the Z3 and 507, there was an aura of controlled drama that had been lacking for so long in modern automotive design. In standard guise the car comes with an electrically-powered soft-top but, in true German tradition, a hard-top, with a heated rear window, is available at extra cost.

The hull of the car is an aluminium space-frame-cum-monocoque, with bolt-on body panels. The sill panels, incidentally, contain the radio, navigation and telephone aerials, a typical piece of modern BMW innovation, but at the same time likely to result in astronomical repair bills if the car is involved in an accident.

trends . . . the product of the passionate enthusiasm of dedicated designers and engineers.

Publicly debuted as the Z07 concept at the 1997 Tokyo Motor Show, and again at the Detroit Auto Show the following year, the car drew great enthusiasm from fans of sports cars and of BMW. With its long bonnet and classic sports car dimensions (4.4m long, 1.83m wide and just 1.31m high) the Z8 looked powerful and tantalising. With large-diameter wheels, long front end, short overhangs and a relatively short cockpit, there is no mistaking its masculine and traditional appeal.

The Wick

Fitted with BMW's oily-smooth 5-litre 32-valve V8, there is no less than 400bhp (at 6,600rpm) available under the right foot. Maximum torque, produced at 3,800rpm, of 369lb ft is equally elephantine. Variable camshaft adjustment (double-VANOS) is carried over from the M models, along with an intake system with electronically controlled throttle butterflies for improved torque at low and medium speeds. A central computer-brain

'Stumpy' rear end is cute to some, but unfinished to others. Natural competitors are from Lotus, Mercedes and Porsche.

(part of the engine management system) is able to execute in excess of a million commands per second, technology that BMW also uses on its Formula One engine.

With traction control and sports tuned DSC (Dynamic Stability Control), the immense power of the engine is transmitted through the rear wheels without drama. With the engine also placed a long way back in the chassis, the front-to-rear weight distribution is a perfect 50:50.

With a best 0–60mph time of 4.7sec, the standing kilometre in 23.4secs and accelerating from 50 to 80mph in 4.3sec, this is an extremely quick sports car. Top speed is electronically governed to 155mph, which BMW's press literature describes as a 'sensible limit'. Unrestricted, there is little good reason for the Z8 not being able to top 180mph, which BMW, one presumes, does not consider 'sensible'.

Z8 (2000–)	
Body style	Two-seater sports coupé
Engine	
Cylinders	8
Bore × stroke	89 × 94mm
Capacity	4,841cc
Compression ratio	11:1
Fuel injection	BMW MS S 52
Max power	400bhp at 6,600rpm
Max torque	369lb ft at 3,800rpm
Gearbox	Getrag D 6-speed
Ratios	First 4.23
	Second 2.53
	Third 1.67
	Fourth 1.23
	Fifth 1.00
	Sixth 0.83
	Final drive 3.38
Suspension and steering	
Suspension	(front) MacPherson struts, with aluminium links, and track control
	(rear) Integral four-arm rear axle
Steering	Power-assisted rack and pinion
Wheels	Cast alloy
	(front) 8J×18
	(rear) 9J×18
Tyres	(front) 245/45ZR18 96Y
	(rear) 275/40ZR18 99Y
Brakes	Power-assisted discs/discs with ABS as standard
Dimensions	
Track	(front) 1,552mm/60.5in
	(rear) 1,565mm/61in
Wheelbase	2,505mm/97.7in
Overall length	4,400mm/171.6in
Overall width	1,830mm/71.4in
Overall height	1,317mm/51.4

Range-topping 3-litre Z3 is a classic, with shattering performance, comfort and road-holding, but has too many creature comforts to be considered as a sports car in the traditional mould.

Correct Pitch

Aluminium-alloy was used extensively in the Z8's sophisticated suspension system. The front 'axle' was made entirely from alloy with the usual spring/strut configuration at the front, and integral four-arm axle at the rear. Multi-spoke 18in diameter alloy wheels (8in wide at the front and 9in at the rear) are shod with specially developed run-flat tyres (245/45 ZR 18 96Y at the front and 275/40 ZR 18 99Y at the rear) capable of running at speeds of up to 50mph for 300 miles after suffering a puncture. BMW have so much faith in these tyres that the Z8 is not fitted with a spare wheel and tyre.

Braking, with ABS and CBC (Cornering Brake Control) as standard, is taken care of by vented discs at the front and rear, the most powerful ever devised for a BMW road car. At 60mph, the car is capable of stopping dead within 2.5secs (or 35 meters) of hitting the pedal.

Driver and passenger safety is enhanced by airbags in both doors, dashboard and steering wheel hub, the latter inflating with varying volume depending upon the force of impact.

Added crash protection is provided by two racing-style roll hoops at the rear of the cockpit. The cabin, incidentally, has everything anyone would expect to discover in a car costing £80,000. The only real surprises are the steering wheel which, with its multiple spoke design, harks back to vintage days, and instruments, which are placed in the centre of the dashboard instead of being directly in front of the driver.

Scrap Book

Since 1962, Ian Fleming's character, James Bond, has been the subject of no fewer than 19 feature films – the twentieth is due for release in 2002. Down these many years the great Bond hero has driven a number of 'star cars'. They have included cars from Aston Martin, Toyota, Lotus and latterly in *The World is not Enough*, a metallic silver BMW Z8. As an agent for the British Secret Service, an Aston Martin DB7 might have been more appropriate. That a BMW was chosen speaks volumes for BMW's image at the beginning of the twenty-first century.

The Z8's performance and drivability cannot be faulted; some commentators consider the tail-lamps to be odd, but it is a design that grows on you.

BMW's exclusive and very expensive Z8, also with 'retro' styling from the 1950s, was smart enough for James Bond in *The World Is Not Enough.*

One intentional step backwards, and many huge leaps and steps forwards, a Z8, an open road and a breezy landscape are all that anyone really needs for living motoring life to the full.

As *BMW CAR's* report in December 2000 pointed out:

> You need to understand the Z8. Where the Z1 was a technical forum for BMW, the Z8 is all about image. There is no doubt BMW's designers have created a set of clothes which are nothing short of eye-popping, but it takes time to appreciate them. There are just so many elements to it, you just don't know where to start. Your eyes jump from detail to detail in a hurried pupil-straining stare. There's never enough time to take it in.

The same magazine criticised the car's ride quality for being 'too hard and uncompromising' and 'too stiff, with the slightest imperfections finding their way into the Z8's cabin, and ultimately through to you.'

No-one has yet criticised the Z8's performance, for it is, by any standards, quite startling. Of this BMW, CAR commented:

> If its looks are the overwhelming factor to those who will only ever get to admire a Z8, then for those lucky few who will drive one, it will be the Z8's performance which knocks them for six. Just as the V8 will pull you around town in any gear,

when the scenery goes from grey to green, there is nothing stopping those 400 horses from running wild. Nail the throttle in any of the first three gears, and you'll be hitting the rev limiter before you have time to think.

In conclusion the same writer remarked:

> On looks alone, it would take something very special to steal the Z8's thunder. Though for some, it will remain as an over styled, retro cash-in on the classic 507.

By contrast, BMW's conclusion of the Z8 is as follows:

> In all the Z8 is an attractive driving machine created not merely to move people and their baggage – but also to move emotions. The BMW Z8 therefore focuses on sheer driving pleasure at its best, particularly with the roof down in beautiful weather. Introducing its own unique concept, the BMW Z8 ranks high in the super sports car league. And built in an exclusive, small series in Dingolfing and Munich, the Z8 is truly a unique driving machine for the genuine connoisseur, a car that makes automotive dreams come true.

Index